Smart Companies, Smart Tools

Smart Companies, Smart Tools

Transforming Business Processes into Business Assets

THOMAS M. KOULOPOULOS

VAN NOSTRAND REINHOLD

I(T)P® A Division of International Thomson Publishing Inc.

New York • Albany • Bonn • Boston • Detroit • London • Madrid • Melbourne
Mexico City • Paris • San Francisco • Singapore • Tokyo • Toronto

Printed in the United States of America

Visit us on the Web!   http://www.vnr.com

For more information contact:

Van Nostrand Reinhold
115 Fifth Avenue
New York, NY 10003

Chapman & Hall GmbH
Pappalallee 3
69469 Weinham
Germany

Chapman & Hall
2-6 Boundary Row
London SEI 8HN
United Kingdom

International Thomson Publishing Asia
60 Albert Street #15-01
Albert Complex
Singapore 189969

Thomas Nelson Australia
102 Dodds Street
South Melbourne 3205
Victoria, Australia

International Thomson Publishing Japan
Hirakawa-cho Kyowa Building, 3F
2-2-1 Hirakawa-cho, Chiyoda-ku
Tokyo 102 Japan

Nelson Canada
1120 Birchmount Road
Scarborough, Ontario
M1K 5G4, Canada

International Thomson Editores
Seneca, 53
Colonia Polanco
11560 Mexico D.F. Mexico

1 2 3 4 5 6 7 8 9 10 QEBFF 02 01 00 99 98 97

Library of Congress Cataloging-in-Publication Data

Koulopoulos, Thomas M.
    Smart companies, smart tools : transforming business processes
into business assets / Thomas M. Koulopoulos.
        p. cm.
    Includes bibliographical references and index.
    ISBN 0-442-02496-7
    1. Reengineering (Management)–Case studies. 2. Communication in
organizations–Technological innovations–Case studies.
3. Industrial efficiency–Case studies. I. Title.
HD58.4'063–dc21   97-19345
                                                          CIP

Production: Jo-Ann Campbell • mle design • 213 Cider Mill Road, Glastonbury, CT 06033

For Mia
The Smartest Person I Know

CONTENTS

PREFACE

This book is about the inextricable relationship between business process and business assets, which, if understood, can provide quantum competitive opportunity for savvy organizations.

Global competition and the craze to transform business into an agile, adaptive, and constantly changing enterprise has put enormous pressure on workers and managers to rethink traditional management methods and tools. Virtual organizations, free-agent workers, and unprecedented downsizing have created an imperative for a new type of management, based on new organizational models. Coupled with new technologies to capture and automate work processes, this has led to the evolution of Smart Tools and the ultimate connected enterprise.

Smart Tools may well be the white-collar equivalent of the industrial revolution; transforming knowledge work through radically new methods that are as important to the front office as industrial automation was to the factory. But the principal difference is that unlike the early days of factory automation, when workers were persecuted and enslaved by their jobs, Smart Tools liberate employees.

There are legions of consultants and reengineering gurus who want to convince you that process change requires the charisma of Theodore Roosevelt, the will of Attila the Hun, and the resources of the sultan of Brunei. Don't believe it. Process change is most often a matter of applying the right tools to the right problems. And these tools, what I will call *Smart Tools,* are being used in thousands of cases already. Becoming a Smart Company means ferreting out the many ways in which simple changes can amount to quantum improvements. Success stories are not built on overnight turnarounds and crisis. They are built on a track record of success and buy-in from users, sponsors, and technologists. That's the theme of this book. So before you get out the artillery, bulldozers, and wrecking crew, stop and consider the arguments and the examples shown here. It may just save your company, your job, and your sanity.

Why have we been so lax as to let these opportunities go by? It's a long story that began about two hundred years ago when the attitude toward labor began to shift away from craftsmanship toward mass production. In short, everything was replaceable and reproducible, including people. That attitude did not stop with the white-collar workforce. Today we find ourselves at the end of a revolution rethinking these fundamental assumptions. Companies have become white-collar gluttons, using an ever-increasing labor pool as a spoiled child might use a trust account, for meaningless and often trivial applications.

But the trust fund has started to run dry. The labor pool can no longer perform the trivial. It has to shift to the craftsmanship that so clearly epitomizes skill and the creative application of knowledge.

In this new era, individuals and enterprise no longer have the luxury of wasting the human resource. You will need to define value and apply people to those tasks that are most worthy of them— apply technology to what remains.

But this does not justify or support the cowardly leadership that has resulted in the dumbing down of American management through rampant downsizing. This book is not a prescription for the zealous pursuit of job elimination. It is not a manifesto for short-sightedness. It *is* a basis for vision and brave leadership into the next millennium.

Consider these apparently unrelated facts:

- During the 1970s and 1980s, the British manufacturing economy barely increased its output. In the same period almost 40% of the labor costs were eliminated, the largest increase in productivity during those years among industrialized countries, other than Japan. That legacy is now being applied to white-collar workers as their ranks thin with increasing cuts in the knowledge workforce.

- Since 1900 American productivity has nearly doubled. So has consumption.
- Forty-five million people out of the U.S. workforce now work at home.

As disparate as these statistics may seem they are intimate components of the economic, cultural, and organizational fiber of the next century. Productivity increases must be supported by a healthy workforce. During the 1900s the commensurate increase in both has resulted in a higher standard of living for the industrialized nations of the world.

Suddenly, however, we find ourselves at the precipice of an economic collapse as unemployment and underemployment subverts our ability to prosper from productivity.

When rampant downsizing ravaged the factory the service sector served as a safety net. It absorbed the productivity backwash of unemployed created by factory automation in to office and administrative work. No surprise that Manpower Inc., the largest U.S. temporary placement agency, now employs more people than General Motors. But as these same productivity gains were realized in the service sector of the economy, the safety net began shrinking.

Yet the workforce is suddenly enabled with new technologies and communications infrastructure that can reapply the skills of knowledge workers, in home work settings or as free agents, in ways that were entirely incomprehensible just a few decades ago.

In factories, workers used manual skills which were finite and could be replaced by machines and automation. In the knowledge enterprise, workers rely on intellectual capacity, which is limitless and can be expanded far beyond current capacity. But this will require using technology to remove the mundane and monotonous that impede creative innovation. These technologies are what I call Smart Tools.

What's needed is an awareness and an acceptance of management's role in using these Smart Tools to apply human intellect and value in ways that increase opportunity and innovation. We cannot manage costs alone without sending the global economy into a death spiral.

We need brave managers who are willing to take advantage of

Smart Tools, not as a means of exploiting workers and pacifying stockholders, but rather as vehicles for providing long-term opportunities and prosperity for both. We need managers who are not simply responsive but strategic. Managers must have confidence in their ability to create new paradigms for work and the value of the worker. Smart managers can use Smart Tools to build Smart Companies.

As you read, keep in mind the common power of paradigms, such as those we will discuss, to change the world in dramatic and unpredictable ways. We can form a basis for understanding the genesis of the change, but we can never fully estimate or predict the actual events that will bring change. Nor can we anticipate new paradigms before they come into existence. But that is the beauty of human progress and achievement. In the process of attempting to understand change and the forces that cause it, we are actually effecting the change and shaping it to meet our perspective of the problems it will be addressing. And in that change, we also plant the seed of new paradigms, requiring more change and growth.

Lastly, in today's global market, adaptive organizations are not those organizations that empower their employees—but instead those that educate them. Start thinking about how you can educate. And here's the good news: if you are reading this, you have already started.

T. Koulopoulos
Boston, Massachusetts

ACKNOWLEDGMENTS

There is great delusion in writing a book—even if you have written before. In my case it began innocently enough with a singular, clear vision. Yet the illusion (and it is one that every author shares) is believing that simple concepts can be easy to articulate. The reality is much harsher. As I delved beyond the concepts floating on the surface the obvious conclusions and the steady stream of insightful thoughts and prosaic text quickly threatened to become stream of consciousness. In short, the many ideas that had taken shape in the subjective depths of the mind dissipated quickly as they made their journey from synapse to keyboard. All of this would be the end of any book were it not for the invaluable assistance of the many people who provide the support and honest commentary needed to shoulder the author's ideas (certainly this author's). It is on this foundation of support that I have been able to write *Smart Companies, Smart Tools,* and it is with these people that I must share any measure of insight that it brings to the reader.

But before naming the many people who I can recall, I have to acknowledge the thousands of people who I cannot recount individually, but who have been involved in shaping my thinking about *Smart Companies, Smart Tools.* These are the tens of thousands of attendees at the seminars and presentations I have delivered over the past nine years. When someone tells you that your presentation has helped them to better understand their own predicament, inspired them to go back to work with new ideas, or simply affirmed what they already believed—but were afraid to say, you are given an extraordinary satisfaction in your own work. The innumerable insights, comments, anecdotes and kind words from these people are the bedrock of this book.

As for those people I can recount there are many I would like to acknowledge individually. John Boyd, my managing editor at VNR believed in the project from the start. He provided both the vision and tenacity to proceed with a project that was defined much clearer in my own mind than on paper and he also brought to the project the much needed creative structure of the book. John is halogen when it comes to cutting through the fog. Also on the VNR team was Chris Bates who skillfully coordinated the myriad of tasks needed to pull together the final books production and Jo-Ann Campbell, at mle design, who did her standard, excellent job of layout. Marc Sperber, my development editor, was an outstanding resource for filling in the "holes" and rearranging otherwise fragmented ideas to make the book flow from past to present. Marc was also willing to do much of the research for the historical chapters—something unlikely for most development editors to take on and even less likely for someone who was simultaneously studying for his bar exam. Patrice Maye assisted in researching and keying in hundreds of footnotes and quotations. Although only a small fraction of these ended up in the book, her assistance was invaluable in providing the foundation and substance of the arguments made. Mark Armstrong, contributed extensive material on the subject of resistance to roles and his three beliefs, which are found in chapter three. His insightful perceptions were valuable in helping me to reconcile the important human elements of roles in Smart Companies.

The many companies such as Sandia Laboratories, Aetna, Home Box Office, Nordic Track and others whose case studies illustrate the Smart Company should be acknowledged for their forward thinking and innovation. I am especially grateful to individuals at companies that I and others at my company, Delphi, have worked with to apply the methods discussed in this book. My ideas have benefited considerably from the involvement of many of these individuals, including Mark Tucker at National Life of Vermont, Stacie Burnham at Lockheed Martin Energy Systems, Dave Jones and Kemp Bohlen at Hewlett-Packard. In addition there were a number of technology vendors who provided the basis for many of the case studies, which offer the evidence of Smart Companies in action, including; Roger Sullivan at Keyfile, Matthew Graver at DST, and Sumi Shohara at Action Technologies. Dave Shorter at IBM who first introduced me to the idea of a Business Operating System several years ago, has given me food for thought to fill many pages and countless discussions on the topic of BOS. Kian Sanaii, at FileNet, has also given me the benefit of his own perspective on how Business Operating Systems will impact the shape of technology and work management in the future and has been a sounding board for the evolution of the BOS concept.

MaryAnn Kozlowski, my incredibly reliable and persistent public relations manager, has been there to push the project along from its outset and to make sure that hardly a stone was left unturned when it came time to promote the book. The entire team at Delphi whose own spirit and attitudes reflect the very essence of what a Smart Company should be, have lent their energies and collective experience to the project and often provided the critical viewpoints during the formative portion of the book's development. I am especially grateful to those individuals who have helped form the core Delphi team over the past nine years, including long-time team members Nathaniel Palmer, Carlene Foreman, and Mike Muth. Their support has provided the lookout point from which to formulate many of the ideas in this book.

Included in this team is someone whose professional and personal support have accounted for much of my own motivation, my business partner, Carl Frappaolo, who has more stamina and personality than any one person deserves. Carl has helped to solidify the methods and tools discussed in the book during his countless consulting engagements. His work proves that Smart Companies are indeed built by the tools and hands of craftsmen.

Finally, I am grateful for the enduring wisdom and support of my family—the people whose judgment and honesty I value most. My brother Nick, whose quick wit and creative energy have been at the core of building the Smarts at Delphi, has believed in me enough to support Delphi's mission despite the fact that, as he puts it, "The first child is always an experiment. It's the second time around that parents get it right." Nick is the younger one. My father helped me to form the true essence of a Smart Company after a brief lesson on the Greek meaning of the word "Exotaxio," which roughly translated means "the factory that moves," or the place where work is moved to the people. After reading five manuscripts, he is still eager to read the final book. The first copy will go to him and my mother, whose support and faith is simply endless. My wife, Debbie was the first to read *Smart Companies, Smart Tools*—long before it was suitable for human consumption. She was behind the project even with full knowledge of the toll yet one more book would take on our time. Yet that has been an ongoing theme for us. I come up with a great new idea (at least in my mind), Debbie supports it, then braces for the impact. Fortunately, for me, her devotion, intuition and uncommon good sense add balance and sanity to an otherwise crazed schedule and life.

And after everyone else has been mentioned there is my two-year old daughter, Mia, for whom this book is really being written. Mia shows me everyday that being smart is not about what you have learned or how much you already know. It is about how much you can learn and how much you want to know. For the hours that this book has taken me from her I can only hope in return that it helps, in some slight way, to create a world that is more deserving of her and the countless smart children who will someday inhabit tomorrow's Smart Companies.

PART I

WHAT IS A SMART COMPANY?

INTRODUCTION

Two hundred years in the making, the Industrial Revolution is being turned on its head. Concepts that were central to the formation of organizations, employment, and work itself are being challenged as a new breed of Smart Companies and Smart Tools are making possible unparalleled advances in their ability to innovate, compete, and connect with the customer.

Describing these Smart Companies is easier to do by describing what they are *not*. The Smart Company is not static. It is not bureaucratized. It is not shackled by the credo "But this is the way we've always done it." It is not afraid, or disdainful of, change—constant change. Most important it is not driven by a monomaniacal vision and the toil of countless workers. Instead, it is driven by the democratic access to new technologies and tools throughout the organization.

In short, a Smart Company stands in sharp contrast to the types of organizations that grew out of the Industrial Revolution and are with us today.

The organizing principle of the Smart Company is that the work, and the tools needed to do that work, are moved to the workers—wherever they are. Smart Companies understand the distinction between human aptitude and technology value. They recognize that technology can be used to support and liberate people, freeing them up to use their creativity, energy, and initiative to the fullest. Technology is employed not for its own sake, but as an *instrumentality* in maximizing the human potential of the organization.

Simply put, in Smart Companies *everything revolves around the people.*

This is not a revolutionary concept when applied on a small scale, but when considered in the context of today's information-based economy and society it directly challenges what is perhaps the most salient feature of modern capitalism and the cornerstone of industrialism: the growth of the centralized enterprise, in which workers *came* to the work.

Since the first water-driven looms of the late eighteenth century, workers have trooped off to foundries, mills, mines, and offices. The idea of the factory—often an empire unto itself—looms large in the collective consciousness in the history of the United States and the nations of Western (and later Eastern) Europe. This industrial ethos was captured perfectly in the 1936 film *Modern Times.* Who can forget the image of the hapless Charlie Chaplin tightening bolts on a large flywheel? Along with his fellow workers, Chaplin had become a cog in the machine.

A number of factors made this possible. The development of interchangeable parts by Eli Whitney and other inventors in the late 1700s and early 1800s meant that goods both large and small could be produced with benchmark levels of consistency and quality. James Watt's steam engine, first put to use in the 1760s pumping water out of mine shafts, was joined by the electric motor and the internal combustion engine.

In a very real sense, these developments paved the way for Henry Ford. Ford understood the movement of work and used it to its fullest. He did not create new technology, or even radically change existing technologies. Rather, Ford's genius lay in the simple application of existing tools and methods in novel ways.

Ford's innovation was not mass production, nor the principle of interchangeable parts. Both had been in use for at least 100 years before the invention of the Tin Lizzie. In fact, Ford did not even *create* the assembly line. While many historians believe that Ford conceived of the assembly line after observing the practice in slaughterhouses of hanging carcasses on hooks and slings to move them through the meatpacking process, Ransom Eli Olds and the Cadillac Motor Company were already using complex interchangeable parts and assembly lines in their manufacturing processes.

Ford's innovation was so simple as to be overlooked even in most history books. His assembly lines, like the meatpacking plant lines, *moved*—work was transported to the worker, not the other way around.

Most Smart Tools are just as straightforward in their application of existing technologies. It is their obviousness—with the benefit of hindsight—that makes them so popular and yet so difficult to predict. After all, if it were that simple, why wouldn't someone else already have done it? That is certainly what mainframe users were saying in the late 1970s about the PC when it began to emerge as an industry force. Or, for that matter, what the same users are saying two decades later when the World Wide Web takes over their desktops and catches even technology monoliths like Microsoft by surprise. Smart Companies do not create Smart Tools; they simply apply them in innovative ways.

That is precisely what Ford did as he perfected the assembly line concept—to extreme measures. For example, he realized that by manipulating the speed of the line and the rate at which work moved, he could manipulate the output of workers. But Ford's real genius lay in his conception of work itself. As the writer E.L. Doctorow noted about Ford:

> He'd conceived the idea of breaking down the work operations in the assembly of an automobile to their simplest steps, so that any fool could perform them....Thus, the worker's mental capacity would not be taxed. The man who puts in a bolt does not put on the nut.[1]

From these principles, which today strike us as archaic, Ford established the final proposition of the theory of industrial manufacture—not only that the parts of the finished product be interchangeable, but that the men who build the products be themselves interchangeable parts.

Ford began to implement the assembly line system in the spring of 1913. The first component to be manufactured on the line was the magneto coil assembly. Before this, a single worker assembled a magneto from start to finish, a process that took 20 minutes. A good employee could produce 35 or 40 units per day. Ford divided the process into 29 discrete steps, to be performed by 29 different workers, and time for producing a magneto fell to 13 minutes.[2]

Ford then extended the concept to the assembly of motors and transmissions. The first *moving* assembly line was installed in 1914. Where assembly of a car took 728 hours of one man's work (43,680 minutes) several years before, the new system allowed a Model T to be assembled in just 93 minutes.[3]

The efficiency of Ford's system was undeniable. But, as we shall see, this concept of divorcing the worker from the totality of the product or process is the very opposite of one of the seven crucial traits for a Smart Company: *process intimacy*. A worker in the door panel division of Ford's River Rouge factory would have known nothing about the way in which those doors were attached to the chassis; that was the job of another worker "down the line."

Today, a worker in a Smart Company must know something about *all* aspects of the company's products or services. Clearly, it is not possible for a person to know everything down to the smallest detail, but in an environment in which job titles and organizational boundaries are fluid, and the competition is fierce, the average worker's baseline of knowledge must be high. Stated another way, an organization full of people who say "Sorry, that's not my department, you'll have to talk to…" or "That's not in my job description" clearly hasn't gotten the message.

Hard on the heels of Ford's early developments, Frederick Winslow Taylor developed scientific management principles for industrial work. He attempted to create near-perfect harmony between workers and their tasks. Soon, the science of "time-motion study" had employers taking motion pictures and stop-action photographs of their workers to determine exactly how many strokes of a hammer it should take to place a nail, or how many twists of a wrench were needed to join two parts of a widget. Absolute efficiency—not a single wasted moment or movement—was the goal.

Compiling their massive study of *Middletown* (in reality, Muncie, Indiana), sociologists Robert S. Lynd and Helen Merrell Lynd observed in 1929 that the "cog-in-the-machine" philosophy had strongly taken root and supplanted "the cunning hand of the master craftsman." The most salient feature of Middletown's economy was the "batteries of tireless iron men doing narrowly specialized things over and over." The modern technological innovations were "merely 'operated' or 'tended' in their orderly clangorous repetitive processes by the human worker.[4]

It was no surprise, then, for the Lynds to find that for most workers in Middletown, "the amount of robust satisfaction they derive from the actual performance of their specific jobs seems, at best, to be slight."[5] As we will see, this is the precise opposite of the Smart Company, where the *prosperity* of the worker is of primary importance.

By the middle of the twentieth century, American business culture was marked by very high levels of bureaucratization, organizational segmentation, and impersonalized—indeed, *de*personalized —environments. Hordes of writers and social scientists warned that the average worker, whether blue- or white-collar, felt trapped in stultifying jobs, toiling away only because there were bills to pay and mortgages to be met. Books chronicling this alienation, especially William Allan Whyte's *The Organization Man* and Sloan Wilson's *The Man in the Gray Flannel Suit,* were bestsellers in the 1950s.

But a handful of analysts and management theorists was beginning to point out what was wrong, and steps that could be taken to reverse the decline. One of the first people to analyze the dysfunction prevalent in American businesses was the M.I.T. professor Douglas McGregor. In the 1950s and early 1960s, he observed that most organizations simply did not *motivate* employees; rather, workers were "kept in line" with elaborate systems of punishments and rewards, and there was little or no effort to unleash creativity and individual thinking.[6]

The high-water mark of this trend was perhaps the Ford Motor Company of the 1950s, when Robert McNamara was the president. Until the late 1940s, when Henry Ford's grandson, Henry Ford II, took over the reins, the company was in a shambles. The senior Ford had stubbornly continued to produce the Model T until 1927. Its replacement, the Model A, was not well received. And Ford kept workers in line through the use of intimidation and strikebreakers, courtesy of the company's "Sociology Department" and its thuggish chief, Harry Bennett.

What Henry Ford II found upon assuming the top post was a company with ossified management structures and obsolete products that reflected absolutely no awareness of the changing market ("You can have any color you want as long as it's black").

And as Detroit went, so went American manufacturing. American businesses reigned supreme in the decades following the Second World War for the simple reason that there was no competition. But by the 1970s, American cars were perceived as shoddy and unreliable, and sales of foreign cars soared. The steel mills of the Midwest began to lose market share to upstart competitors from South Korea and Japan. In the consumer market, people began to realize that the quality of U.S. goods was usually sacrificed to cost control. With planned obsolescence and advertising imagery so firmly embedded in the national culture, we came to expect that the things we bought would fall apart, wear out, or quickly become unfashionable.

At the same time, the nations of Europe—and especially Asia—had recovered from their total devastation and were becoming important players on the world market. More important, many of the new enterprises were doing things *differently*. Their employees seemed more involved in planning *how* to do their jobs; management and labor worked together; and an obsession with quality went beyond sloganeering. Americans began to hear stories of Japanese workers gathering before the workday to exercise and sing company songs.

The market share held by American companies in many industries—steel, electronics, automobiles, shipbuilding, to name but a few—was shrinking. Moreover, there was a sense that most companies just didn't *work;* they were inefficient, fragmented, and resistant to new ideas.

Perhaps the epitome of this trend was the decline in the quality of American cars. Certain companies became a joke, their brands used to denote popularly accepted acronyms of disdain. Ford, it was joked, stood for *F*ix *O*r *R*epair *D*aily. Chrysler, on the verge of collapse, sought a federal bailout. People began to turn to Japanese companies for well-made and reliable cars. Where once a foreign car (save for a European sports car, perhaps) was considered an odd sight, by the 1980s it was quite possible to see many more Toyotas, Nissans, and Hondas in an average parking lot than Fords, Chryslers, and Buicks.

What had started as a very smart way to run a company soon became the ball and chain of American industry.

Then, in 1982, two relatively unknown management consultants, Thomas J. Peters and Robert H. Waterman, Jr., published *In Search of Excellence: Lessons from America's Best-Run Companies,* which pointed out that those organizations thriving in a brutally competitive environment seemed to share a set of common values and practices, despite their wide variations in size, mission, product, and customer base.

In 1992 Michael Hammer and James Champy published *Reengineering the Corporation,* their manifesto for a reengineering revolution. The crisis was so desperate that only "obliteration" seemed an adequate antidote for the American corporation, according to Hammer and Champy. They were right, but they provided only the wake-up call. So much of this was dogma and charismatic "vision-building." CEOs and stockholders bought into the charisma, and short-term gains resulted as quality and then reengineering movements raced through corporations and hatchets came down en masse on the front office workers. But the pathology of industrialization remained. Not because people lacked the desire to change, but rather because the *tools* for effecting changes were still embryonic. The technology, communications, and methods of the industrial era continued to loom large over corporate infrastructure and culture.

From this very brief—and admittedly selective—history of the evolution of the modern, industrial business environment, we can now turn to the structure of the Smart Company, and the tools that make it smart.

END NOTES

1 Doctorow, E.L., *Ragtime* (New York: Bantam Books, 1976), pp. 154–155.

2 Halberstam, David, *The Reckoning* (New York: Avon Books, 1987), p. 73.

3 Ibid.

4 Lynd, Robert S. and Helen M., *Middletown* (New York: Harcourt, Brace & World, 1929), pp. 39–40.

5   Ibid., p. 73.

6   Heil, Gary, Parker, Tom, and Stephens, Deborah, *One Size Fits One: Building Relationships One Customer and One Employee at a Time* (New York: Van Nostrand Reinhold, 1997), pp. 194–195.

CHAPTER 1

THE SEVEN TRAITS OF THE SMART COMPANY

Smart Companies differ in many ways: by industry, size, age, and life-cycle, but they are always alike in two ways:

- their seven most basic traits;
- their organizational structure.

In this chapter we will first look at the seven traits exhibited by Smart Companies and then discuss the new *perpetual* structure, supported by these traits, that Smart Companies are adopting.

The seven traits of the Smart Company are building blocks for any organization that intends to use the tools and methods we will talk about in this book. They are both technology-based and cultural, but all are ultimately supported by specific Smart Tools, which are discussed in later chapters.

All of these traits focus on increasing communication and collaboration between people and processes. Only through increased intimacy and understanding of the processes that we inhabit can Smart Tools help us to dramatically improve our work environments.

9

The seven Smart Company traits are:

1. An *integrated rhythm of work independent of organizational structure.*

2. Fostering a high degree of *process intimacy* among employees.

3. The use of *asynchronous communications* to bridge time and geography.

4. Applying technology to *leverage, rather than eliminate,* people.

5. A strong emphasis on *return on time* as the principal success metric.

6. An extended enterprise that encourages *nontraditional employment.*

7. Heavy technology investment in *"Touch Point" both inside and outside the organization.*

By its very definition, there can be no one-size-fits-all description of a Smart Company. What is important—essential, really—is to keep in mind another concept discussed in the introduction: that each organization is a unique entity with specific and often shifting interrelationships among its employees, the technologies it utilizes, and the method by which it adapts to meet change and growth.

Thus, it would be folly to assume that *all* Smart Companies *always* display *all* of the seven traits discussed in this chapter at any given time. Nor will the traits that Smart Companies do possess necessarily be in equal proportion. A small retail business, serving customers in a small or well-defined geographic area might not stress asynchronous communication as much as it does process intimacy. By comparison, a multioffice or multinational company will, by nature, need to rely more on asynchronous communication, and it may well be possible that the across-the-board level of process intimacy displayed by its employees is lower. Put simply, the mom-and-pop grocery store and General Motors have very different needs, and will exhibit very different traits.

The order in which the seven traits are listed is designed to spur the method of thinking that Smart Companies requires. For example, consider how the seven traits work in harmony:

It is only in an organization in which there is an integrated rhythm of work (Trait 1) where employees have the organizational—and emotional—freedom to become intimate with processes and products (Trait 2). An organization where people and processes are in a dynamic state needs convenient and asynchronous communication (Trait 3).

Once the intelligence, enthusiasm, and potential of employees in an integrated business environment is recognized, human capital can be maximized by using technology (Trait 4) to further blur boundaries, eliminate boring and repetitive tasks, and explore new avenues of opportunity. When an organization grows comfortable with the process of becoming a Smart Company, it can begin to take empirical measurements of its efforts, using return on time as a principal success metric (Trait 5).

This can lead to an acceleration of flexible management and job structures (Trait 6), as the organization adjusts its internal operations to meet its goals. Finally, an organization well on its way to becoming a Smart Company will be able to identify its touch points, both within and without, and will invest in the technology (Trait 7) to facilitate communication, collaboration, and cooperation.

With this in mind, consider each of the seven traits discussed below as "jumping-off" points for an extended analysis of your organization and how it functions. And while each trait is discussed separately, remember that there is a gestalt at work: the traits interact with one another, and what is ultimately created is greater than the sum of its parts.

TRAIT 1: AN INTEGRATED RHYTHM OF WORK

The most profound effect of all of the structural changes that have occurred within organizations is on the employees and the *rhythm of work* both inside and outside the workplace. We have become so much better at transferring work to any location than we have been in coordinating its performance. Virtual workplaces infiltrate our lives at all times and places, often wreaking virtual havoc. *Smart companies invest heavily in tools that ease this burden by helping employees control and manage their work, in the face of ever-increasing and portable work.*

It wasn't that long ago when we associated distinct places and times for working, family life, and personal leisure. An eight-hour workday was the norm Monday through Friday. Evenings and weekends were "off limits" for work; they were times for family and home life, and leisure fell somewhere in between.

As our society and its technologies have changed, however, the lines of demarcation among these three areas have become increasingly more vague.

For better or worse, our work lives and our personal lives are entwined through electronic connections, telecommunications, and networks. Many employers expect—or even mandate—that their employees' work will be boundaryless. For example, one large East Coast law firm requires, in the employment contract, that attorneys be available around the clock and carry a modem-enabled laptop, cell phone, and pager at all times outside of the office.

Vacation? What's that? A change of scenery? Alvin Toffler originally noted that technology would allow us to work "anyplace, anytime." If there is a phone line nearby, work awaits.

Amid all this, we hear in the hallways of global corporations the familiar themes of virtual enterprises and a new workforce of free agents. Yet all of these connections do little to add quality or even productivity to the enterprise we work for if there is not a mechanism by which to coordinate the myriad tentacles in such a way that they can become part of a sane work ethic.

So how can the demands on workers in a personal enterprise be balanced with more traditional concerns of family and private life? Connections to work can become a maddening treadmill if they are not managed properly. There's a mordant quip that expresses the problem: The good news is that companies are constantly creating new jobs; the bad news is that these new jobs are just being piled up on top of the old jobs, already stacked two and three deep for most workers.

The problem is simply that managing the priorities of ever-increasing workloads is becoming more and more difficult. Our desktops lie under a deluge of information. We are our own administrators, support staff, managers, and workers. With ten million fewer secretaries since 1989 in the U.S. workforce alone, it's easy to see how this is a problem gaining momentum. At the same time, companies are requiring their workers to wear multiple hats and change them frequently with ease.

Is this a technology problem, you ask? It seems to be more a problem for the social rather than the computer scientists. The problem is simply that managing the priorities of ever-increasing workloads has become the property of nearly every professional. Technology is, in fact, the only way to solve the problem that technology has created.

So what can be done? Can Smart Tools help? The answer is yes, through the application of one of the most important Smart Tools: *workflow*. As a discipline, a technology in and of itself, and as a management tool, workflow provides the foundation for far-flung change in the way we work. More important, it allows this change to occur in ways that increase the general quality and rhythm of our lives.

Workflow automates the steps that go into a business process by capturing the rules, routing instructions, and roles required to perform work. Once a workflow is defined, the work progresses automatically from one task to another, avoiding the inherent delays associated with manual workflow.

If we shift our focus from the *delivery* of work to the *coordination* of work, technologies such as workflow may actually make our lives more pleasant by proving that work is best accomplished when it is integrated intimately with our lives.

If all of this sounds a bit too Orwellian for your taste, consider how basic technologies like the fax machine, cellular technology, pagers, and e-mail have already altered the rhythm of your life. Like it or not, you are accessible. The question is not how to break away, but rather how to better integrate and manage the accessibility. Smart Companies take care to acknowledge this and create environments that provide tools for coordination and work management.

TRAIT 2: A HIGH DEGREE OF PROCESS INTIMACY

One of the most basic problems in today's highly specialized workforces is that of process intimacy. It's actually better phrased as a *lack* of intimacy. Simply put, increasing task specialization in complex organizations tends to isolate workers from one another, and one's knowledge of what others in the organization actually do is scant, or perhaps even nonexistent. Where once the isolation was structural (i.e., built into the organizational structure of the workplace), today it is more likely that space, distance, and time are the factors that work against process intimacy.

Henry Ford designed a system in which each worker on the assembly line was concerned only with his or her highly specific, highly routinized task. It worked—but with high social costs. But the compartmentalization of job knowledge is fundamentally unsuited to the needs and mission of the Smart Company. In the Smart Company, everyone will know, at least to some degree, what the person in the next office, down the hall, or at another site, actually does within the organization.

For the better part of this century, most large organizations *discouraged* process intimacy. The theories of Ford and Taylor held that a worker need know very little about the production process as a whole. Guidance of the organization and decision making on all matters—even the most minute—were left to a management cadre, which was invariably composed of people who had very little idea of what workers actually *did* in the performance of their jobs. Strict lines of authority and bureaucratization kept the average employee confined within the boundaries of a strict job description or grade. Management and labor were separated not only by class and educational attainment, but by philosophy as well.

THE LEGACY OF McNAMARA AND THE WHIZ KIDS

The high-water mark of this trend was perhaps the Ford Motor Company of the 1950s, when Robert McNamara was head of the Ford division, and later president of the company. McNamara had come to Ford shortly after the end of the Second World War as part of a group known as the "Whiz Kids." These men, with mathematical and scientific backgrounds, had invented systems analysis for the Army Air Corps, and were eager to test their theories in a business setting. Led by Charles "Tex" Thornton (who later went on to found Litton Industries), the group offered its services to the ailing Ford Motor Company, which was then on the brink of collapse. As the writer David Halberstam notes in *The Reckoning,* his study of the postwar American and Japanese automobile industries, this would have profound consequences for Ford, as well as other American car makers, when they later were forced to compete with the Asian automobile juggernaut.[1]

Empiricists to the core, the Whiz Kids believed that an organization—*any* organization, from the military to the smallest local business—could be managed efficiently through the application of statistical control, centralized accounting procedures, and strict adherence to metrics. The "soft" variables—such as employee-management relations, morale, job satisfaction, and reflecting on the organization's mission—were largely, if not totally, ignored, for the simple reason that human emotions cannot be reduced to numbers. Productivity was still very much a matter of speeding up the assembly line.

Most of the Whiz Kids eventually left Ford for other pursuits, but McNamara stayed, rising through the ranks. He was named president in November 1960. Several months later, he was summoned to Washington by President John F. Kennedy to become secretary of defense, which, as we shall see later, had dire consequences for the country. Yet through all of his years at the company, McNamara showed not the slightest interest in overcoming his own personal lack of process intimacy. As Halberstam notes, "He was at once a man who soon knew everything quantifiable about the business and who had absolutely no feel for it."[2] He had grown up in California, not Detroit. After coming to Ford, McNamara did not mix with his industry peers in Grosse Pointe; he pointedly chose to live in the college town of Ann Arbor, 60 miles and a world away.

In the Detroit of the 1950s, Halberstam notes, you were either a "car guy"—with a feel for design, engineering, and the buying public—or you were not. If you were not, you could never understand the emotionally complex and often ineffable aspect of the business.[3] Cars then were more than a simple tool for transportation; they were embodiments of freedom, adventure, sophistication, and sexuality. At General Motors in the 1950s, it was Harley Earl, the chief stylist, who was the most powerful executive, not its president, Harlow Curtice. Alfred Sloan, GM's chairman of the board, imbued Earl with the concept of the dream car and then gave him organizational carte blanche to achieve it.[4]

McNamara, on the other hand, with his fetish for choreographed meetings featuring charts and graphs, cared little about Ford automobiles, how they were made, and whether they were being received well by the buying public. He was interested only in whether "the numbers added up." The chasm between the manufacturing divisions and the enormous management structure was immense. Ford's plant managers took to devising their own procedures for meeting the accounting department's daunting cost criteria while still producing a solid automobile. As Halberstam notes, Ford's products suffered for the simple reason that people from different departments were discouraged from talking to one another.[5]

McNamara's failure to appreciate the nature of the product was highlighted during a meeting convened to investigate production bottlenecks. The paint ovens in Ford's plants were old, outdated, and too small to accommodate larger cars. At a meeting convened to examine the problem, an executive from the manufacturing division explained to McNamara that there was no way to expedite the painting process.

According to Halberstam, McNamara then suggested that a car chassis be built in two parts, painted, and then welded together into one piece. The executive told McNamara that such a plan wouldn't work; the welding could not come after painting, and even if it could, the chassis would be greatly weakened. Yet McNamara insisted that the manufacturing division find a way to speed up the painting. At this point, the executive shouted at McNamara, "The problem with you is that you don't know a goddamn thing about how our cars are actually made!" After the meeting broke up, McNamara turned to the executive's superior and said, "I don't want that man at any more meetings."[6]

McNamara's "by-the-numbers" approach, which left little room to assimilate the *actual* state of a problem, would have tragic consequences a decade later during the war in Vietnam. Field commanders had to ignore, or at least transmogrify, the truth in their combat reports in order to satisfy "body counts," the Pentagon's metric for measuring military success.

And as Detroit went, so went American manufacturing. Competition from manufacturers in Asia and Europe and planned obsolescence at home put U.S. industry in crisis. People complained that the United States was no longer a country that "made things," and those things that were made were not worth buying.

CREATING PROCESS INTIMACY

As we said earlier, fewer organizations now have a structural lack of process intimacy. It's more likely that the problem is caused by space, distance, and time. But the result is the same.

When two people are separated by several days in performing their respective tasks on a particular value chain of activities, the reality is that they are less likely to understand the impact of one another's work than if they were separated by hours or minutes. Why? In a word, *iteration*. The longer it takes to iterate a task, the less likely it is to be iterated. In other words, if it takes you two days to get a response to a question as opposed to two minutes, you are less likely to ask the question. By the same token, you are less likely to try to understand or change a process if you are removed from its components by significant intervals of time.

Smart Companies close the time intervals by eliminating the inherent transfer times in routing information and work from one person to another. But it's useful to note that this is not a problem that can be solved by a communications network alone, no more so than it can be solved by the evolution from paper memos to e-mail. Electrons may travel at the speed of light, but work does not.

If you don't believe that, ask yourself this question: "When did I last read my e-mail?" If it was two hours ago, then you could say that the e-mail messages waiting for you have taken at least that long to get from their sender to you, although the actual message traveled at the speed of light and probably took nanoseconds to be delivered. The same is true for work of any sort being delivered electronically. Part of the problem is that organizations have focused for too long on the delivery of *information* and not on the delivery of *work*. Work, by its definition, is not delivered—it is performed. No matter how fast the information assembly line runs, the work will always end up waiting without the right tools to connect it with the performer of the work.

Smart Companies go beyond networking of information alone by using sophisticated mechanisms to route work and deliver it in the fastest possible period of time. This may include using *roles* to route the work instead of a specific person. In such a case, if one person, who would normally do the work, is not available to act on the work, the workflow will find someone else with similar qualifications to perform it. The key is getting the work done—not just transferring the information. This is often referred to as a *pull* model, as opposed to a *push* model of work.

In the pull model, a manager doesn't have to hunt down the right person to get the work done; instead the workflow manager "goes after the role." For instance, in one large software support organization, the workflow system identifies how incoming support calls are routed to individuals based on predefined skill sets. In another case, a major defense contractor uses workflow to route approvals for proposed contract changes. The workflow is intelligent enough to know that a number of people can fill the role of approver and routes the approval based on availability.

The other effect that roles tend to have on an organization is that of increasing the critical analysis of any process. In the same way that a single role can be filled by a number of people, a single person may have multiple roles, since it is entirely likely that a single person can have multiple skills. As a result, work tends to be distributed across a broader range of individuals within the organization, creating less parochialism and thus avoiding the "this is the way it's done" syndrome that makes so many processes stale.

Ironically, the traditional push model works best for employees who perform relatively poorly and worst for those employees who are most productive and responsive. The reason is simply that work tends to congregate around productive people, creating an incredible imbalance. Knowledge is punishment in this model, since the rewards for work well done are an ever-increasing workload. Pull models tend to distribute work more equitably among all workers defined by a particular role. Additionally, the pull model can be used to create more equitable forms of compensation for workers, as we will see in the case studies discussed later in the book.

Smart Companies believe strongly in this equity and create work environments that recognize it. By doing so they are reaffirming the value of the individual by increasing process involvement, critical analysis, and process intimacy across the organization.

TRAIT 3: ESTABLISHED PATHS FOR ASYNCHRONOUS COMMUNICATION

There are two fundamentally polar means by which humans communicate, synchronous and asynchronous communication.

Standard interpersonal communications occur in a synchronous mode. That is, when two or more people conduct a discussion, they are able to communicate at the same time and possibly (but not necessarily) in the same place. A face-to-face meeting or telephone call are perhaps the most common settings for synchronous communication. A benefit often attributed to synchronous communication is the ability to address issues as they arise without delay.

The explosive growth in global communications technology and software for communication, including the World Wide Web, e-mail, and groupware, has allowed companies to take advantage of asynchronous communication; that is, the ability to communicate serially, without interaction and interruption, thereby bridging the constraints of time and distance.

For centuries, the only form of asynchronous communication was that of the written word or image. The cave paintings of Lascaux, Egyptian steles, and the Dead Sea Scrolls, for example, have communicated ideas and thoughts across social and political chasms spanning thousands of years. The most common form of asynchronous communication in modern times has been the letter: One person writes to another and then waits for a reply. Synchronous communication, on the other hand, has, until very recently in the history of mankind, been limited by the confines of distance; quite literally, how far one's voice could be heard.

A quantum leap in asynchronous communication came in 1844, with the invention of the telegraph. As a result, the speed of asynchronous communication was vastly increased. Moreover, distance became largely irrelevant; as long as wires could connect Site A to Site B, communication could take place. At first, telegraph lines crisscrossed the United States and were a critical factor in the development of railroads.

When the great railroads first established transcontinental lines, one of the most serious problems to be overcome was that of head-on collisions. At that time it was not very cost-effective to put two lines in services for each route, so a single line handled both directions of traffic. Coordinating this before the telegraph presented a serious workflow problem.[7]

Although the telegraph brought us closer to continental synchronous communication, it was still limited by geography and the basic requirement of a telegraph operator who could translate the electronic gibberish. True synchronous communication was still limited by shouting distance.

By 1869, however, much of this had been resolved. With the first transatlantic telegraph cable, linking North America with Great Britain, and the invention of the telephone in 1876, distance became irrelevant to synchronous communication.[8]

Since then, telephony has remained the mainstay of business communication, enhanced by such innovations as satellite transmission and fiber optics. Although aided by common modes of asynchronous communication, including e-mail and voice mail, the process of communication has never achieved the most important aspect of true synchronous communication, which is its connection with the underlying process being communicated. This linkage is a difficult but essential point in understanding the creation of a Smart Company.

In a global context, asynchronous communications are often associated with delays, since each party is waiting for the other before continuing the communication. For example, if a number of people are engaged in a common task using groupware, each communication may require a response from each user. This can be especially problematic if the parties communicating are separated by several time zones. The following example shows the effect this will have on a simple global task involving several communications.

When the Boston office of an organization sends a message to the Hong Kong office at 9:00 A.M. local time (10:00 P.M. Hong Kong time), workers in the Hong Kong office will not receive the message until coming in to work the next day, at 9:00 A.M. local time (8:00 P.M. Boston time). Although staffers in the Hong Kong office may work all day on the task and make significant progress, their counterparts in Boston will not be aware of the progress until the task is complete and they receive a communication from Hong Kong. If Hong Kong sends this message on the day following its initial receipt from Boston, the total delay from Boston's perspective is at least two days. The total task time, however, is only eight hours of the total elapsed business cycle time. That means that the business process is only 16.6% efficient.

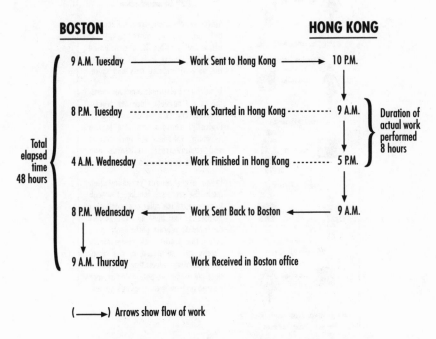

Figure 1-1: Asynchronous Communication

This may seem like an insurmountable problem. After all, Smart Companies cannot alter the laws of time and physics. But they can eliminate the fundamental obstacle in asynchronous communication, the lack of concurrence of human communication. With an automated workflow system, the asynchronous communication can continue even though the people are not working on a synchronized schedule. In the example with Boston and Hong Kong, Boston would be able to communicate with the "task" or the "process" at any time. This is referred to as P2P communication, where the Ps stand for process or person. Thus, there are three types of P2P communication: person to person, person to process, or process to process. In this third type, two information agents, equipped with the rules by which to make a decision, can execute a process-to-process communication and proceed to the next task.

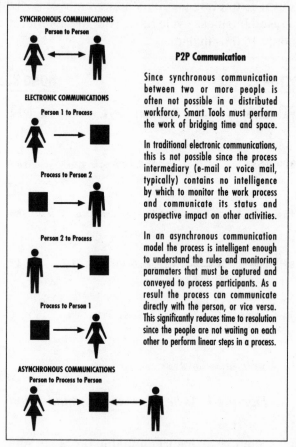

SYNCHRONOUS COMMUNICATIONS
Person to Person

ELECTRONIC COMMUNICATIONS
Person 1 to Process

Process to Person 2

Person 2 to Process

Process to Person 1

ASYNCHRONOUS COMMUNICATIONS
Person to Process to Person

P2P Communication

Since synchronous communication between two or more people is often not possible in a distributed workforce, Smart Tools must perform the work of bridging time and space.

In traditional electronic communications, this is not possible since the process intermediary (e-mail or voice mail, typically) contains no intelligence by which to monitor the work process and communicate its status and prospective impact on other activities.

In an asynchronous communication model the process is intelligent enough to understand the rules and monitoring parameters that must be captured and conveyed to process participants. As a result the process can communicate directly with the person, or vice versa. This significantly reduces time to resolution since the people are not waiting on each other to perform linear steps in a process.

Figure 1-2: P2P Communication

This is a fundamental change in the nature of communication, since a person is no longer necessarily communicating with other people, *but with the process itself.* It should be noted here that "communication" in our definition requires that there be real-time interaction between the two parties. (The parties, in this case, could be any combination of person and process.) Without an automated workflow system, this can only be accomplished if two individuals are both available at the same time. Workflow captures the process in such a way that this communication can continue at any time. This fundamental shift from person to process is one of the most significant aspects of Smart Companies, and similarly one of the most profound advances in global process automation.[9]

TRAIT 4: APPLYING TECHNOLOGY TO LEVERAGE, RATHER THAN ELIMINATE, PEOPLE

Far too often we look to technology as a replacement for people. Although it is clear that there are many tasks in any organization that can be automated, Smart Companies view technology as a method of augmentation to best leverage the people, skills, and products of the enterprise.

The current mania in many industries to focus on head-count reduction is the product of a shortsighted mindset that lacks the creativity to consider how technology can free people and organizations to explore new avenues of opportunity, new products, and increased leverage of their human resource.

Smart Companies do not rank well when compared on the basis of people eliminated by the application of technology. They do, however, win the prize for rate of job obsolescence due to technology. The difference? Job definitions should and will change in Smart Companies as they constantly adapt to competitive markets, and their employees can move into new roles and new jobs as the old ones are left behind.

For instance, at Town and Country Mortgage, profiled below, Smart Tools are being used to augment the roles of mortgage brokers by expanding the traditional banking model to bring service to the customer's location.[10]

CASE STUDY

Town and Country Mortgage: Leveraging the Human Asset Through Innovative Use of Technology

Summary: Process intimacy requires immediacy and accessibility. Town and Country Mortgage delivers both by using workflow to put loan agents and computer-based branch offices in real estate brokers storefronts.

The 1990s have not been kind to the mortgage banking industry. The savings and loan crisis, a recession, and a refinancing binge precipitated an industry shakeout that has driven many players from the field and forced others to consolidate with competitors. Yet even as some in the industry have retrenched, others have grown—seizing new opportunities both in technology and the bank regulatory environment.

Such is the case of Town and Country Mortgage, a Kansas City, Missouri, mortgage brokerage firm that was founded in 1992 and saw its volume of new mortgages go from zero to over $100 million, and from zero loans to 1,200 in less than two years.

Town and Country's strategy was to leverage mortgage lending closer to the customer—by moving loan origination into the real estate agent's office, a proactive business model made possible in 1993 when federal law was changed to allow real estate brokers to originate loans for the first time.

More important, the law approved the use of computers as a means of taking loan applications. Town and Country already had a computer infrastructure. In other words, the basic tools were in place, and Town and Country was smart enough to seize upon them and enter new markets.

To best exploit the opportunities afforded by new law, Town and Country needed an efficient way to set up a "virtual branch" within the real estate agent's office. One problem: The lending office is wherever the mortgage paperwork happens to be located. Unless the paperwork stays with the real estate agents, the best the agents can do is what they already do—send in paperwork and talk to workers in the "real" mortgage office on the phone. Without direct access to the paper, they could not originate loans. Thus, Town and Country faced an age-old problem: how to be in two places at once. It needed to have the paperwork in two places simultaneously—at its headquarters and out at the real estate agency.

Actually, as a broker Town and Country really needed the paperwork in *three* places at once. Brokers do not actually lend money (that is done by a bank or a savings and loan association). Brokers process applications, shop around for the best rate, and then send the application to a financial institution for approval. Thus, the application paperwork had to be accessible to the real estate office, Town and Country's office, *and* the financial institution considering the loan application. And movement of documents among the three locations would have to be immediate.

A complicated task, to be sure, but the goal was immensely attractive—not only could real estate agents have a mortgage broker in their offices, they could also have access to whichever bank offered the best deal to the home buyer. But how was this to be accomplished?

SOLUTION

Unlike some of his competitors, Town and Country's president, Michael Ellis, discarded the notion of simply setting up computer terminals in real estate offices and hooking them into his network. Agents did not want to be bothered with learning a lot of complicated software, nor did they want to be responsible for explaining computer glitches to their customers. Ellis's idea was to put a Town and Country employee *inside the real estate office* along with a PC that could manage the electronic images of the mortgage documents. Those documents could be easily scanned or faxed into the system from anywhere, and they could also be accessed simultaneously from any PC, regardless of physical location.

Besides simplicity, document management also had the advantage of novelty; none of Town and Country's competitors had tried it yet, and Ellis anticipated he would have a head start of at least three years. The technology needed to accomplish the task was already well established. Scanners and fax machines were reliable and inexpensive. So were the optical and magnetic media required to store the massive amounts of data that digital images produce. The networks necessary to tie his operation together would also not be difficult or expensive to install. The critical piece was how to manage all those digital images once he had them in his network.

Ellis chose workflow software to address this part of the equation. Workflow guides the mortgage through the sometimes arduous approval process. "The workflow aspect is the real 'value added' of the whole system," notes Ellis. "It alerts the user to the fact that key documents are missing or incomplete and routes the application to the right person so that these gaps can be filled in."

With transfer time virtually eliminated Town and Country cut about three weeks out of the loan approval cycle. Customers now get an answer in five to seven business days, as compared to an industry average of 25 days. That means that there is much less chance the home buyer will see his or her mortgage rate rise while waiting for the application to be approved. It also leaves less time for a competitor to undercut Town and Country with a lower bid.

Currently, Town and Country has ten loan originators covering about two dozen real estate offices in the Kansas City area. These originators are supported back at headquarters by two "loan processors" who ensure that applications are properly assembled, completed, and forwarded to the correct lender. Ellis notes, "Before [workflow], the ratio of originators to processors was 2.5 to 1. Now it is 5 to 1."

Yet Town and Country is adding—not laying off—staff. "With the rest of the industry failing, we've developed a product and a business concept that's growing," says Ellis. "We're hiring the best people in the industry away from our own competition because we're expanding. We put a person in an office with people to sell to—a group of home buyers and agents who are excited about his being there. That's unusual in an in-

dustry where people tend to compete against the other people
they work with."

TRAIT 5: A STRONG EMPHASIS ON RETURN-ON-TIME AS THE PRINCIPAL SUCCESS METRIC

Everyone talks about return on investment; Smart Companies talk
about return-on-time. Ultimately, all costs hinge on time. One way to
look at a business process is to consider how much value is being
returned for a given interval of time invested. (This concept is discussed in greater detail in Part II, which covers time-based analysis.) In the case of an individual, that time is measured in a literal
sense—the number of heartbeats invested. Return-on-time is increased by creating a continuous process. In other words, if the
process is spread out over time and the work performed in incre-
ments, there is more time spent waiting, queuing, and correcting
work.

A vivid example may be seen in the approval cycle of a large Fortune 50 manufacturing company. Vouchers for parts ordered by
shop-floor machinists required approval by the accounting department. In a typically regimented fashion, accounting would periodically review orders on a batch basis—two times per week—then
send the order to the originator for approval. Since machinists were
busy working other machines during the day, the orders vetted by
accounting were often delayed by at least another day, since the
machinists generally would go through their in boxes only at the
end of each day. In total, as many as four days would go by for a single approval iteration. In many cases, more than one iteration was
required, leading to a worst case scenario of two weeks to get approval for a part.

When the organization installed an automated workflow system,
accounting could immediately route the approval request to the
shop floor, where machinists could periodically check any one of
several networked computers during the day. The approvals were
now integrated with the work, rather than impeding it.

Return-on-time is a measure of how well an organization balances
its investments in Smart Tools with its critical success factors. If fill-

ing customer orders in less than 24 hours is essential for success in your particular industry, then your investment in timely order fulfillment is easy to assess. This may be called the "escape velocity question." Escape velocity is the speed which any object must attain in order to escape gravitational pull and enter earth's orbit. A slightly lesser speed simply will not work. In the same light, there are many success factors that are measured in these terms since no less than a specific measure will attain customer satisfaction, or competitive parity. The amount invested has nothing to do with success if the particular success factor is not attained.

In other words, no matter how much you invest, you will have failed if the fulfillment cannot be accomplished in 24 hours. It's all or nothing—25.5 hours, 28 hours, or 36 hours are all unacceptable. No matter what the investment, it has been largely wasted.

In large part the challenge of changing job definitions without eliminating people, or better yet while creating new positions, is a function of how quickly a company can innovate. And innovation relies primarily on a companies Return on Time. Return on Time measures the speed of innovation. Most important it is a measure that almost always takes precedence over the cost of innovation.

Although that sounds odd at first, it makes good sense when you consider the cost of not innovating—obsolescence. Preemptive innovation which invests heavily in fast response to market shifts and new markets will always establish a dominant position during a market's cycle.

Unfortunately most of us are accustomed to market cycles that were measured in decades. When market cycles are measured in these time frames sustained investment and development to extend and protract product life cycles could easily outperform the demans of the market for change.

However in short market introduction and growth cycles, which are today becoming the norm, fast and repeated investments in innovation are necessary to meet the market and outpace competitors.

This sort of innovation requires moving closer to the customer in order to increase the organizations understanding and awareness of the market's changing needs. But moving closer is not just a marketing metaphor. In a literal sense this means actually moving workers out of traditional office environments and into the market, shoulder to shoulder with the customer. Although not a novel proposition for certain functions such as sales, the problem in moving workers out to the customers often lies in moving the work with them. This can be especially challenging when the work involves access to extensive computer-based tools and information.

Clearly, networking and low cost portable computing have made this easier but also required is a fair degree of change in attitude about what is an inside job versus and outside job. In a sense, Smart Tools ultimately make every job as likely for being outside of the company. And by doing so accomplish two objectives: they increase customer intimacy and immediacy; they create new jobs as the number of opportunities to do business with customers increases.

CASE HISTORY

How 360° Communications Uses Smart Tools to Set the Benchmark for Cellular Service[11]

Summary: Return-on-time is often best measured by customers. In the case of 360° Communications, a provider of cellular telephone services, customers had set what seemed to be an unreasonable benchmark for responsiveness that the company had to meet in order to succeed. 360° Communications used Smart Tools to meet and exceed expectations.

To retain its leadership position as the fastest growing cellular carrier in the United States, 360° Communications (formerly Sprint Cellular) must go where the customers are. This means using a network of independent dealers to reach potential customers at thirty processing centers located in malls, department stores, appliance stores, auto shops, and a variety of other retail outlets throughout the country.

These dealers are the *touch point* between customers and 360° Communications. The fact that the dealers are physically removed from the service provider should make no difference to new customers. That's especially true if one considers the impulse nature of mall and retail shoppers. Once a prospective customer has decided to apply for service, the worst thing that can happen is any sort of delay in satisfying that impulse.

To close a new deal, the independent dealer had to fax a signed customer service agreement to 360° Communications' headquarters for processing. Since one-third of new accounts required additional back-and-forth faxing of deposit agreements or service plan information, the delays represented a significant amount of lost business opportunity. With the increasing popularity in cellular telephone service in some regions of the country, 360° Communications procedures were being taxed to the limit. Inbound fax traffic at the company headquarters jumped by as much as 70% in a single year. Additional fax machines did little to alleviate the backlog of service agreements waiting to be processed. Each application had to be reviewed and the new account data entered into an IBM mainframe computer. The cycle time to activate a new account was unacceptably long, taking as long as twenty-four hours or more. After signing up, new customers returned to the service centers to pick up their phones, but couldn't make calls until hours afterwards—it was like giving a child a Christmas toy, but not including the necessary batteries.

While it may seem unreasonable that a wait of hours or a few days would be so intolerable, that intolerance is dictated by the competitive alternatives available. 360° Communications realized that it had to either set the bar for cellular service or be forced to jump over someone else's benchmark.

Customers were becoming impatient. "The first seventy-two hours of service is critical to customer satisfaction," says Jeff De La Mar, 360° Communication's information technology manager. "New customers want to use their phones immediately. We need a cycle time of thirty minutes or less." De La Mar understood that simply adding staff wouldn't solve the problem. The cellular industry's explosive growth demanded a smarter solution.

SOLUTION

Now, 360° Communications' incoming service agreements are given an account number, and job folders are automatically created for new accounts, forming an inbound work queue for approval and service activation. New service applications automatically appear on a service representative's data entry screen. At the same time, customer service agreements are automatically archived. The manual and mundane tasks of fax delivery and paper shuffling, once a significant impediment to new growth and employee creativity, have now been eliminated.

Customer service representatives can retrieve an archived service agreement in less than ten seconds. If a new account requires special forms or agreements, those files are faxed to the dealer directly from the customer service representative's computer desktop.

The key in all of this is that the workflow, like all Smart Tools, lets the customer service representatives stay at their desks and telephones and do what they do best—provide service and support. Now, when the telephone rings, customer inquiries are answered more efficiently, because there are more customer service representatives available. It's important to note that the CSRs are "available." Smart Tools increase the *availability and the accessibility of people,* without the need to add more staff.

The most important benefit to 360° Communications is, of course, the competitive advantage. The company is now able to significantly differentiate itself from the other cellular providers through better, faster customer service—the number one concern of all cellular customers (and perhaps *all* customers). "Access for Everybody" is De La Mar's motto.

TRAIT 6: FLEXIBLE MANAGEMENT AND JOB STRUCTURES IN AN EXTENDED ENTERPRISE

The evolution of virtual workgroups has been fueled by at least three major trends: the increased availability of floating consultants (that is, white-collar workers who do not work in the confines of traditional office environments); inexpensive portable and home-office computing; and fast, reliable communications. As a result, more and more companies are opting for nontraditional work environments, which includes a significant number of workers outside of the corporate office. Smart Companies have been especially quick to embrace the opportunity presented by these flexible structures.

Although telecommuting or work-by-wire, have quickly caught on, they are fraught with potential coordination and collaboration problems such as the lack of immediacy in communication, which are causing Smart Companies to look at ways to minimize the technology investment in remote setups while still realizing many of the benefits of an extended workforce. These are solutions that beg for Smart Tools. Companies that master the power of a remote workforce are not simply using work-by-wire, however. In many cases, the key is using core personnel in the most effective way, while simultaneously also relying on nontraditional workers to shoulder much of the responsibility for certain core functions. A prime example is NordicTrack, a leading manufacturer of home health and fitness equipment.[12]

CASE STUDY

NordicTrack: The World Is Its R and D Lab

Summary: Using an extended enterprise, NordicTrack is able to deploy one of the largest R and D networks in the home health and fitness equipment industry with almost no overhead.

NordicTrack, based in Minneapolis, Minnesota, is undoubtedly one of the most successful and visible makers of health and fitness equipment. Its flagship cross-country ski machine is known worldwide. Incredibly, of the thirty-three new fitness products introduced in 1993, NordicTrack developed all but five. Yet, surprisingly, this remarkable success counters the fact that the company doesn't even have an internal R and D department!

In a dramatic example of the virtual enterprise in action, NordicTrack's new product innovations stem primarily from an ever-growing network of independent inventors. Amazingly, the company solicits these inventors through classified ads in magazines such as *Popular Science* and *Design News*.

As a result of its unique R and D method, NordicTrack receives about one hundred invention submissions a week, ranging from sketches on cocktail napkins to complete computer-aided design (CAD) files and multimedia presentations. According to Wes Cutter, NordicTrack's vice president of product planning. "The inventions we get are just as diverse, spanning everything from pogo stick–driven bicycles and perpetual motion machines to ideas that resulted in some of our most successful products, like the Flex Gold isokinetic strength training system, and the downhill skier machine."

To support its growing inventors' network (and to ensure that a good idea doesn't get lost under a mountain of unprocessed submissions), NordicTrack established a policy to review and respond to every inventor within ten days. But with its existing manual procedures, achieving this ten-day response time would have required legions of additional staff just to manage and route all the paperwork. "Our only solution was to automate the business processes in our product development group," notes Dave Janiszewski, manager of office automation services at NordicTrack.

SOLUTION

To this end, NordicTrack used an innovative application of Smart Tools using workflow technology. Only a handful of product-planning staff is needed to review and respond to the thousands of new invention ideas that flow into NordicTrack each year.

All inventors' submissions are scanned into an electronic imaging system (which also imports electronically submitted documents, such as CAD drawings and multimedia presentations) and are quickly routed between the key product-planning personnel on an ad hoc basis. These "decision makers" can instantly retrieve all the relevant documentation on a particular invention—including digitized images of the inventor's design, drawings, photographs, product submission forms, the inventor's curriculum vitae, legal documents, patent information, and even dictated comments—all of which are stored in an electronic "folder."

Each person "in the loop" has one day to review all the new folders routed to his or her electronic in box; if it sits there any longer, the system automatically sends an alert to take action, or the folder will be automatically routed to an alternate person. The decision makers can mark up the documents with electronic pen (or mouse) and typewritten annotations; add printed, faxed, and dictated comments; and do just about anything else that they used to do manually.

Potentially promising ideas are routed deeper into the product-planning group for more in-depth evaluation, debate, engineering, and cost analysis. All of these functions are done in the same workflow system. If a design is accepted, all ensuing documentation—such as patent, contracts, and correspondence—are also stored in the workflow system.

If a submission is rejected, it is routed to an administrator who will respond to the inventor with a gracious letter. It's important to note that the workflow system does not automatically generate a generic rejection letter. Remember, the premise is that Smart Tools do not replace the human value of an organization, they augment them. And rejecting someone's dream idea is certainly a *human* issue to be handled with care and tact.

The bottom line? According to Janiszewski, "People in an or-

THE SEVEN TRAITS OF THE SMART COMPANY 35

ganization such as ours seldom notice the technological underpinnings that make their work possible." As with all Smart Companies, NordicTrack uses its technology to support its people by making the technology a natural, almost invisible, part of their work.

TRAIT 7: TECHNOLOGY INVESTMENT IN ORGANIZATIONAL TOUCH POINTS

There seem to be limitless possibilities in any organization for the application of technology. A frequent question asked by many companies is, "Where to begin?" Smart Companies typically pick from three priority areas: interactions with customers, interactions with suppliers, and interactions with employees. These are referred to as a company's *touch points,* since they involve the interface between the organizational structure and a person or persons.

Each touch point represents a significant area of potential process or quality improvement, and competitive advantage. Most importantly, touch points represent areas where human interaction is often at its most intense.

Touch points can be regarded as the periphery of an enterprise's central nervous system. As in human anatomy, it is the extremities that define the efficiency of our interaction with the world around us. Dexterity, mobility, and adaptability depend primarily on the nimbleness of our peripheral nervous system; fingers, toes, hands, feet, arms, and legs define how well we can react to events around us. Granted, the genesis of all reaction is in the brain, but actions are not expressed there; the brain sends messages to the appropriate extremity.

In this same way an enterprise may have outstanding strategies, plans, and tactics, but they must be *enabled* through actions taken to satisfy customers, educate and leverage workers, and negotiate trade with suppliers.

If the fundamental premise of Smart Tools is the liberation of human potential and their application to the areas of greatest value, then Smart Tools must increase *human* interaction at these touch points while simultaneously streamlining the tiresome and repetitive tasks that otherwise consume employees' time and energy.

Even a slight application of the right technology in these areas can have extraordinary impact on a company's processes.

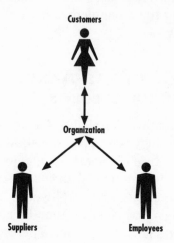

Figure 1-3: Application of Smart Tools to Touch Points Within and Without the Organization

Smart Tools are most often applied to the areas within an organization that can most significantly reduce the distance, in time, between the organization and its three key touch points: customer, suppliers, and employees. The ultimate purpose of a Smart Company is to constantly work toward moving work and work product (service, hard goods, in-process goods) between these three touch points in the most expeditious way.

It could be argued the most important touch point is that of company/customer, and this often is reduced to the contact between a customer and a customer service representative. But what does a company do if the customer service staff turnover is high and training opportunities are minimal? It's easy to take an academic stance and say that it simply needs to retain employees in their particular posts. But the truth is, many, if not most, customer service jobs are stepping stones to higher positions.

In addition, customer service has always been a difficult position because the accolades are often nonexistent. When a customer is happy, he or she rarely sings the praises of the customer service department; it is when the customer is irate that customer service will first hear about what is on the customer's mind. Creating an environment that both rewards and recognizes customer service, while also facing the reality of staff turnover, is a momentous challenge. The solution has to combine Smart Tools and smart management. An example is Momentum Life's Customer Service application.

CASE STUDY

Momentum Life Uses Smart Tools to Achieve Peak Customer Service*

Summary: At Momentum Life, an insurance company based in South Africa, customer service was becoming an area of increasing concern to management. More than 70% of the employees in the customer service department had fewer than twelve months of service experience.

Soon after acquiring a large company called Lifegro in 1989, Momentum Life realized that the merged business' existing systems could no longer support any of the products. In addition, the staff was far from being ideally suited to the commercial challenges facing the newly formed company.

These inherent problems were further exacerbated by the findings of an industry-wide survey that identified other widely held perceptions and customer grievances about the insurance industry. The survey indicated that:

- Customers experienced no continuity when communicating with service representatives. When attempting to resolve an issue, customers prefer to speak with the representative they first spoke to regarding the issue.

- Service was both inadequate and inappropriate for customer needs.

---

* Case study courtesy DST, Inc.

- Promises regarding responses were not being met, and representatives were unable to adequately track correspondence and find the appropriate representatives to solve issues.

- Turnaround time on customer requests was too long.

- Senior management was spending up to 80% of its time fighting fires, instead of taking a proactive role in improving processes.

Correcting all of these problems was one side of the equation. The other was motivating the customer support staff.

SOLUTION

Momentum Life realized that solving both sides of the equation required Smart Tools that would achieve at least three objectives: (1) allow the customer service department to focus on the customer contact; (2) allow management to focus on process improvement; and (3) involve management in an intimate understanding of the successes and failings of customer service representatives.

The solution Momentum Life chose was a controversial one that has garnered much attention among work management thinkers.

Momentum Life is using a workflow application that routes, monitors, and audits work and performance. Customer service representatives receive work and all of the customer information at their desktops, what may be termed point-of-access computing. The work is delivered to each representative based on preconfigured rules which maintain continuity between customer and selected representatives. On its face, this sounds neutral. But the controversy set in when that work was monitored and quality tested.

Supervisors review work performance in two ways. First, a

preset frequency interval is established, which determines how often a customer service work package is routed to the supervisor. For example, a new CSR might forward every fifth customer resolution to a supervisor for review, whereas a tenured worker might have only one out of one hundred resolutions forwarded to a supervisor.

But Momentum Life has gone far beyond simply using Smart Tools to route information. They use them to compensate people—something which sounds, admittedly, antithetical to the culture of a Smart Company. In most cases it would be the wrong way to use a Smart Tool, but Momentum has challenged conventional wisdom in two ways: by using the Smart Tool to track performance and, most importantly, by not allowing management to be the ones who design the detailed metrics of performance.

On a regular basis, each representative's performance statistics are reviewed against the group as a whole to determine how well he/she is performing. At Momentum pay for performance is based on three elements: the number of transactions completed, turnaround time, and quality rating. Detailed audit trails and quality reporting features allow the customer service team to accurately assess its results in these three areas and be compensated based on the performance of each specialist.

Admittedly, that does not sit well with many people. It did not sit well with many workers at Momentum. However, if the metrics are ones agreed on by the entire customer service team—and in the case of Momentum Life they were—then there is little basis for argument. Contrast this with a compensation system that may be determined arbitrarily by management alone.

At Momentum, teams determine the metrics and the specifics of how work is routed and audited. The rules are open and accessible; they are not hidden criteria intended for persecution. The position taken by the workers is that these are not just metrics developed by Momentum Life, but are established by the industry.

In the eighteen months after implementing the system the results speak for themselves:

- Productivity gains exceed 33%.

- An intensive internal training course lasting fourteen weeks has increased skill levels of the staff. Fifty of the highest-rated associates were placed in client services and are fully conversant with all aspects of the company, as opposed to having a narrow range of skills.

- The length of time dedicated to performing technical conversions, such as policy changes, have been reduced from fifteen days to three.

- An indexed work queue intuitively routes work items to the entire workforce. Once a representative completes a work item, the automated workflow immediately delivers the next piece of work that he or she has been approved to complete, therefore enhancing productivity by eliminating the need for representatives to leave their desks to find work.

- Ninety-eight percent of transactions are now completed in less than three days, and 99% of all policy applications are completed within one day.

- Loan and surrenders, which once required twelve days to complete, are frequently turned around in one day and never require more than three.

- Cross-selling opportunities have increased because all customer information is presented at the workstation upon retrieving a customer file.

THE STRUCTURE OF THE SMART COMPANY: FROM THE VERTICAL TO THE PERPETUAL ORGANIZATION

The Tower of Babel is said to have been created by legions of people who all spoke the same language. Their ability to communicate in a single tongue gave them the basic tools with which they attempted to build a structure that would touch the Heavens—spanning the chasm from mortals to the divine. This blasphemy to God did not go unpunished by the Creator, who in His rage destroyed the tower and scattered the legions across the world into separate and isolated communities where they were each forced to use differing tongues to communicate among their individual tribes. So was born the nation state, according to the biblical prophets, and thereafter humans were relegated to miscommunication and misunderstanding, which prevented them from ever again easily sharing a glorious common vision.

As technology has evolved and made possible new lines of communication within organizations, the standard organizational models have changed dramatically. Arguably, the role of technology in flattening and democratization is the single most profound factor in organizational change over the past fifty years.

This much is clear: the structure of a Smart Company should be simply a tool for promoting communication—both within and without the organization. Hierarchy for hierarchy's sake has no place in the philosophy of a Smart Company.

If you consider the value of a hierarchy it can be summarized in one word: *communication.* Hierarchies are vehicles of communication. This is especially true in the absence of adequate communication technology. But as noted before, communication is not collaboration and collaboration is necessary to be agile and adaptive.[13]

The structure of an organization also has profound effects on its people and their perception of potential for success. As David Packard, co-founder of Hewlett-Packard, once noted:

The way an organization is structured affects individual motivation and performance. There are military-type organizations in which the person at the top issues an order and it is passed on down the line until the person at the bottom does as he or she is told without question or reason. This is precisely the type of organization we at HP did not want...and do not want. We feel our objectives can best be achieved by people who understand and support them and who are allowed flexibility in working toward common goals in ways that they help determine are best for their operation and their organization.[14]

One way to understand the changes that have taken place in enterprise structures is to look at the distinct periods of evolution of the modern enterprise. Although one could profile dozens of organizational models, all organizations fundamentally boil down to at most four structures:

- vertical;

- horizontal;

- virtual;

- perpetual.

THE HIERARCHICAL CONFINES OF THE VERTICAL ORGANIZATION

Unfortunately, the vertical organization, a fixture of the Industrial Revolution and the hallmark of many of the world's largest businesses, is still the most prevalent type of management structure among medium- and large-scale organizations.

The vertical organization is characterized by extensive hierarchies, approval committees, and often snail's-pace decision making. Long response times are required to send information up-line and back down-line in order to make even basic decisions.

The vertical organization also exhibits resistance to change due to the inherent justification process necessary for investment, and to the political strife caused by the isolation of hierarchical structures. The management theorist Peter Drucker refers to these many layers of management in a vertical organization as "boosters, amplifying the very faint signals that come up and down through the organization."[15]

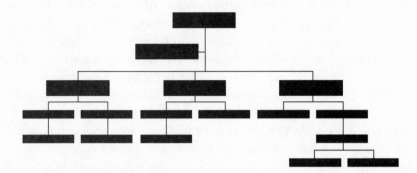

Figure 1-4: The Structure of the Vertical Organization

Hierarchies are the best way to segregate people within functions and ultimately create distrust and isolation. Worst of all, hierarchies close the door to new experiences and evolution by reducing the opportunity for process mutation.[16] If you lock the process up within a confined ecosystem, it will never keep pace with the shifting market climates it inhabits.

This is why nature fundamentally abhors hierarchies.

Yes, this sounds peculiar. Most of us expect that nature is basically hierarchical. Yes, if you are referring to complex fractal patterns or the building blocks of matter. But we're not referring to inanimate objects but to communication among beings. Consider every species of the animal kingdom, except humans. Flat organizations are the norm; there is a leader and the pack. Humans, on the other hand, need to communicate greater complexity in their interactions. The reason for a hierarchy is precisely that. It facilitates complex communication. However, as the technology tools evolve to facilitate that communication, the need for the hierarchy goes away.

In the same way that instinct among a pack of wolves reduces the need for complex communication of administrative details, Smart Tools can reduce the need for time-consuming administrative communication among workers in an organization and increase collaborative communication and creativity. This is the essence of what may be termed *corporate instinct.* Why does every anthill and beehive look identical (even though their creators don't have policy and procedure manuals, building codes, or consultants)? Because they have a process memory which is innate.

This is not to suggest that Smart Companies require humans who have evolved into beings with innate corporate instinct. But what we have done for the past five decades is capture more and more information without considering the foundation of that information from an organizational standpoint, which is, to process intelligence. How do you create that corporate instinct? How do you share it? And the more your organization changes, the more volatile it is, the more often you have to reorganize, the more important it is to preserve that corporate instinct. Not in policies and procedures, by the way. They grow old. They get stale. They grow cobwebs. We're talking about being able to share that process dynamically among the people.

So how do you change the hierarchy? By corporate memo?[17] How often can you do that? Once a year? There are some companies that do. Once a year, like clockwork, an executive memo comes from the CEO's desk mandating change—here's what we change, here are the new players, here are all the new rules by which we play the game.

Can you do that twice a year? How about three times? You certainly can't do it more than four times a year because it takes three months just to understand the latest corporate memo and assimilate it into the organization. And even if you had the fortitude to reorganize this often, what toll would it take on the people? No one has calculated the cost of constant reorganization, but in terms of downtime and lost opportunity it may well be one of the greatest productivity barriers.[18] If for no other reason, hierarchies don't work because they simply cost more than they are worth, especially in times of frequent change.

Hierarchies are outdated and simply do not move fast enough. Even the hierarchical archetype, the Roman Legion, was divided into units that were interchangeable enough to allow teams to form and then be assigned as needed to the particular task or battle at hand. But in the creation of the factory and its rigid work models, we lost that flexibility in order to ensure that the flow of commands and instructions moved from manager to employee.

In a modern-day example, the military operation Desert Storm in

Kuwait created unparalleled diffusion of authority and decision making by enabling front-line personnel, fighter pilots, and tank commanders to make decisions that would have normally traversed the military hierarchy.[19] Responsiveness equates to survival, but only if it is supported by the right technology.

Today both the communication and the interchangeability is hampered by hierarchies.

THE HORIZONTAL ORGANIZATION, OR, THE MINOAN PALACE

As hierarchies are dismantled, most companies move to the horizontal structure, epitomized by networks, matrix management, and teams. The horizontal organization has been lauded by many as the organizational structure of the future. But it is more problematic than one might think. The horizontal organization runs the very high risk of becoming like the Minoan Palace (the palace of King Minos in Crete), a structure that in Greek mythology was laid out like a maze and housed the Minotaur. People who went into the Minoan Palace would never find their way out, their ultimate fate to be eaten by the Minotaur, whose labyrinth only he knew. Could the ancient Greeks have been telling us something about the frustration of workers in a horizontal organization?

The problem with the horizontal structure has to do with the difficulty in identifying who is responsible and accountable. After all, how often do you find yourself referring to an organization chart instead of relying on your knowledge of the skills and capabilities needed to perform a task?

The team approach emphasized by the horizontal structure can work very well, but only if teams remain stable. They degenerate into chaos if there is a high turnover of team members. People move into new jobs within an organization, they transfer to other locations, or they leave the organization. The free agency of workers is inimical to forming stable and long-lasting teams. Thus, maintaining any sort of institutional memory is difficult, if not impossible.

A team manager is likely to spend a great deal of time simply tracking down necessary information, as well as the last person to have had it or been responsible for it. Playing bloodhound becomes a large part of the manager's job; huge amounts of time are spent trying to navigate through the maze—the process maze and the information maze. Often, information on a particular project has been passed around from team to team, like a disagreeably wet infant.

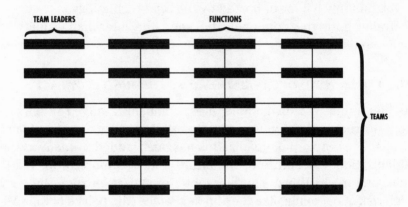

Figure 1-5: The Structure of the Horizontal Organization

While the team concept has a nice aura of collegiality about it, teams are hardly immune to the politics of turf warfare. Teams often form long-term functional alignments. For example, the new-technologies team aligns with the information systems department. The customer support team aligns with customer support; and so on. There is an implicit fragmentation of justification in this type of enterprise. Redundant investment thrives and systems become ever more fragmented. Turf warfare and technology fiefdoms run rampant.

There are certainly differing schools of thought on the effectiveness of teams, but the key to any successful team is the combination of the proper technology and culture. A network and an e-mail system alone do not a good team make. As Michael Schrage, author of *No More Teams!*, notes:

There is a huge difference [between communications and collaboration]. The sad fact is, however, that many managers think there is a close relationship between the two, that if you fix one then you'll automatically get the other. 'If only we had better communications,' they say, 'then we could empathize more, we could be more effective in our collaboration.' This is demonstrable nonsense. It's one of the biggest fallacies in management today.[20]

Schrage's observations strike at the core of a problem that plagues many organizations: the use of technology as a crutch for human collaboration. The application of Smart Tools is not an excuse for poor management or the absence of a common vision. If anything, technology can exacerbate a pathology of mistrust and increase the opportunities for confrontation. A return on this sort of technology investment may well be negative, causing more problems than it solves.

In *Teams and Technology: Fulfilling the Promise of the New Organization,* the authors describe the empty promise teams have in many organizations:

Teams and Information Technology are two of the most important developments in organizations today. Vast amounts of time, money, and effort are spent with the expectation that their impact on the bottom line will eventually justify their costs. But many organizations are disappointed in the results. Few are getting the bang from the many bucks they spend each year to create teams and to develop new information systems. The challenge facing these organizations is how to fulfill the potential of these two promising and complex developments.[21]

The fundamental problem, it seems, has to do with the nature of how teams are formed in many organizations. Instead of being part of the organizational fabric and culture, they are a crisis-intervention vehicle. Forming a team—much less imparting a sense of urgency to its members—in a time of crisis is perhaps the worst way to introduce or promote the benefits of a team or team-based technology. The authors of *Teams and Technology* note that engaging in team building under these circumstances is like rearranging the deck chairs on the *Titanic.* "[22] But then, in the case of the *Titanic* there was no better use of those last few moments. Most organizations are far more fortunate, but no less chaotic, when it comes to aligning how their teams support the overall mission of the enterprise. The bottom line is that teams and technology both need alignment with organizational vision and direction. Horizontal structures often lack these features, which are, in large part, the reason for command and control hierarchies. In sum, horizontal structures are appealing and may work well over limited time frames, but soon turn chaotic without the backbone of a hierarchy.

And so it would seem to be a no-win situation. Both the horizontal and vertical organizational models have grave flaws.

THE VIRTUAL ORGANIZATION

The shortcomings of both the vertical and horizontal organization have been transcended by Smart Companies, whose business models are moving toward structures that promote a more integrated rhythm of work.

Recently, we've heard a lot about the virtual organization, a concept often touted as the preferred, technology-based enterprise architecture of the future. A virtual organization is a modified form of the horizontal organization. While difficult to comprehend in the context of today's well-defined organizational models, one can find the beginnings of virtual enterprises in those companies that adopt a "recombinant structure," pulling resources together quickly to solve a particular internal or external problem.

For example, in a virtual corporation, managers might rely on electronic communications, such as e-mail and groupware, to gather an ad hoc team to address an immediate problem.

According to William Davidow and Michael S. Malone, authors of *The Virtual Corporation,* the hallmarks of the virtual organization are:

- formerly well-defined structures begin to lose their edges;

- seemingly permanent things start to change continuously; and

- products and services adapt to match consumers' desires.[23]

The benefit of virtuality is the reduction of organizational response time. The liability is the cultural impediment created whenever an enterprise adopts any structure; namely, that markets change faster than the ability of most enterprise cultures to respond.

Many managers and workers misconstrue the virtual corporation, believing that it has no structure and everyone has access to everyone else. It's a wonderful vision, but it's not reality. A CEO in even a medium-sized company can't be involved in every process on an ongoing basis. It's just not possible. There has to be some structure.

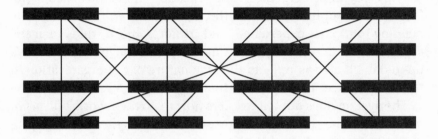

Figure 1-6: The Structure of the Virtual Organization

THE PERPETUAL ORGANIZATION

So which is the right organizational model? Is it vertical? Horizontal? Virtual?

It's all of the above, and it can change radically from one moment to the next. It should. It shouldn't be based on a piece of paper stuck on the wall and called an organization chart.

Rather, it should be based on the competitive forces, the customers, the suppliers, the roles, the talent, and skill base within the existing organization. Creating flexibility requires creating the *perpetual enterprise.* Even the term *perpetual* indicates a change from the spatial structure of traditional organizations to the time-based essence of this new model. Perpetual enterprises go beyond simply adapting to change by altering culture and management structure. They do more than simply become virtual by sharing systems and information with suppliers and customers, and they certainly do not settle for basic networking and distributed computing technology to connect their people and processes. *Perpetual enterprises create value in their enterprise by establishing an entirely new asset base, that of a process memory that allows instantaneous adaptability.*

But the perpetual organization requires a foundation of what we have called *corporate instinct*. One can't simply say "Poof!" and create it. It requires process knowledge to be captured, stored, and constantly, continuously updated. It creates what many have termed *knowing* organizations.[24] These are organizations that are organized around processes and information, not functions and management layers.[25]

The rules for structuring the organization should be based on information about how people in the organization work together. Depending on past experience and results, those rules can be changed, live, in real time. Real-time project management is always up-to-date. It always reflects the true nature of the organization in the marketplace. That's a perpetual organization.

The system does not tell workers how to do their work, only *what needs to be done*. This is an important contrast to the approach proposed by Frederick Taylor. His emphasis was on telling a worker *how* to do his job, not on *what* to do.[26]

Change at this pace is not a function of vision or charisma; it is the ability to move faster than the market. It's a matter of having the tools that enable the organization to constantly understand the market forces at work and take appropriate responses.

When you visualize a perpetual organization, don't think departments. Don't even think teams necessarily. Think *workcells*. A workcell is a collection of roles. And people fill roles. If you define the method by which people fill roles, you then have tremendous adaptability and *permeability* between functions, allowing you much greater flexibility in your workforce.[27] The workcell concept is discussed at greater length in Chapter 4.

In the perpetual organization, the foundation of technology removes much of the knowledge workers' burden, effectively allowing them to be more creative and more innovative. For example, at NordicTrack, workers are able to focus on the creative aspects of defining new products, rather then be mired in the drudgery of paper shuffling and paper flow.

In short, we can say that the only structure that will survive change is one that never stops changing. A perpetual enterprise can take the form of any structure, based on the market demands at the moment.

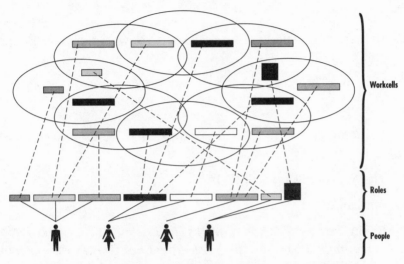

*Figure 1-7: People, Roles, and Workcells in the
Perpetual Organization*

So how do we break free of the cultural impediments that hamstring our current organizational structures and create a perpetual enterprise? The key here lies in understanding how an enterprise ultimately changes its form from vertical to horizontal to virtual.

In almost every successful case, it is the imposition of a subjective initiative, such as a CEO who anticipates a market trend, a large customer who demands change from a supplier, the expectation or realization of diminishing profits, or other quantifiable indicators of change.

Take heed, however, that there have been many unsuccessful cases, too. The business landscape is littered with the remnants of enterprises that realized their predicaments long after any change could be instituted. Planning for change is much like blocking a penalty shot in soccer: if you wait until you know the direction in which the ball is coming at you, then you have waited too long.

For a perpetual enterprise, the rate of change becomes a competitive weapon. The faster change takes place, the more opportunity there is to compete and win. In perpetual enterprises, success is measured in volume of innovation—not volume of production.

END NOTES

1   Halberstam, David, *The Reckoning* (New York: Avon Books, 1987), p. 201.

2   Ibid., p. 205.

3   Ibid., p. 204.

4   Halberstam, David, *The Fifties* (New York: Villard Books, 1993), p. 123.

5   *The Reckoning,* pp. 212–214.

6   Ibid., p. 241.

7   Rifkin, Jeremy, *The End of Work: The Decline of the Global Labor Force and the Dawn of the Post-Market Era* (New York: G.P. Putnam's Sons, 1995), p. 93.

8   Eventually, all trains carried a telegrapher who was armed with a relay box that could be attached to telegraph wires by the roadbed in order to receive instructions from a dispatcher or call for assistance. Brown, Dee, *Hear That Lonesome Whistle Blow: Railroads and the West* (New York: Touchstone Books, 1977), p. 179.

9   Koulopoulos, Thomas, *The Workflow Imperative: Building Real-World Business Solutions* (New York: Van Nostrand Reinhold, 1995), pp. 53–54.

10   Town and Country Mortgage Case study courtesy of Keyfile Corporation.

11   360° Communications case study courtesy of Keyfile Corporation.

12   NordicTrack case study courtesy of Keyfile Corporation.

13   For more on the importance of collaboration in work, see Schrage, Michael, *Shared Minds* (New York: Random House, 1990).

14   Packard, David, *The HP Way: How Bill Hewlett and I Built Our Company* (New York: HarperBusiness, a division of HarperCollins Publishers, 1995), pp. 127–128.

15 Drucker, Peter F., *Managing for the Future: The 1990s and Beyond.* (New York: Truman Valley Books/Dutton, 1992), p. 329.

16 McGill, Michael E., and Slocum, John W. Jr., *The Smarter Organization: How to Build a Business that Learns and Adapts to Marketplace Needs* (New York: John Wiley & Sons, 1994), p. 96. The authors see moving from a functional organization as the key to creating a learning organization.

17 For more on this, see Smye, Marti, Ph.D., *You Don't Change a Company by Memo: The Simple Truths about Managing Change* (Toronto: Key Porter Books, 1994).

18 Ackoff, Russell L., *The Democratic Corporation: A Radical Prescription for Recreating Corporate America and Rediscovering Success.* (New York: Oxford University Press, Inc., 1994), p. 168.

19 Helgesen, Sally, *The Web of Inclusion* (New York: Currency/Doubleday, 1995) pp. 26–27.

20 Interview with Michael Schrage, *Virtual Workgroups,* September–October 1996.

21 Mankin, Don, Cohen, Susan G., and Bikson, Tora K., *Teams and Technology: Fulfilling the Promise of the New Organization* (Boston: Harvard Business School Press, 1996). p. ix.

22 Ibid. p. 36.

23 Davidow, William H., and Malone, Michael S. *The Virtual Corporation: Structuring and Revitalizing the Corporation for the 21st Century* (New York: HarperBusiness, a division of Harper Collins, 1992), p. 4.

24 McGill, Michael E. and Slocum, John W. Jr., *The Smarter Organization.* Used somewhat out of context, the term is used to describe organizations that have well-defined models of doing business. Examples are Walt Disney, Toys 'R' Us, and Blockbuster Video. These are companies that have solid market positions and perception. The *knowing* comes from the fact that they have an ingrained corporate memory, what we call corporate instinct, to guide their actions. Similarly, a perpetual organization has a mechanism by which to commit this instinct to a collective memory.

25 Drucker, Peter F. *Managing for the Future: The 1990s and Beyond.* p. 30.

26 Ibid., p. 97

27 McGill, Michael E., Slocum, Jr., John W. *The Smarter Organization. Permeability* is a term used to describe the loosely defined boundaries within today's organizations.

CHAPTER 2

SMART TOOLS: MOVING THE WORK, NOT THE WORKER

INTRODUCTION

So what are Smart Tools, and what are the engines driving today's Smart Companies? Well, let's ask this a different way. "What Smart Tools are being used to free the workers of today's organizations from the menial and the mundane?" The list may appear to be immense. The explosive growth in computing power over the last two decades, and the proliferation of communications technology, would seem to make that an overwhelmingly voluminous answer.

Don't believe it. As overwhelmed as you may feel, the basic tools are few. One Smart Tool can an entire litany of technologies make, and the inverse is equally true. The telephone, for example, is credited with fueling everything from the expansion of the railroads to creation of high-rise buildings, the suburbanization of America, the factory, and the divisional structure of the modern business enterprise. Conversely, you could ask, did all of these create the need for the telephone?

High-rise buildings were difficult to imagine without reliable communications tools by which to communicate with workers beyond shouting distance. The same is true in creating management systems as organizations become increasingly more geographically dispersed so that different functions are in different locations—often in different countries.

Identifying each new generation of Smart Tools is also a challenge, often due to the technology noise that surrounds eras of innovation and ferment. Smart Tools create a chain reaction that is much easier to trace *backwards* in time than forward.

Radar, for example, was thought of as little more than a curiosity when it was first invented in the 1930s, but during the Second World War it became a milestone technology, and quite literally saved Great Britain from being conquered by the Third Reich.

During the Battle of Britain in the spring and summer of 1940, England's Royal Air Force was outnumbered by a factor of four to one and its planes were technologically inferior to those of the German Luftwaffe. But thanks to a network of twenty-one long-range radar stations (constructed, in no small degree, at the urging of Winston Churchill), the R.A.F. knew *when* and *where* enemy planes were coming from. With this advantage in information, British pilots could lie in wait for German planes and then attack. Thanks to the efficient coordination between radar operators at Fighter Command and the R.A.F. pilots, Germany's air offensive was stymied. In September 1940, Hitler called off Operation Sea Lion, his planned invasion of Great Britain. Praising the R.A.F. pilots in a speech before the House of Commons, Churchill noted, "Never in the field of human conflict was so much owed by so many to so few."[1]

Radar has clearly been one of the most profound tools of the twentieth century; as a keystone for air and naval transportation it has enabled the global village.* Smart Tools are trivial on the one hand, but on the other hand they change the world.

---

* It is interesting to note that one of the scientists instrumental in developing radar at M.I.T.'s Radiation Laboratory, Vannevar Bush, went on to head the National Defense Research Council, which quickly grasped the significance of the discovery of uranium fission in 1939, and recommended that the U.S. government launch a program to develop atomic weapons. Bush also was the inventor of another contemporary Smart Tool that has become a foundation of the Internet, *hypertext,* which he created to amass and arrange the huge volumes of scientific data generated by wartime research.

So what do all Smart Tools have in common? Simply put, they are *the technological embodiment of preexisting metaphors, and they are specific responses to current social phenomena.* The telephone, for example, succeeded because it did more than provide fast communication; it succeeded because it was the cornerstone of no less than one hundred other significant technological and social trends.

In other words, Smart Tools are *people-centered technologies and methods that enable quantum increases in prosperity and fundamental change in the social fabric. And Smart Companies are those companies that employ Smart Tools to increase the prosperity of their workers and customers.*

By prosperity, we are referring to the tangible effects on quality of life, as measured by an increase in financial incentive, ownership, or opportunity relative to the existing work paradigm. It's important to keep in mind that retrospective analysis does not work well in this regard. If we look to the turn-of-the-century textile industry in Lowell, Massachusetts, from today's vantage point, we see sweatshops and unacceptable work conditions. Yet the inhabitants of those mills—mostly poor immigrants from southern and eastern Europe—saw boundless opportunity along the teeming shores of the Merrimack River.

Prosperity is a relative term. Keeping this in mind helps us to not only be less judgmental when we look backward but also be more open-minded about future possibilities for changing current work paradigms. You may have noticed an obvious omission in the definition of a Smart Company: the prosperity of the owners. The reason is that an owner's prosperity—whether a singular owner or a multiplicity of owners—will always go up if the prosperity of workers and customers rises.

Today, all too often, an owner increases his or her prosperity without a concomitant increase in that of either customers or workers. Most notable is the recent phenomenon of increased market value and executive bonuses in the ranks of those companies that downsize radically to cut costs, what we will later describe as "denominator management." Long-term prosperity cannot work in this way; it has to be shared, or else it will simply be an illusion.

Fundamental change in the social fabric refers to the way in which Smart Tools alter the very perception of not only work, but also the way in which we interact and behave as individuals, communities, and nations. The telephone did more than fuel mobility, suburbanization, and transportation; it also created a societal infrastructure to support social institutions ranging from the family to government organizations and multinational corporations.

But Smart Tools are a double-edged sword. Because of the radical way in which they change society, we need to consider their effects on employment and the dark side of increased productivity.

For example, technology that boosts productivity can—and historically has—thrown large numbers of people out of work. As a United Nations official once asked the author at a conference in Geneva, "Isn't there a technology that will reduce productivity?"[2] His point, which was received with curious looks from other members of the audience, was valid. The countries of the third world, in which unemployment is rampant, may not need greater productivity; they simply need to employ people—for both economic and social reasons. A huge class of unemployed and dissatisfied citizens can be a potent catalyst for social unrest and revolution.

Is this point so absurd? We seek perpetual productivity increases yet, when we realize them, unemployment invariably follows. As Hamel and Prahalad tell us "If you don't become more efficient, you'll lose your job. By the way, if you do become more efficient, you'll lose your job."[3] We could just as easily say, "If you work smart, you lose your job."

Should we be looking to reduce productivity to reemploy people? Are we creating what Jeremy Rifkin, in *The End of Work,* calls "the cult of efficiency"? Truth be told, it is a hollow question for the free market economies of the world. Competitive pressure does not afford the luxury of even contemplating the possibility. As long as Smart Tools are available, companies will use them. The question is, will their use increase or decrease human dignity and prosperity, not just productivity?

Our era is not the first to be confronted with the issue of technology that threatens to restructure the workforce—a delicate way of saying that lots of folks will be losing their jobs. In 1912–1913, as Ford's Model T production doubled, so did his workforce. But in the next model year, as production again doubled, Ford cut 1,500 jobs, the result of enormous productivity increases brought on by the assembly line.[4]

But what we often fail to see is the long-term redeployment of the jobs and people purged by technology. The tremendous success of the automobile, and the industries it created, reabsorbed these workers (if not at Ford, then at the myriad other companies that benefited from the same Smart Tools and technologies that were initially the villain). Moreover, the myth that technology in manufacturing industries has decimated the workforce appears to be largely untrue. Although industries periodically experience large scale job destruction, for example, automobile manufacturing as the result of robotics, concurrent job creation restructures these same industries and reallocates displaced workers.[5] The term of displacement for unemployed workers is what causes the greatest social turmoil. If the period of displacement can be reduced, as it is with Smart Tools which allow workers to quickly redeploy their skills, the destruction of jobs does not result in massive long term unemployment.

Today we find ourselves in an era of enormous entrepreneurial expansion. Smart Tools are not only making it possible for large companies to realize greater opportunity, but also for small companies and individuals to work outside the confines and perceived insecurity of a corporate job. Although traditional employment may be experiencing its slow demise, employability is increasing as individuals are able to more precisely focus their contributions to an enterprise as free agents.*

Thus, the United Nation official might have asked a better question: Can Smart Tools help underdeveloped countries and their people enter the free market? Absolutely. Countries such as India and Russia are already becoming enormous labor pools for companies that can easily transport information-based work electronically.

Finally, it is worth repeating that Smart Tools are *not* replacements for people; they replace tasks, and the most mundane ones at that. Automation usually implies the automation of people when it is, in fact, the automation of only parts of what people do. Where Taylorism told workers *how to do* their work, imposing standardization on everything from the most menial to the most complex tasks, Smart Tools tell workers *what to do* and leave the how up to them. *Smart Companies realize the distinction between human aptitude and*

---

* Free agency is discussed in greater detail in Chapter 6.

the value of technology, and apply technology where it can be used to support and liberate people.

Our focus on automation has been misplaced. A better way to look at the use of Smart Tools may be described as what the authors of *Teams and Technology* describe as augmentation.

"One of the prerequisites for productive tinkering is the use of information technology to *augment* rather than *automate* work tasks. Instead of designing systems that simply replace what people do with a computer routine or program, they can be designed so that they enable users to do what they have not been able to do before. The kinds of labor savings realized from systems that automate tasks are in any case rarely enough to justify the costs of the systems themselves."[6]

Uncovering the Smart Tools of today requires looking at the most basic trends, challenges, and opportunities that we are facing, and then following them to the intersection of technology, society, and industry.

WORKFLOW: THE SEMINAL SMART TOOL

If there is one tenet that is central to the concept of Smart Companies, it is workflow. But what exactly is it?

Workflow is defined as a tool set for the proactive analysis, compression, and automation of information-based tasks and activities.[7] The basic premise of workflow is that an office environment is a process factory. The process, which can exist in a range of formats, from paper to electronic, provides the basic raw material of every office task. The connection of these office tasks creates a *value chain*—a unique combination of activities that together create competitive value-added products or services for a company—that spans both internal and external task boundaries. Workflow attempts to streamline the components of the value chain by eliminating unnecessary tasks and automating the remaining tasks that are necessary to a process.[8]

But "task" in this use of the term is not synonymous with person. Unlike the typical factory at the turn of the century, in which each line worker had one and only one task, people in modern office settings typically have many tasks.

Workflow applications are designed to automate the routine tasks, eliminate the redundant tasks, and ensure that the right information gets to the right person at the right time, based on the specific conditions. The decisions that determine the right information, route, and person can usually be predetermined. But the decisions made by that person, based on that information and the conditions of the instance, still afford the participant a large degree of freedom. When the burdens of clerical paper pushing are removed, an individual is free to do what he or she does best—be innovative and make knowledgeable decisions.

Workflow may well be the most important Smart Tool of this century. Like Ford's assembly line, it has a simple and yet profound effect on the relationship between workers and work. But unlike the assembly line, it is as variable and as dynamic as the conditions of today's fast-changing markets and as flexible as the workers it enables.

Workflow represents a massive swing in the tools and methods used to support a business process. So massive, in fact, that it is doubtful any organization will be able to keep pace with the metronome of change if its processes are not enabled with these new technologies and methodologies. Not unlike the tremendous competitive pressure to invest in factory automation and quality assurance techniques during the second half of the twentieth century, workflow systems will become a cornerstone of competitive advantage as we move toward the full bloom of postindustrialism in the next millennium. Such an edge is desperately needed in the white-collar work force, which, despite the monumental investment in information systems, has apparently yielded no increase in productivity over the past two decades.[9]

Although the factory environment may seem a long way from the domain of the knowledge worker, both are part of the same value chain of activities. Within the factory we have already embraced a new information-based paradigm, where techniques such as mass customization and just-in-time production are achieving economic order quantities of single units.

The mass-production legacy of the last three centuries, however, is a constant progression toward ever-increasing work fragmentation and specialization. What this meant in the office is that each new pairing of specialized process steps required a corresponding element of time and effort to transfer information from one step to the next. This problem is mitigated in factories due to the constant rhythm of the assembly line, but in the knowledge worker's domain, miscommunication thrives as specialization leads to more tasks, more people, and more points of control in the process.

The modern office is still very much like the Minoan Palace we described earlier, with corridors that wind and turn in myriad directions. Specialization and highly distributed operations have created monstrously complex interactions between knowledge workers. The walls we have placed between the parts of an organization, its people, its suppliers, customers, and all participants of the value chain are artificial. As Michael Porter, author of *Competitive Advantage,* has said, "Organizational structure in most firms works against achieving interrelationships."[10]

Bringing productivity gains from the factory to the front office should not be regarded as a leap across a divide, but rather a bridge that acknowledges the importance of bringing discrete processes within organizations closer together. The ability of Smart Tools such as workflow to bring these pieces together will change the fundamentals of the office and knowledge work. Not only will technology and organizational infrastructure change, but the *very nature of work will be transformed.*

The most vociferous critics take the analogy of the factory too far, and assume that workflow imposes unswerving conformity on knowledge workers. It is generally recognized that an office environment thrives on some measure of creative chaos. Periods of high productivity are often preceded and followed by what would be considered idle time on the assembly line. Workflow, according to its detractors, would make an office as bloodless and efficient as the model assembly line dreamt of by Ford and Taylor. As Ronnie Marshak, a notable workflow expert, once noted:

I was somewhat surprised to learn that several of my colleagues in the industry are completely baffled by my support of workflow—technology they consider rigid and an enemy to

worker empowerment. The way they see it, workflow, by definition, takes away *any* freedom of choice on the part of the participant. After all, in a structured workflow, work is delivered
to you when the system dictates, not when you are inclined to
do it. Further, they believe that innovation is stifled because all
the options (rules and exceptions) are predefined and you are
restricted to following those predefined rules.[11]

This line of thinking throws the baby out with the bath water.
Workflow systems deliver work to the worker when the *business
process*—not the *workflow application*—dictates. And, yes, there
are rules to be followed, sometimes pretty stringent rules. But these
rules should be followed whether or not they are enforced by a
workflow system. Business rules and processes are in place for important reasons. It simply isn't practical to reinvent the way you do
business for each situation. There must be guidelines and requirements. But is this technological fascism? Are we really limiting freedom and creativity? Most reasonable people would say no.

However, we must acknowledge that a transformation of this
scale will not come without a human cost and an added measure of
social responsibility. We have seen vivid evidence in the drastic impact of downsizing on our blue-collar workforce, and recently we
have been seeing the same effects in the front office. When technologies are used only as a means to accelerate downsizing and increase productivity, they do not also increase prosperity. If we
ignore the call to social responsibility, and do not apply process automation technology to *enhance* the role of the knowledge worker,
we face the potential for tremendous social upheaval.

THE TENETS OF WORKFLOW

As with all Smart Tools, workflow is part technology, part management discipline, and part methodology. Exploring this broad spec-
trum of capabilities and applications of workflow requires
understanding its basic characteristics and benefits.

One of the easiest ways to do this is to compare and contrast
workflow with other technologies and methods with which you may
be more familiar, such as TQM, workgroup computing, value chains,

and extended or virtual enterprises.

Much of workflow's uniqueness, however, hinges on a simple distinction: its focus on *process* over *information*. As a result, one of the most important aspects of the advent of workflow during the past decade is the impact it has had on the changing concept of information as an organizational asset. The premise that information is a tangible asset that must be preserved and valued does not change. What does change is the concept of *information management*. In the traditional view, information management was represented by the data and documents used in the support of a business process. With workflow we add a new dimension to information management—that of the *process asset*.

This is also the principal difference between workgroup computing and workflow. Workflow enables organizations to capture not only the information but also the process, including the rules that govern its execution. These rules include schedules, priorities, routing paths, authorizations, security, and the roles of each individual involved in the process.

Before tremors of fear begin to resonate in those readers who see this as yet one more way to downsize the workforce, they should stop and think about the flip side of downsizing. All too often we attribute downsizing to technology. Though technology, incorrectly applied, may cause downsizing, it is typically external economic and global factors that drive the downsizing, cost-cutting, and the wholesale reengineering of organizations. Whether we like it or not, most organizations will have fewer office workers burdened with performing more and more tasks in less and less time.*

Without a means by which to validate, compress, and augment work roles, downsizing has no long-term benefit. Downsizing alone would send industry into a death spiral of ever-increasing inefficiency as knowledge workers are burdened beyond their abilities and capacity to cope. By way of example, England achieved amazing productivity increases of up to 40% during the Thatcher years, while actual output rose only 10%. This was achieved by using drastic downsizing in factory production. Applying the same principle to knowledge work would be catastrophic. Knowledge work cannot

---

* This is not a bleak outlook, as we will see in the last chapter.

be as easily, if at all, replaced by a machine's intelligence. As a result, focusing on decreased body count across the board can produce an exceptionally dangerous scenario.

Workflow is a survival response mechanism. It not only stems the downsizing spiral, but can actually improve the standard of work environments by minimizing miscommunications among heavily burdened workgroups. More important, it can increase the ability of an enterprise to capture new opportunity without displacing workers by opening up new possibilities for collaboration that did not exist.

For example, Town and Country Mortgage, the company profiled in Chapter 1, could now make a case for hiring loan officers to put in every real estate office throughout its service area.

It is also worth pointing out that if external factors were different, the perception of workflow as the knot in the hangman's ligature would be equally different. For example, during a boom period of abundant opportunity—think of the 1980s—any technology or method that helped expand capacity and convert opportunity to revenue was extolled as beneficial, even though it often raised head count and costs well above what long-term opportunity could support—a legacy we are now working hard to expunge.

In this section, workflow will be compared and contrasted with six other areas. These are not exclusive technologies or concepts. For example, we will see that value-chain analysis and workflow have a great deal of synergy, as does Total Quality Management and workflow. Clearly, Smart Tools can leverage each other and help create even greater value in the process. The six areas explored in this section are:

- Workflow versus workgroup computing

- Workflow as a development environment

- Workflow and TQM

- Workflow in the extended/virtual enterprise

- Value chains and value streams

- The impact of time-based analysis on the value chain

WORKFLOW VERSUS WORKGROUP COMPUTING

One of the most often asked questions when the subject of workflow comes up is "What is the difference between workflow and workgroup computing?" The distinction is actually a simple one. It is the difference between communication and collaboration. Workgroup products facilitate the transfer and sharing of information from workgroup to workgroup or individual to individual. The key ingredients are communication and information. In a workflow application the *process knowledge that applies to the information* is also managed, transferred, shared, and routed. The key ingredients are collaboration and process.

This may appear to be a subtle distinction. It is not. Process knowledge involves capturing the roles, schedules, and resource descriptions and then defining these as part of the workflow application. Many workgroup applications provide a minimal level of process functionality, for point-to-point workflow or ad hoc processes, similar to an e-mail system, but only workflow products focus on the issues and problems inherent in process automation, such as the analysis of processes and the definition of role relationships. For example, how does a credit analyst work with a salesperson in any one of a dozen interactions?

WORKFLOW AS A DEVELOPMENT ENVIRONMENT

Workflow is caught up in the maelstrom of activity generated by the evolution of desktop computing, groupware, the Internet, and the general trend toward increasingly sophisticated development tools for applications. Although a critical part of workflow is its use as a development platform, it is important to understand that workflow represents a significant step toward the elimination of complex development staffs and programmers.

As we have already seen, reflective desktop computing environments will allow users greater access to process logic and its modification. One way to look at this is to categorize Smart Tools, including workflow, into four distinct layers of technology.

In simplified version, these categories are:

- Off-the-shelf tools such as spreadsheets, e-mail, groupware, and other basic desktop applications;

- Programmable scripting tools, such as C++ or Visual Basic languages used by developers;

- Object-oriented tools such as current generation workflow products;

- Knowledge-based tools that can monitor a process and learn from it.

As applications development technology evolves through each of these categories, it follows the path shown in Figure 2.1 where cost increases as the complexity of the business solution increases. With new-generation object tools, however, costs begin to decrease as the factor of reusability comes into play. Finally, with knowledge-based tools, the cost of development actually begins to retreat significantly as the system learns how to modify itself to achieve the optimal capabilities of the business process.

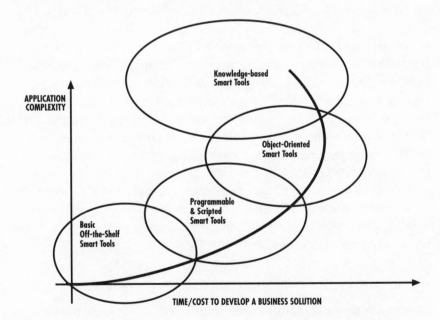

Figure 2.1 Relationship of Cost to Complexity for the Evolution of Smart Tools

WORKFLOW AND TQM

Total Quality Management is a broad-based model for evaluating and redeploying every aspect of the organization toward the ultimate goal of increased service and product quality. Information moves quickly and directly to the individuals closest to the process. The presumption is that these individuals are best able to determine what problems may exist and what measures need to be taken to improve quality in a timely fashion.

Another key element of TQM is its focus on preventing, rather than simply measuring, defects. The organization moves from a reactive mode to a proactive one. This goes back to our earlier point that it is much easier to prevent problems than to rectify them once they are discovered.

Workflow facilitates TQM by providing tools to bridge any gaps between layers of management. In fact, in some cases, the approach is so effective that the ultimate result is a flattening or restructuring of the organization to eliminate layers of inefficiency. In these new organizational models, workers are empowered with information and the authority to actively contribute to the quality process.

In turn, the TQM environment generates a much higher need for ongoing communication and coordination at a peer-to-peer level, because the traditional management hierarchy no longer provides top-down coordination. Tools such as workflow can ensure the integration of these tasks through automation of the information-transfer process. The benefit is improved communication and better responsiveness. The result is a more competitive model for a quickly changing marketplace than that provided in an extensive and tedious management hierarchy.

Workflow also helps to focus effort on the real-time identification of process problems. This helps to ensure a quality process by correcting slight inefficiencies in the process before they become defects in the product or service.

WORKFLOW IN THE EXTENDED/VIRTUAL ENTERPRISE

Recent advances in technologies such as EDI (electronic data interchange) and electronic commerce have brought about a new model for describing the structure of an organization's information systems. This new model, called the extended or virtual enterprise, which we discussed earlier, has far-reaching implications on workflow technology because it causes the workflow application to extend beyond internal data.* In the extended enterprise, an organization's information systems are no longer limited to internally generated data and documents. Instead, they are redefined to include *all* documents and information that apply to a particular task or process. This could extend well beyond the enterprise into outside organizations, such as suppliers and customers.

Extended enterprises also have the benefit of maintaining a close proximity to customers by creating a transparent organization. In other words, it makes no difference to the customer where the functions of the company are located, as long as the organization is serving the customer's needs. Davidow and Malone see this as an essential ingredient of virtual corporations:

> The virtual corporation...will abhor distance. If it can find a friendly environment close to customers, it will want to locate there. Being close will enable it to be more responsive. There will be more opportunities to deal face-to-face with customers, to understand their problems, and to design products that precisely meet their needs, and there will be less chance of something going wrong as the product moves from the factory to the customer."[12]

In using the term "being close," Davidow and Malone are referring to both electronic closeness and physical proximity. It should be noted, however, that they emphasize actual physical proximity.

An excellent example is the case study of Town and Country Mortgage. By putting its loan officers in the real estate broker's office and equipping each with a remote office, the bank was brought to the customer rather than bringing the customer to the bank.

The idea of an extended enterprise is not a new one in concept or in practice. The *kanban* system (providing inventory control by

---

* Before Davidow and Malone's coinage of the term "virtual corporation," the EDI community had used the term "extended enterprise" to describe organizations that used electronic communication of information to join suppliers, customers, and employees as a single business or process unit.

physically attaching slips of paper to batches of parts), devised by Taiichi Ohno of Toyota, was principally a vehicle for extending processes outside of an enterprise in order to create just-in-time inventory capability. Ohno got the idea to use kanban from a visit to the United States, during which he was struck with the speed of supermarkets in restocking shelves. He took this idea back to Japan for use in automotive factories and inventory management.[13]

The difference today is that the paper slips used in the original kanban system that were attached to the parts, which were then delivered to the factory floor, and then returned to the parts supplier in time for a new order to be filled, have been replaced by electronic communications.[14]

It is hard to imagine that sophisticated functions now handled by electronic communications were once performed with paper. Until the mid-1960s, almost all air traffic control in the United States was managed manually. Paper slips containing an airliner's flight number, navigational bearing, and destination were handed from controller to controller. In the period from 1945 to 1955, the number of domestic airline passengers rose from 6.7 million to 38 million per year. Yet only two radar-controlled air route systems were in place.[15]

A prime example of the extended enterprise is the use of EDI in situations where business information is shared among trading partners—and thus crosses organizational borders—to expedite transactions. Trading partners share certain common information with access privileges that allow direct access to each other's information.

Through the EDI extended-enterprise model, for example, an order placed by Ford for tires supplied by Goodyear would give Ford direct access to Goodyear's inventory information. Ford may be able to initiate a manufacturing process at Goodyear that corresponds to Ford's manufacturing schedule, based on production times and schedules at the Goodyear factory. This in turn may trickle down to Goodyear's raw material supplier, who is indirectly affecting Ford's manufacturing schedule based on seasonal inventory cycles.

The challenge posed by this model is establishing parameters and rules for integrating the two or more business partners' manufacturing activities. Workflow becomes a major factor in establishing an effective extended-enterprise model. It provides the tools for defining these parameters, the integration of discrete applications, and the transactional rules. In addition, the workflow model would work just as well with a system that integrates office functions, such as sales and marketing, as it does on the shop floor.

CROSS-PLATFORM SMART TOOLS AND INTRANETS: A NEW WORLD ORDER

It may seem odd to include a specific technology, like the Web, on a list of Smart Tools, but the Web is more than a graphical environment; it represents a dramatic shift in the way work is performed and a quantum increase in the *capacity for intimacy* offered by the touch points of an enterprise with its customers, suppliers, and employees.

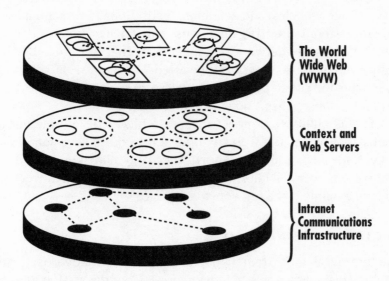

The World
Wide Web
(WWW)

Context and
Web Servers

Intranet
Communications
Infrastructure

Figure 2.2 The Three Layers of the Internet

It may be helpful to clarify here the distinction between the World Wide Web (also known as the WWW or the Web) and the Internet. The Internet provides the infrastructure for the Web. The Web is the system for delivering and connecting graphic and multimedia content over the Internet—that's hypertext. In other words, the Internet is the network, and the Web is the connectivity. The Web connects and delivers information to a person using a browser, such as Netscape or Microsoft's Explorer. There were methods of navigating the Internet and extracting information before the introduction of hypertext, but they were primitive and not user friendly. And early Web browsers were text-only and uninteresting to look at. Web browsers as we know them today give you the ability to click on a graphic in one document and be transported halfway across the globe to another document on a different part of the Internet.

The three layers of the Internet and the Web include, from bottom to top, the Internet communications infrastructure, which allows information to be transferred across a global network of servers and service providers; the content, which resides on individual Web servers, such as those created by many companies, government agencies, and academic institutions to disseminate information about their organizations; and finally, the World Wide Web, which is the network of connections that bind together the many content sources across the varied Web servers. It is this last layer (the top) that people most often associate with the Web, browsers, home pages, and surfing the Internet.

It is this ability to connect disparate pieces of information instantly that makes the Web so important to our discussion of intimacy and innovation. In short, the Web allows us to make connections between information and ideas at speeds that were not even imaginable just a few short years ago.

AN OVERVIEW OF INTRANETS

The Internet is an extremely useful Smart Tool in advertising and reaching distant customers. More central to our discussion here are the concepts of the intranet and the extranet.

An *intranet* is an internal network built on the same technology as the Internet, which comprises the World Wide Web, specifically HTML (hypertext markup language) and HTTP (hypertext transfer protocol). Intranets may be run over private WANs (wide area networks) or public networks, such as the Internet.

Despite its limitations in the areas of security and programmability, the intranet is a valuable tool for breaking down barriers that have stood for decades between divisions, departments, and workgroups of an enterprise, all using different computer platforms.

Given the runaway commoditization of the Internet, the Intranet has emerged as the value proposition of choice. Today, intranet server applications are outpacing Internet servers by a factor of two to one. The impact of this can't be overstated. With the enormous growth of global organizations, the merger mania of the 1980s, and the rise of platform-specific applications, fragmentation is possibly the greatest single barrier to productivity and competitiveness in the modern enterprise.

The key to creating a boundaryless enterprise lies in sharing not only information but also *processes* across the entire value chain of activities, from production to consumption, through a single universal computing interface. Transfer times can be collapsed, thereby creating new levels of intimacy with customers, suppliers, and teams. That, in essence, is the intranet. It is, simply put, the strongest process glue ever invented.

One of the keys to defining and understanding the impact of intranets, however, is understanding the new definition of an "enterprise." Under the old definition, enterprises had walls and boundaries that were used as guideposts for defining internal and external communications. Information did not translate well across these boundaries. With the advent of smart tools such as EDI, the boundaries started to fade. Suppliers, customers, partners all melded into one extended process and extended enterprise. With the advent of the Internet (and later, the intranet), the boundaries all but went away.

COMBINING SMART TOOLS: WORKFLOW AND THE INTRANET

Consider what the intranet can do to redefine the office and the mobility of the user. With the intranet, work is transportable—work can be shipped to any place, at anytime. A connected Web browser becomes the definition of "the office."

But if we are going to maintain any semblance of control and management over the business process in this new business model, a tool such as workflow becomes critical. What document management means to the integrity of information, workflow means to the integrity of process.

Workflow uniquely provides functionality over the information-based business processes that cannot be replaced or surpassed. Workflow takes the business intelligence that comes from experience and embeds it into the document. Using workflow technology, documents are transformed into self-directing and managing objects that streamline and control the business process.

Through tighter control and a just-in-time approach to information availability, workflow can provide increased productivity, increased communication, and increased process integrity to an organization. This level of control becomes imperative as the walls of the organization become thinner.

But consider this other facet of workflow and what it can mean to the widely dispersed, fast-paced environment of the intranet: Workflow creates a dynamic history or audit of the business. Herein lies the foundation to a new knowledge base, a keen insight into not only process mechanics, but also to the daily experiences of running the business. In an environment as loosely defined, and as dynamic, as the intranet, how else could the capturing and controlling of the process be done?

Workflow is not only a tool to automate a process, but also a *means* to better understanding the process. It provides a means to make changes to the business dynamically and intelligently. Workflow facilitates your ability to spot trends in the execution of a business, identify and locate hurdles and bottlenecks, and make warranted changes to the process centrally in a controlled manner.

With workflow, the business model can be altered with the same dynamics that have come to personify the intranet itself. Properly utilized workflow transforms the lethargic organization into a living, thinking, and thriving enterprise. The integration of the intranet and workflow is the foundation of wide area workflow (WAW). If your current intranet strategy does not include a workflow component, it soon will. The competitive atmosphere has been changed forever.

TYPES OF INTRANETS

Today there are four fundamental intranet classifications:

1. document-based
2. process-based
3. commerce-based
4. knowledge-based

Although intranets will increasingly represent a mix of two or more of the four application types, successful pilot applications are typically focused around only one.

Document-based intranets are concerned with the archival and/or distribution of internal documents. These applications take advantage of the broadcastlike qualities of HTTP, allowing updates to documentation and other information to be replicated across multiple sites simultaneously.

Process-based intranets focus on automating processes within an organization. Although not exclusively workflow-based, this type of intranet often incorporates ad hoc workflow management, or other event-driven applications.

Process-based intranets allow the establishment of corporate command centers. Typically, a command center is composed of a Web page, or collection of pages, that contain links to a variety of administrative processes. From within an HTML form, users can initiate a process (for example, a requisition request).

Commerce-based intranets facilitate business-to-business information exchange. This type of intranet may eventually replace EDI.

Knowledge-based intranets are principally concerned with the management and presentation of the corporate knowledge base. Serving as a single point of access to various databases, generated reports, and other information, these applications bring together knowledge that is otherwise locked up in disparate applications.

It is important to keep in mind that *both* internal and external users can access your intranet, should you so choose. Put in a larger context, the only real difference between the Internet and intranets is one of *access to information.* Internet theorist Richard Gascoyne describes it in this way:

Customers and business partners may not need to view information available to your employees. The information to which your banks, law firms, and accountants have access is likely to be different than the data your suppliers need. Similarly, you may want to offer different degrees of access to customers, depending on their interests, needs, and buying habits.[16]

According to Gascoyne, the intranet may be viewed as a pyramid with correspondingly higher levels of access. The base—the lowest layer—is public access. The second layer, community access, is open to *certain groups* of users, such as existing customers. The integrated access layer is open to *business partners and strategic customers.* The organizational access layer is open to *employees of the organization* (either remotely or locally). Finally, the strategic access layer—the apex of the triangle—is open to a limited *strategic group of key customers, employees, and business partners* (internally and externally). The level of security rises with the level of access (see Table 2-1).[17]

Table 2-1 *Levels of Access in an Internet/Intranet System*

Access Layer	Characteristics	Sample Applications
Public Access Layer	Open to public; no security	General marketing; customer service (e.g., FAQs)
Community Access Layer	Open to *certain groups of users* (e.g., existing customers; moderate level of security	Services/products available to registered customers; on-line delivery of subscription-based products (e.g., newsletters, bulletins)
Integrated Access Layer	Open to *business partners and strategic customers;* high degree of security	Supply-chain management; product planning; partner-specific information services; joint product development
Organizational Access Layer	Open to *employees;* high level of security	Employee manuals; interoffice communications; branch/HQ communications; forms; requisitions; HR guidelines; directories

(continued)

Table 2-1 *(continued)*

Access Layer	Characteristics	Sample Applications
Strategic Access Layer	Open to a *limited* strategic group of key partners and customers; highest level of security	Private information sharing between executives and select outside partners and customers (e.g., bank, level of security law firms, accountants)

From: Gascoyne, Richard G., and Ozcubukcu, Koray, *Corporate Internet Planning Guide: Aligning Internet Strategy with Business Goals* (New York: Van Nostrand Reinhold, 1996), pp. 95.

An example of the integrated access layer might be the intranet established by McDonnell Douglas's commercial aircraft division, Douglas Aircraft. This document-based system is used to distribute aircraft service bulletins to its customers around the world. Each bulletin runs approximately twenty-five pages in length, and four or five bulletins are issued each day. Clearly, a system of electronic distribution is preferable to duplicating and mailing four million pages annually. Since confidentiality is a primary concern, McDonnell Douglas uses a standard encryption system, and customers must enter passwords on the intranet's home page. Upon validation, the system downloads each requested service bulletin.

In the functioning of a Smart Company, employee interaction with the organization access layer may save time and money. The case study below illustrates a process-based intranet in which employees use the organizational access layer of the organization.

CASE STUDY

Sandia Laboratories' Intranet Workflow Architecture Accelerates Business Process Transactions

Summary: By implementing its travel authorization system over a secure intranet, Sandia Laboratories has cut the approval cycle for staff travel from two weeks to three days. The change has improved employee effectiveness throughout Sandia.

Sandia Laboratories, based in Albuquerque, New Mexico, and

Livermore, California, is a U.S. Department of Energy national laboratory engaging in engineering, research, and development in the national interest. It conducts research on stewardship of the nation's nuclear weapons stockpile, energy options, and environmental site remediation technologies.

Sandia has been providing data to its eight thousand employees via a private intranet since the summer of 1995. In 1996, Sandia began to explore the use of this intranet as an interactive work management backbone linking employees and lines of business at three primary sites.

The foreign travel request approval process, used by some six hundred people in distributed locations, became Sandia's launching point for intranet-based workflow. With a paper-based process, an individual could wait up to two weeks to get the four signatures required to secure approve of an application. As an intranet workflow process, that cycle is reduced to no more than a few days.

The employee who wants to initiate this process uses his Netscape Navigator Web browser to access a Sandia Web page that includes an anchor pointing to the appropriate form. The Web server returns the initial form, which the user then completes and submits. Inside the form, instructions tell the Web server to invoke the appropriate program to process it.

Since much of Sandia's work is sensitive or classified, security was a top concern, and the lab employed a specific technology to protect data and authenticate users.*

---

* The authentication technology employed by Sandia Laboratories is the Kerberos authentication system, which allows clients and servers to authenticate and communicate securely over an untrusted network. Kerberos uses symmetric-key encryption technology (DES) to avoid sending passwords over the network in the clear. Persons communicating over the network can prove their identity to each other while preventing eavesdropping or replay attacks. The workflow technology used is Action Metro, a product of Action Technologies.

The workflow then validates the transaction according to predefined business rules. If the transaction is successful, the workflow changes the status of the business process and updates the appropriate entries of all participating users.

Each user has an electronic in-box/out-box, or worklist, for requests and commitments to do work. The worklist reports all of the work that user expects from others as well as all of the work that others expect from her. When the user selects an item from her in-box, the workflow automatically reports the status of the request/commitment and shows a selection of next actions that might be taken. Thus, managers who approve foreign travel requests log into the intranet, review the travel requests in their worklist, and by pulling down a menu, approve, decline, or ask for additional information.

With foreign travel approval applications, each of the four people who must sign may approve the travel request, deny the request, or ask for additional information from the applicant. The map for this application is a series of four workflow objects connected by approval events; as soon as the first signature approves, the second workflow is automatically triggered. If the number of signatures is increased or decreased, it takes about an hour to make the change, including testing.

In the case of Sandia Laboratories, the intranet is used to replace a paper-based process that was cumbersome and time consuming. The case study below demonstrates how a knowledge-based intranet can serve as a central repository for information used by various departments of a large organization.

CASE STUDY

Home Box Office Uses an Intranet to Assist Sales Force in Promoting Premium Services

Summary: Home Box Office, a New York-based cable television service owned by Time-Warner, Inc., provides programming via

*both the HBO and Showtime cable networks to nearly thirty mil-
lion viewers throughout the United States. HBO uses an intranet
to provide enterprise-wide access to data needed to assist its
sales force in selling premium television services.*

Previously, the sales force learned of new marketing campaigns only once a month, when HBO's marketing department
would send large boxes of marketing materials, video tapes,
and promotional data to its two hundred to three hundred
sales representatives nationwide. Now this information is
rolled out via the intranet, eliminating costs for printing and
video duplication. But perhaps more important, the intranet
provides the sales force nearly instantaneous access to time-
sensitive market intelligence. This information often took
weeks to receive under the previous system.

HBO employees use the intranet to access crucial information in the company's corporate database, which contains information on virtually every movie ever made (as well as those
in production). A database tracks various data related to each
movie, including its cast, director, distributor, gross earnings,
and details of HBO's rights to show it. This database is also
linked to a Nielsen database that tracks ratings of each show.

Previously, this information could only be accessed as paper reports. With HBO's intranet, users can submit queries to
the database directly. A graphical representation of the requested data is then automatically generated.

HBO's ultimate goal is a single point of access to all the line-
of-business data spread throughout the organization.* In its
present state, this information is locked up within a mixed environment of Macintosh and PC users. The intranet will eliminate the multiple, noncommunicative desktops and provide
one common interface to all corporate information, including

---

* Single point of access (SPOA) is discussed in Chapter 6.

network programming, HR policy manuals, the employee database, organization charts, the cafeteria menu, conference room availability, and the internal newsletter.

MULTIMEDIA AND THE INTRANET

The intranet is uniquely suited to manage multimedia repositories, as the limits on how material is used tend to fall away. For example, the intranet created by the United Nations Food and Agricultural Organization combines printed matter in numerous languages (e.g., studies, reports, and databases), video material, and real-time, interactive features.

EXTRANETS

Yet another permutation of Internet/intranet technology is the *extranet*. This may be thought of as a heuristics-based network that can develop profiles of repeat customers and dynamically tailor Web pages to meet each customer's needs and preferences. In other words, an extranet is an intranet with selective nonenterprise access. Customers and partners can check on the progress of their applications directly, or conduct business on-line. Through the universal browser, virtually anyone can be included within the extranet.

Currently, the rate of deployment of extranets is minimal, but given the relative newness of intranets, it is reasonable to expect that great strides will come in this area in the next few years.

CASE STUDY

Aetna Retirement Services' Customer Service Extranet Alters Paradigm for Investment Account Management

Summary: Most companies are using the World Wide Web as a marketing platform. Aetna Retirement Services sees it as a service platform. In taking this strategic direction, Aetna's management recognized a number of opportunities: the competitive advantage of being the first to market with self-service investing;

better customer service; and cost advantages. In a short twenty business days from the time senior management gave the IS department the green light to proceed, Aetna was offering Web-based self-service investing to college and university retirement fund participants in the state of Texas.

Aetna Retirement Services, Inc., of Hartford, Connecticut, is a wholly-owned subsidiary of Aetna Life and Casualty Company. Variable annuity contracts are issued by Aetna Life Insurance and Annuity Company. Securities are offered through Aetna Investment Services, Inc.

A NEW PARADIGM FOR CUSTOMER SERVICE

Two trends fueled Aetna's pilot for Web-based self service investing—the dramatic rise in popularity of the Internet, and a client base of individuals who are increasingly more knowledgeable about both technology and their investments. Based on successes with its Web home page as a customer-service interface, Aetna foresaw the potential to use the Internet as a vehicle for direct and secure access to personal account information. This strategic direction was supported from the outset by senior management, including the president, the vice president of customer service, and the chief information officer.

In May 1996, Aetna Retirement Services introduced its first self-service Internet site, giving plan participants a more personalized way to assess and plan their retirement investments. After identifying themselves by Social Security number and a PIN number, participants were able to view an informational account statement in a *read only* fashion—an account statement anytime, anywhere. Customers liked that, but wanted more. In November 1996, Aetna took another step forward, blending legacy systems, the Web, and secure transaction capabilities to enable plan participants to transfer allocations among the mutual funds within their pension plan.

Aetna has had a home page up and running since September

1995. There, one finds information on the various services and financial vehicles offered by Aetna, recent press releases, newsletters, and a way to communicate with a client services representative. The Web site was proving an effective interface, allowing customers to get a general overview of products and services and to interact with Aetna staff via e-Mail. Aetna was averaging about twenty to twenty-five calls a day, or about one hour per day of a customer service representative's time.

By extending its use of the Web as a vehicle for personalized account information delivery, Aetna had three key questions to answer:

- How can we offer clients fingertip access to personal account information without compromising the confidentiality of that information over the Internet?

- How can we protect plan participants from unauthorized access to and viewing of sensitive financial information?

- And perhaps most important, what would offering two-way access do to the security and integrity of the corporate legacy systems that comprised Aetna's asset base?

SECURE ACCESS TO UPDATED ACCOUNT INFORMATION

The migration to self-service account management required few changes to the network and systems already in place. The security mechanisms already in place for the telephone service were linked with the Web server. Authentication is provided through a PIN number and server-side digital certificate. Firewall protection allows just this one application through a protected port in the firewall.*

DECISION POINTS

The use of the intranet as a vehicle for customer service was clearly endorsed from the start by senior managers, who saw

---

* A firewall prevents unauthorized access to an intranet.

it as a way to provide more timely customer service at a lower cost. Aetna launched the new Internet-based service as a pilot through an Aetna Web site in Austin, Texas. During the first month, the service was available only to Aetna's college and university participants in Texas, a defined and controlled pilot group.

The market for 403(b) nonprofit institution retirement plans, heavily populated by college and university staff, was chosen for the pilot because of this group's extensive use of the Internet. Texas was a logical pilot market because of the large number of plan sponsors and participants with Internet access there. Aetna Retirement Services has nearly 670 plan sponsors in Texas, with more than 30,700 plan participants.

Two months after the initial test, the Internet self-service was opened to all Aetna's 403(b) and defined contribution plan participants, more than five hundred thousand individuals. Aetna then offered the Internet service channel to life insurance, individual annuity, 401(k) plan, and mutual fund customers. Plan participants access personal account information through the customized plan sponsor's Internet or intranet home page (or directly from http://www.aetna.com). The participant signs on with a Social Security number and a proprietary identification number (PIN). Participants are able to retrieve account information, make changes to future contributions, make transfers between existing options, and maintain their own account information.

THE CHALLENGES

The most prevalent concern with this or any Internet service involving personal and financial information revolves around security. Recognizing that its customers had selected Aetna in part for its high commitment to financial integrity, the company was very careful to select tools and procedures to ensure confidentiality of the customer's information before making this service public. Aetna relies on two high-level protective barriers—encryption and authentication. Precautions have been taken to ensure the integrity of the individual's information through encryption, and server-based digital signatures, along with Aetna's proprietary security features. All entry to this one application is through a protected and dedicated port through the firewall. Before offering the service as a pilot, Aetna tested its firewall extensively internally, and then hired outside security experts to stress test the system.

LESSONS LEARNED

Aetna expected the Web-based services would be well received by its plan participants. The high level of enthusiasm for account information anytime, anywhere has created a demand for new services that Aetna now has to satisfy. IS implemented the first self-service offerings quickly to give plan participants the access they had been seeking. Time and experience have shown the Web to be a viable new service platform that now has to be supported and institutionalized with formalized internal structures to ensure timely response to inquiries and management of responses.

Aetna is also developing additional marketing elements, including Web-based educational programs and interactive planning tools for individuals looking at financial and retirement instruments. Next on the horizon are programs that will give institutions a comprehensive view of the employee benefits picture.

THE MAGNA CARTA OF THE INTRANET

It's as if you've inherited computers from at least three dynasties. They're all different sizes, shapes and capacities, and sometimes they don't seem to like each other very much. On the other hand, you really need them to get along.

—From an advertisement for IBM RISC System/6000

On June 15, 1215, a group of barons met King John of England on the plains of Runnymede and presented him with a list of demands to be recognized and confirmed by his royal seal. The thirty-eight chapters of the Magna Carta defined temporal and ecclesiastical jurisdictions, guaranteed certain personal liberties and property rights, and limited the powers of the monarch. It was a perfect irony that to survive, the monarchy had to open the door to its own radical restructuring.

Today, the World Wide Web has opened the way for a new Magna Carta, and like the courageous barons of the thirteenth century, corporate IS has penned its own bill of rights and served it to the present-day monarchs of technology.

After decades of being told that platform independence was impossible; that applications must live in strictly defined organizational silos; that information systems were doomed to fragmentation; and that monolithic dominance by benevolent technology vendors was the only way to achieve near compatibility, an alternative has appeared—the intranet.

As with most revolutions, the power base is being shaken. The intranet does not bode well for many of the software technology vendors who are so clearly behind it. The problem that traditional technology vendors will find with this great new charter is that it signals the death of single-vendor dominance over the desktop and opens the door to commoditization, "componentization," and interchangeability of software applications unimaginable just a few years ago. But Smart Companies, on the other hand, see this as the key to creating an enterprise without boundaries.

THE INTRANET MAGNA CARTA

- Software Shall Be Free

- Applications Shall Fade Away

- The Desktop Shall Be Public Domain

- The Business Operating System Shall Belong to the Users

- Commoditization Shall Be King

SOFTWARE SHALL BE FREE

This may seem a difficult concept to fathom. But no more so than it would have been for a telephone user of fifty years ago to imagine that phones would be throwaway technology today (in other words, it is the *service* that the user pays for, not the equipment). Nor could most people have foreseen just a few short years ago what would happen to the cost of cellular phones.

The ability of the Web to act as an instantaneous delivery vehicle for dissemination of applications is far too tempting for most software providers. By infiltrating business enterprises with their particular products, these vendors hope to be able to go back and provide the back-end services that enable their client's applications. To invert a popular analogy, "The money is not in the blades, but in the razors."

APPLICATIONS SHALL FADE AWAY

When Microsoft asks, "Where do you want to go today?" most users respond, after looking at the chaos that typifies their computer desktop, "Where the hell am I to begin with?" Applications create islands of automation. They separate and segregate functions that are intuitively part of the same process. This is paramount to using a different type of phone for every state you want to call. Computer users have suffered the absurdity of the need to use discrete silos to launch applications in silence, because there was little alternative, other than proprietary desktop computing environments, until the advent of the Internet.

Today, it is not outrageous to predict that within a decade, at most, all talk of applications will fade away. Word processing, spreadsheets, and databases will all become part of a single integrated business environment, known as the business operating system.* Users will no longer launch or care about applications.

How will this be done? The Intranet provides a common ground, namely HTML, for stitching together work in a single interface

---

* The concept of the Business Operating System (BOS) is discussed at greater length in Part III.

(page) format. Where it once required extensive programming to integrate separate pieces of information into a single presentation, the Web is inherently integrated.

THE DESKTOP SHALL BE PUBLIC DOMAIN

Follow this logic: Proprietary interests in the desktop create fragmentation of platforms; processes cut across platforms; organizations are using virtual structures as one of the key competitive forces; and virtual processes must be supported by a ubiquitous universal platform. Ergo, proprietary platforms must go away. Even if you don't subscribe to that line of reasoning, there is a simpler, more compelling reason: Given an option between uniformity and platform diversity, users won't put up with the more complicated system. The intranet is the option.

How? Intranets act as windows to old legacy computer applications, as well as contemporary solutions. But users only see the surface, they do not see the complexity of integration going on behind the scenes. And since nothing exists at the surface (interface) other than the intranet browser, users see simplicity.

THE BUSINESS OPERATING SYSTEM SHALL BELONG TO THE USERS

Users refuse to be held hostage by technologists and technology interests. Operating systems have, until now, reflected the underpinnings of computers—the internal gibberish of file structures, directories, platform nuances, and procedural logic. If you are intimately acquainted with the minutiae of information technology, this makes perfect sense. If you are one of the millions who is concerned less with the how of computing than the what, it doesn't. All of this should be transparent to the user. The rules, roles, and routing of the business process must be expressed in means that are compatible across platforms and plainly obvious to the most naive of end users. The Business Operating System acts as an intelligent broker that coordinates work and information across business processes using intuitive metaphors such as icons that illustrate the work being done. And these metaphors are identical without regard to the underlying computer platform. Workflow and groupware vendors are already providing a wide array of tools compatible with intranets and Web browsers that can create the foundation for the Business Operating System.

COMMODITIZATION SHALL BE KING

Good technology is that which weaves its way into all aspects of the socioeconomic fabric. This can only be done if the technology is affordable to every strata of society, and if the technology is, for all practical purposes, identical in function. For example, consider the basic operation of an ATM machine. There is no training, ramp-up, or machine specificity that cannot be overcome by even the most basic user. Applying this same benchmark to a computer-based business system may seem odd, but that is precisely the objection many banks had to the use of ATMs—how could a complex task that differed from bank to bank be made so simple? Well, the fact was that it did not need to differ substantially; it could be made simple. And people flocked to ATMs. The same is happening with the advent of simplified and highly commoditized software tools.

How is this done? Applets (small pieces of applications distributed over the Internet), free clients, click/usage-based pay schemes, and standardized interfaces will make commoditization possible. These applets will create the equivalent of a universal dial tone for computing—no matter where you are or what computer desktop you are using, the business process you are working on will look exactly the same. As long as you know the process, any training, ramp-up, or complexity will be negligible. Hard to believe, isn't it? But the tools to do all of this are here—today.

So where will all of the enormous change being brought on by the Internet take us? A few things are clear: The silos are being torn down; desktop dominance by any single vendor is speculative; commoditization and componentization are fact; and the Internet, which cannot be claimed by any single vendor, will finally offer the alternative that no single vendor ever could have.

Twenty years ago most of us would have thought it patently absurd to believe that PCs would take over enterprise computing. Today we wonder how we could have been so shortsighted. The same trend that drove PCs into the mainstream is also driving the Internet. The Internet is the embodiment of the most important trend in the computing industry today—the trend toward connectivity. Connectivity creates a single point of access to all of the information that workers need to get their jobs done. It does what computers have always done best: deliver work to the worker.* Intranets do more by delivering both the work and the tools to the worker. Henry Ford would recognize their significance in a heartbeat, as would any Smart Company.

END NOTES

1   Buderi, Robert, *The Invention that Changed the World: How a Small Group of Radar Pioneers Won the Second World War and Launched a Technological Revolution* (New York: Simon & Schuster, 1996), pp. 89–97.

2   International Management Congress, 1995.

3   Hamel, Gary, and Prahalad, C. K. *Competing for the Future* (Boston: Harvard Business School Press, 1994), p.10.

4   Stamp, Daniel, *The Invisible Assembly Line: Boosting White-Collar Productivity in the New Economy* (New York: AMACOM, 1995) p. 3.

5   Davis, Steven, J., Haltiwanger, John C., and Schuh, Scott, *Job Creation and Destruction* (Cambridge, MA: MIT Press, 1996). The authors have analyzed data on manufacturing industries collected by the U.S. Bureau of the Census as part of the Longitudinal Research Database.

6   Mankin, Don, Cohen, Susan G., and Bikson, Tora K., *Teams and Technology: Fulfilling the Promise of the New Organization,* p. 13.

7   For more on workflow, see Koulopoulos, Thomas, *The Workflow Imperative.*

---

* We will discuss this as third paradigm computing in Part III.

8 Ibid, p. 12.

9 Strassman, Paul, "Will Big Spending on Computers Guarantee Profitability?" (*Datamation*, February 1997), p. 75.

10 Porter, Michael E., *Competitive Advantage: Creating and Sustaining Superior Performance* (New York: The Free Press, 1985). p. 365.

11 Marshak, Ronni T., *The Workgroup Computing Report* (Boston: Patricia Seybold Group, 1996) vol. 19, no. 7, p. 2(1).

12 Davidow, William H., and Malone, Michael S., *The Virtual Corporation*, p. 137.

13 Ohno, Taiichi, *Toyota Production System* (Cambridge, MA: Productivity Press, 1989).

14 For more on this, see Masaaki Imai, *Kaizen: The Key to Japan's Competitive Success* (New York: McGraw-Hill, 1986). Kaizen is a trademark of the Kaizen Institute, Ltd.

15 Buderi, Robert, *The Invention that Changed the World*, pp. 458–460.

16 Gascoyne, Richard J., and Ozcubukcu, Koray, *Corporate Internet Planning Guide: Aligning Internet Strategy with Business Goals* (New York: Van Nostrand Reinhold, 1996), p. 91.

17 Ibid., pp. 94–96.

CHAPTER 3

ROLES IN THE SMART COMPANY: WHAT SMART EMPLOYEES DO

"HOW TO WORK" VERSUS "WHAT TO DO"

Smart Tools create organizations that do not tell people how to do their work, but rather what to do. This is an essential distinction with knowledge workers.

How involves creative reasoning, judgment, and human knowledge. *How* cannot be replaced with automation in the context of knowledge work. *What,* on the other hand, augments the knowledge worker in an administrative capacity. A facility that defines *what* helps to make the work less tedious and, in the case of knowledge workers who juggle multiple roles, it also makes the multiplicity of tasks easier to manage.

The key here is understanding that the environment of the knowledge worker is in large part an exercise in the coordination of tasks, many of which are unrelated, and all of which require human value. Without a facility with which to perform the coordination, the onus of process integrity is entirely on the shoulders of the worker.

The human mind has limitless capacity for creativity and rational thought. Computers have limitless capacity for administration and coordination. Smart Tools use each to leverage the other.

This aspect of becoming a Smart Company hinges on the use of Smart Tools to define roles rather than job definitions. This is a concept deeply rooted in Japanese companies, which defy the creation of job definitions, but instead rely on the ability of workers to apply their collective wisdom and skills to solving problems. The difference is subtle—but imperative—for a Smart Company. Job definitions limit the ability of not only the person, but also the organization to fully leverage its human capital. Roles, on the other hand, provide greater flexibility by allowing each individual to fill limitless roles, or having any single role performed by limitless individuals.

This adaptability provides a foundation for creating what we earlier referred to as a perpetual organization. Perpetual enterprises are able to focus on areas such as *mass customization* of services and goods since they can quickly adapt to market requirements without the limitations of internal structure and job definitions.

Mass customization is the ability to produce large volumes of product in small lots—ultimately in lots of one to address the myriad needs of individuals in a market space.[1] The structures of perpetual enterprises allow them to quickly take on differing forms to meet such changing and diverse market requirements. Examples exist in both the hard goods and soft goods markets. For instance, Gateway Computer set the standard for delivering custom-configured personal computers overnight. Similarly, Hewlett-Packard is able to customize its popular LaserJet printer for different markets. A core engine, manufactured in Japan, can be matched with a country-specific power supply (e.g., 110 volts or 220 volts). Distribution centers customize the product and package it with the appropriate manuals and instructions.[2]

But the more dramatic examples are now occurring in the area of information services and Web-based providers of goods and services. Amazon.com, the on-line bookstore that bills itself as the largest bookstore in the world, uses mass customization to present repeat buyers with customized lists of books they are interested in. Through its personal notification service, it will also inform a user when his or her favorite authors publish new works. By gathering heuristic information (that is, evaluating feedback) on buying patterns and behaviors, Amazon.com can customize what a particular customer sees when accessing the Web-based service, based on that person's individual tastes. Moreover, Amazon.com can manage its mass customization program and multi-million-title selection with just several dozen employees![3]

Similarly, Scudder, a mutual fund company, offers its clients a customized "personal page." The page, designed with interactivity and ease of use in mind, provides the client with information on his or her particular asset allocation and performance of specific mutual funds.[4] But the structures needed to support mass customization and the perpetual enterprise work only if the underlying roles that define the interactions of a company's human resource are adequate to coordinate the extensive complexity of related and unrelated tasks that knowledge workers need to perform. This feature of the *role* is a powerful—yet often resisted when confused with job definition—aspect of many Smart Tools, such as workflow.

Role playing is something we do as children as an effective way of developing a sense of self in relation to others. As adults, the roles we take in organizations are equally meaningful, because these roles define the scope of work and relationships we have with co-workers, managers, and parties outside of the organization. Roles allow us to perform activities that make use of and further extend our skills. A promotion to an elevated role category or level is recognized as a validation of our skills and experience. Yet resistance is commonplace as people avoid defined roles in a workplace environment. Employees often express fears of being pigeon-holed.

Why are these defined roles viewed with such suspicion when they could equally be viewed as an opportunity to exercise our skills and as an important means of fulfillment?

THE RESISTANCE TO ROLES

Marc Armstrong, an organizational behaviorist and workflow expert, categorizes this resistance as the three beliefs behind role resistance:

1. The first has to do with the way we view how we should conduct business in the era of increasing

mass customization. It is perceived by workers that there is less and less room for standardized processes when business is increasingly providing individualized services and customized goods.

2. The second has to do specifically with our belief that defined roles impair team performance and successful business execution. Defined roles are perceived to be the straitjackets that impair a team from working together with high levels of communication, innovation, and flexibility needed to adapt to a constantly evolving business environment.

3. Finally, there is a belief that process automation is equivalent to the automation of human resources. The notion of software scheduling activities for people goes against the grain of the current groupware "group think" perspective. Technology's purpose is viewed as enabling people to make better decisions, not scheduling them as if they were on an assembly line.*

Each of these is a valid point, but only if you use the outdated factory analogy of role definition as the basis for these beliefs. Let us now look at each of Armstrong's beliefs in detail.

BELIEF 1: MASS CUSTOMIZATION REQUIRES CUSTOMIZED PROCESSES

Many of us believe that if one of our objectives is to create customized products and services at a high quality, then unique processes are a requirement. These processes are not considered to be standardized, or predictable, since standardized processes are equated with standardized output. By this reasoning, then, Smart Tools, such as workflow, with its requirements that processes be defined and documented and somewhat predictable, are considered to be antithetical to the creation of customized products.

---

* The author acknowledges Marc Armstrong who provided much of the basis for the section on "Resistance to Roles" and the following three beliefs.

The main influencing factor behind this belief is a confusion of terms. Most automated workflow methods use process models that graphically represent flow alternatives as the work moves through an organization. A process model is essentially a map that reflects the workers' understanding of a series of interrelated tasks. This is discussed in greater detail in Chapter 4, which covers the creation of the System Schematic. For many highly predictable processes, such as insurance claims processing, virtually 100% of the alternative flows can be mapped. However, any one execution of the process model may reflect a *unique* route through it. In fact, a single process may have hundreds of unique combinations of routing alternatives, or what are referred to as *instances*. Instances can be highly customized and difficult to predict whereas the process model itself may be highly standardized and predictable.

This is not a contradiction in terms or approach. As we have already said, Smart Tools work with humans in a synergistic fashion—each where it is most powerful. There are many examples of standardized processes which lead to the creation of customized output. For example, operating rooms are the theater for the execution of processes that frequently involve life and death scenarios. Because of this, process work was done decades ago to define how best to provide high-quality patient care while lowering risk. Standardized processes, from preparation of the patient and sterilization of the instruments to procedures for staff scheduling, were developed over time often ad hoc, or by trial and error, but eventually captured as part of a process memory.* This sort of standardization of processes has embedded a consistently high quality of care in most hospitals and has significantly lowered the risk of undesirable outcomes.

---

* The introduction of surgical gloves, for example, was an accident. At some point in the 1890s, a nurse working with William Stewart Halsted, a surgeon and founding member of the Johns Hopkins University Medical School, came to him complaining that the antiseptic used in the operating rooms irritated her hands. Halsted had plaster casts made of the nurse's hands and sent them to the Goodyear Rubber Company, which supplied her with a set of heavy rubber gloves capable of being sterilized. Halsted, who pioneered many of the surgical techniques used today—most notably, local anesthesia and the radical mastectomy—quickly recognized the aseptic value of the gloves, had a set of *bronze* casts of his hands made and shipped off to Goodyear. The company provided him with a set of strong, yet thin, gloves that gave him the required dexterity and sensitivity. By 1900, use of gloves was standard a standard surgical practice.

Admittedly, using health care as an example is fraught with many variables. The patient's condition, for instance, is a variable not under the control of the organization, and response to processes cannot always be predicted. Yet the principles of a Smart Company can often be found in the most obscure places. The knowledge hierarchy of an operating room is flat, with two basic layers, the doctors and the nurses. Job responsibilities are less important than objectives and the skills needed to achieve them. The same should be true of any Smart Company. Moreover, many of these standardized processes are reused for customized outcomes, like surgeries involving new techniques, in order to leverage the investment in process infrastructure. A new cardiac procedure, for example, will still draw upon standardized processes such as heart-lung bypass circulation, general anesthesia, and defibrillation.

Another example involves a manufacturing scenario that is familiar to many of us who buy and wear eyeglasses. It used to be that a visit to the local optometrist was the means by which one obtained a new pair of glasses. This craftsmanlike approach was costly in terms of waiting and expense. Limited choice in frames, lens coloring, and insurance coverage further reduced the value of the purchase transaction. Now, many of us purchase eyeglasses by going to any one of the large number of retailers that allow the customer to design the eyeglasses with custom lenses, frames, and accessories. The eyeglasses are then made in one hour or less. Without a set of standardized processes, these stores would not be able to produce customer-designed eyeglasses at a competitive price. Their internal operations have been standardized for the purpose of creating customized products. For example, most optical stores do not grind their own lenses. Rather, they carry inventories of blanks in a wide range of prescriptions. All that need be done is cut a blank to fit a particular frame.

BELIEF 2: DEFINED ROLES ARE STRAITJACKETS

Roles need not be straitjackets. But they are often uniforms that prescribe certain aspects of our interactions and relationships with processes and people. And the uniforms often vary: Some might be more like a roomy jumpsuit, while others are as highly tailored as a

Savile Row suit. The alternative, however, is severe "adhocracy." Without a doubt, the business environment is constantly changing, presenting us with a unique challenge in the form of a question: "Will we manage organizational change by assumption or by reference to explicit representations?"

John Zachman, creator of the Zachman Framework for modeling organizations and for understanding change management, suggests that organizational change is best managed through reference to models, much like blueprints that serve as the reference point for change management on a construction project. Blueprints serve as the means by which agreements are solicited and change is documented. Models—specifically process models that reflect human resource role representations—can provide the same function.

The core problem with models representing "who" is responsible for "what" within an organization is one of fidelity. How do we know that a particular process model accurately represents actual conditions of the workplace? Using the construction and architect analogy, there usually is one person who owns the database of blueprints and who is responsible for change documentation. The architect is paid to perform the service of ensuring the fidelity of the final product to the drawings. If our business architects do not have this responsibility, or worse, if we have no business architects at all, then of course there will be significant issues regarding the fidelity of our processes, or business models. The roles represented in them will be constricting, because they do not represent the needs of the changing business environment, nor the changing skills of the knowledge worker.

The solution to this problem is to give business architects the responsibility to manage the enterprise process models as a *knowledge resource,* to create a standardized set of representations that effectively communicate how our organizational resources can be viewed dynamically, and to put into place procedures that quickly and easily capture and document process change. The vehicle for this will be tools discussed in Part III, such as the System Schematic and Time-Based Analysis, which provide visualization methods for creating a shared representation of a process.

BELIEF 3: AUTOMATION OF PROCESSES IS AUTOMATION OF PEOPLE

Do people like to be scheduled, whether by humans or computers? On the face of it, most people would say they want to have the freedom to determine their own set of prioritized activities and perform them accordingly. Most people would probably indicate that it is a matter of choice as to *how* they do their jobs and that performance outcomes should be the yardstick by which they are measured. Many would believe that this freedom of choice comes with our jobs, and that our roles are defined at a high enough level so that we are free to choose how best to accomplish our objectives.

If standardized processes are indeed agreed upon by all parties responsible for process execution and if there is a high amount of fidelity of the process model and its role definitions, then there is a major conflict between the implications of process standardization and this last belief. As any process becomes increasingly standardized and automated, there is about as much freedom of choice as to how one performs one's job as there is for the surgical assistant when the surgeon says "scalpel." Of course, the assistant has a limited set of choices as to how this activity is performed, but most choices were set aside when the person accepted the role's responsibilities.

The view of technology's role as enabling people to make better decisions has only limited value when discussing the subject of *what* a knowledge worker is doing. If you were a patient on an operating table, would you want to be taken care of by a series of ad hoc or even collaborative processes involving multiple decisions about *what* should be done? Or would you rather have proven, standardized processes in place, with specialists performing a prescribed set of proven activities, and leaving it to them to decide how it should be done?

Although a delay in a business transaction is not the same as a delay in repairing a burst appendix, you have to wonder how much more effective most organizations would be if they took their touch-point transactions with this same attitude. This, after all, is the defining factor in good service. Any one of a thousand hospitals would go through the same steps as you are led on the gurney from room to room, but the best of these institutions will significantly exceed expectations on *how* the steps are performed. Operating room personnel rarely say, "Well, I've never seen this before. What do we do now?"

Activities, whether explicit or implicit, or categorized by roles, allow us to make use of our skills and talents. Do we have choice? Are we making decisions? Are we automated? Does it really matter? Perhaps not, as long as we are fulfilled by the ability to improve our skills, use our natural aptitude and talents, and gain valuable experience. Acceptance of role definitions is central to this fulfillment.

INCREASING ORGANIZATIONAL DEMOCRACY MAKES ROLES POSSIBLE

When Apple computer first introduced graphical user interfaces, there was an incredible difference in attitude among computer users and software vendors: Vendors were aghast at the notion that such a sophisticated machine could be reduced to a Crayola crayon mentality. Computers were complex and difficult to use because they solved complex and difficult problems.

Much of that was certainly the legacy of technological limitations that preceded the Macintosh and the unforeseen quantum leaps in power, miniaturization, and processing speed. The five-ton monster with vacuum tubes that was ENIAC in 1946, was the image that most people still had of what a computer should be. Simple interfaces would never be an excuse for the lack of a developer's skills, nor could they ever replace the security of a well-built application. Yet the shortsightedness of the computer industry to forecast its own growth potential is legendary. Whether it be Thomas Watson, founder of IBM, who said in 1943, "I think there is a market for maybe five computers," or Kenneth Olsen, founder of Digital Equipment Corporation, claiming in 1977 that "there is no reason anyone would want a computer in their home," the changes brought about in the last decades were pure fantasy when they were first proposed.

Most important, the graphical user interface, originally developed at Xerox's Palo Alto Research Laboratories and then popularized by Apple and ultimately Microsoft, was one of the most significant Smart Tools of the computer industry, allowing mass market use of computing to finally empower users and not just developers.

It's no surprise, in retrospect, that users, on the other hand, were ecstatic, giddy with their new empowerment. Their Apple computers liberated them from the shackles of the proverbial thirty man-year backlog of applications development that had caused them to all but tip their hats and curtsy to information technology (IT) systems (MIS) professionals—in hopes that their application request might someday move up a few years in the backlog. In short, these users were liberated from centralized and chronically backlogged IT MIS departments. Decentralization of computing power and the liberation of the employee removed the computing straitjacket.

At first the radical Apple users were regarded as anomalies, odd ducks who didn't have team spirit. And if ever they needed help to move their puny personal applications into the mainstream of the enterprise, IS would look at them with a combination of incredulity and scorn.

So it went for the first ten years, until the tables began to turn and the Apple users actually proved to themselves and to their IT counterparts that they were actually able to solve their problems without the assistance of the designated "professionals."

As software vendors began to provide ever more sophisticated desktop solutions, and hardware vendors increased the power of desktop computers, the democratization of computing became a reality. With the ability to control their desktops, users now demanded the same control over other enterprise applications. IT departments invariably resisted, noting that the integrity of corporate applications was not the domain of users presumed to be inexperienced in such matters, but the arguments were often mooted. By then, many users were simply going out and making technology investments on their own, short-circuiting the established routes of information control one would find in a vertical organization. For better or worse, the cat was out of the bag.

Clearly this phenomenon is not without its liabilities, which, among other things, includes the lost productivity in maintaining myriad software applications, hardware devices, and utilities at every desktop. As IBM once warned in an advertisement (noted in

Chapter 2), *you* may need your different computer systems to "get along," but, like recalcitrant children, they'd rather fight among themselves. But today, no amount of prodding can separate users from their umbilical attachment to their personal computers. This trend toward democratization of computing is acknowledged by Smart Companies as a necessary part of empowering the knowledge worker for three reasons:

- Work can be transported to any place, anytime (at home, the office, or the beach).

- Business cycles can be shortened through asynchronous communications.

- Workers can observe and alter business processes as they occur.

The third reason represents a new category of Smart Tools, which is called the *self-service desktop*. A self-service desktop has at least two distinct features. It is *reflective* of the process and the worker's role in it, and it allows alteration of process flow in *real time*.

Reflective means that the Smart Tool provides a graphic visualization of the process and the user's role in it. Imagine that this is a view of the organization from 35,000 feet, which depicts all of the tasks and connections between tasks as well as the descriptive narrative that describes the process.

It's difficult to fully appreciate what this view of an organization's process looks like if you have not used a reflective Smart Tool, so let us use a fictitious analogy to demonstrate. By the way, with the exception of the "retina saturation," all of the capabilities described in the following flight of fancy are available and in use today.

MIA'S CYBER-SORTIE:
SEEING THE PROCESS FROM 35,000 FEET

Mia was daydreaming when catastrophe struck.

As process architect for First National Manufacturing in Akron, Ohio, overseeing one of the last manual process networks in the UnFortunate 500, she was accustomed to surprises like this.

The 30,000-node process had come to a screeching halt, and along with it would follow the myriad complaints from users and customers.

She did not turn to her PC monitor to review the process status. Not only was that impractical at the moment, but GUIs (Graphical User Interfaces) had long since been set aside for those with queasy stomachs or poor balance.

Without moving from her seat she reached for a small unit just about large enough to hold a pair of reading glasses. It contained a black metallic glove with a small cylinder attached to the back and thin wires extending to the finger tips, another small cylinder that she held in her left hand, and a tiny set of cordless earphones.

The device, a Single Point of Access Companion (most simply called it SPOC), connected her to an immense maze of information portals. Today she would use it to navigate through First National's arcane process workflow.

With the case opened and placed in front of her, she looked into a pair of thin beams of light that appeared to shine from the case lid directly into her eyes. She took a deep breath and spoke.

"SPOC, set paradigm for translucent structural components, tactile network access, and user-controlled altitude. Begin at 500 meters."

With that she was airborne in a quiet black sky.

Mia could clearly see the company's work being passed back and forth over an immense computer network of cables, nodes, bridges, routers, and external telecommunications shining like the lights of downtown L.A. seen from a low-flying plane. It all looked as it should in cyberspace, with the exception of a small patch of shimmering light that appeared to be pulsing intermittently. Further to the horizon she could see the orders from customers mounting as bars of light reached critical levels of backlog.

Twisting her left wrist, as though holding an invisible joy stick, she dove steeply into the northwest corner of the building, through the walls, skimming above the fiber-optic backbone that was the organization's central artery for data traffic, toward the pulsing light.

Looking at the dual cords of light she grasped one fiber and squeezed. The light stopped as it entered her hand. That meant a break somewhere in the workflow. The other cable, although visible, was dimly lit. She followed the line, never letting go as her hand passed through the network connections that allowed work to flow from person to person, each node causing a slight thump in her palm.

Suddenly she felt a break in the flow of work.

There was no longer any resistance as she grasped for the beam of light. The network connection was gone. Work had come to a halt. She reached up without taking her eyes off of the cable and slid back a door, or what those accustomed to primitive two-dimensional displays called a window. Grasping an illuminated clipboard with a palette of network icons, she went to work. By tapping her pen and dragging a few icons from the clipboard's palette to the network she enabled the secondary redundancy of another fiber-optic backbone. With that she placed the clipboard behind the door, which silently slid shut. As she pulled up and glided above the roof line, she could see the network come back to life and work stream to its many destinations.

Looking down at the maze of light, now intact, Mia spoke again,

"SPOC, log and report repairs. Shutdown."

As the retina saturation dimmed, her cyberworld faded slowly to black. She had three seconds to shut her eyes and avoid the harsh blinding light that accompanied real-entry.

One day away from the job and she had already had her first remote cyber-sortie.

Sipping at her ouzo with toes buried deep into the warm sand, she watched as the sun hovered over the Aegean and wondered if it wouldn't be a good idea to leave SPOC at home the next time she took a few days off.*

The visual alteration of process flow may not yet be quite as vivid as Mia's cyber-sortie, but the basic tools are there to provide the ability to modify the tasks and their connections with a simple click-drag-and-drop interface. Users can literally change the process at will (and in accordance with security or authorization levels) by simply manipulating a mouse. Gone are the days of waiting in line to plead your case with the IT department for even minor changes in programs.

What this all means is that users are becoming involved in defining and redefining the business rules that govern the execution of their applications. This was always the case, although it was through the intermediary of the IS professional. But now the path to change is direct and instantaneous. "Disintermediation" has become the norm in most IS/end-user relationships.

If this strikes chords of fear in you as you consider the havoc it may wreak on applications, you are not alone. Many inside and outside of the IS world believe that this is an untenable situation. But

---

* This fictitious case study is as much about the human factors involved in a round-the-clock work ethic as it is about technology. We will discuss the former in much greater length in the Human Factors chapter later in the book.

such a stark view may not be warranted, since these tools create an opportunity for information systems professionals, business analysts, *and* users to collaborate at a new level that results in extraordinary responsiveness. If the members of an organization's IS department zealously hold onto the old paradigm, they will be rendered obsolete, or their organizations will simply become glaciers in the competition with Smart Companies, which pull ahead by embracing the democratic principles of computing.

What causes the most concern for IS in adopting the concept of democratization is the question of information integrity, or more specifically data integrity. Simply put, that means certain rules about business processes may have a direct impact on the integrity of the business applications that result.

For example, if a mail-order retailer sells consumer goods and has a policy to meet or beat the best price offered by any competitor, then the rules governing discounts cannot be hard and fast. Each transaction between a sales representative or order taker and a customer begins with a blank slate.

Business rules are about how a business process is executed by its participants. Business rules are, and should be, easily understood by users of a business system (i.e., employees—but also outside vendors, suppliers, and customers). In the past they also had to be understood by the developers of those systems, although the developers were hardly business experts. Data rules, on the other hand, were always understood by the developers and rarely, if ever, understood by the users. The assumption made about data rules was that users need not be troubled with the logic of programming applications. The net result was that developers understood everything and the users understood what they were told, mainly by the developers. These were far from *reflective* applications. The job definitions stated clearly that users were responsible for business rules and developers for data rules—and rarely the twain did meet. If there is an opposite to the Smart Company, the Dumb Company, then this separation of responsibilities epitomizes it.

In practice the tools used to develop applications had more to do with the distinction between the two categories of rules than the good intent of developers. When all rules must be embedded into machine language that is indecipherable to the average person, it is clear that users have no chance of understanding any of them without adequate and time-consuming training.

A good example is the horrific combination of codes and keystrokes that a reservation agent at an airline ticket counter must know when booking a ticket. In this case, the business rules and the data rules have been created by developers in a language meant for developers and imposed upon users.

Smart Tools offer an interesting—but often threatening—alternative to this dilemma. Going back to our original point, what if the business rules could be segregated from the data rules in the case of the mail-order retailer? It is easy enough to imagine a solution that provides the sales agent or the self-service order-entry screen used by the on-line customer, the ability to ask for the business rule that applies to the given situation. In other words, "What discount, if any, should be applied to this sale?" Now, how does this differ from a data rule, where it would be hidden from (either the internal or external) user? It doesn't, if the rule is known. But trying to predict and accommodate every contingency creates an indecipherable web of old and outdated rules by which to run the business. The process memory becomes stale becomes it becomes unwieldy.

The fact is that empowerment must be more than lip service. It must also provide the people most likely to understand the process with the tools to change it and modify it as conditions change—in many cases too fast for developers, one step removed from the process, to keep up with the competition.

Part of the problem—perhaps the biggest part—is that many of these process-integrity constraints were put into place during a time when auditing meant sifting through piles of paper and poorly organized archives, hoping to uncover some discrepancy that might indicate fraud or mismanaged processes. In fact, the role of the modern-day auditor is still largely to verify through random checks the validity of transactions.

But this has changed radically, or should have, in organizations that rely on Smart Tools such as workflow and the WWW. For example, Hewlett-Packard's Colorado Springs Financial Services Center processes over ten billion dollars in purchases for HP's manufacturing operations each year. Naturally, the company conducts audits on a regular basis (it is important not to be misled: the role of the auditor has not been eliminated, it has simply been changed). HP, like most other companies, has a rule that all invoices over a certain amount have to be approved and verified manually, without exception. This was an inviolate policy. However, HP realized during a routine process analysis, using the tools we will talk about in Part II of the book, that its internal technology audit capability was so well-honed that the dollar amount, which triggered the approval, could be increased significantly, thereby reducing the amount of manual validation and associated time and costs... The end result would not be the elimination of the audit requirement; but simply a changed business rule.*

The HP example, and many others, show that the business rules need to change as the business model and the technologies available to support it change. Constraining people by forcing them to abide by antiquated business rules is no less counterproductive than forcing them to use antiquated tools. Both result in frustration, poor performance, and dissatisfied workers who know that there is a better way to do things if only they were not shackled to the process by some anachronism.

Another aspect includes reconsidering some of the most basic tenets of accounting and separation of duties. Today, auditing is not an afterthought, but can be implemented as a real-time activity.† That does not negate the principles behind separation of duties, but it certainly changes the degree of separation required. Ultimately, intimacy is the preferred state of any set of process participants. Smart Tools help to create that intimacy by closing the gap between process activities, for example, by moving the audit step closer to the transaction rather than separating it by extended periods of time.

Democratic computing is not simply a matter of soliciting user input occasionally, or frequently. It is much more a matter of giving users Smart Tools, like reflective desktops and real-time process change that can be used to reincorporate their changing views of the organization into the process structure on a continuing basis.

---

* For obvious reasons, we are not disclosing specifics. Suffice to say that the savings resulting from the adjustment far exceed the downside risk.

† Event-driven business solutions.

END NOTES

1   There are four types of mass customization: collaborative; adaptive; cosmetic; and transparent. Collaborative customizers conduct a dialogue with individual customers to help them articulate their needs, identify the precise offering, and then make customized products. Adaptive customizers offer one standard but customizable product, which is designed so that users can alter it themselves. Cosmetic customizers present a standard product in different ways to different customers. Transparent customizers provide individual customers with unique goods or services without letting them know explicitly that those products and services have been customized for them. Gilmore, James H., and Pine, Joseph B. II, "The Four Faces of Mass Customization," *Harvard Business Review*, January–February 1997, pp. 91–101.

2   Feitzinger, Edward, and Lee, Hau L., "Mass Customization at Hewlett-Packard: The Power of Postponement," *Harvard Business Review*, January-February 1997, pp. 116–118. Another example of mass customization may be found in the sweater-manufacturing activities of Benetton. Rather than dyeing yarns into different colors and then knitting finished garments, the company dyes uncolored sweaters either when it receives an order or has a better idea of consumers' tastes during that season. Ibid., p. 119.

3   Gascoyne, Richard, and Ozcubukcu, Koray, *Corporate Internet Planning Guide*, p. 59.

4   Ibid., pp. 56–57.

PART II

TIME-BASED ANALYSIS: MAKING YOUR COMPANY SMARTER

INTRODUCTION

Part I focused on defining the Smart Company and Smart Tools: Smart Companies *move the work to the worker.* Adopting this approach, however, will require significant changes in organizational structure, and *attitudes* toward organizational structure, *creating the seedbed for the Smart Employee.*

Now, in Part II, we examine how to get there. This begins with a discussion of the System Schematic. Discussion of the System Schematic will include the basic issues of: (1) defining the scope of change; (2) interviewing the individuals to be affected by the change; (3) and most important, defining the new unit of workgroup—the workcell.

The System Schematic will form the blueprint for ongoing change that constantly keeps the organization and its workers in the know, with an up-to-the-minute understanding of the organization and its structure.

Once an accurate description of the organization and how its employees actually work emerges, it is then possible to conduct a Time-Based Analysis (TBA), which uses the data from the System Schematic to produce an empirical snapshot of the work process. The TBA then becomes a metric tool, used to benchmark the organization's functioning and measure process improvement.

The true benefit of TBA lies in its ability to optimize the most limited universal resource—time. Whatever your cost structure, opportunities, or competitive stature, time is what you and your customers ultimately pay for. The rationale behind this statement is often lost until one considers that the actual tasks that make up any organization are limited in their efficiency by the fundamental limits of human capability. Irrespective of breakthroughs in computer chip processing speed, massive parallel processing, and artificial intelligence, people can only move so quickly, think so fast, and innovate so often. Save for the lone craftsman working in isolation, a worker's speed in accomplishing any set of tasks is less a matter of how quickly he or she can perform them than it is a question of how little time exists between tasks.

Think of a simple analogy such as the U.S. Postal Service. Its basic tasks, and their associated times, for nearly every form of postal package are identical. Items must be classified, sorted, distributed, and delivered. No matter what class of mail, from bulk to priority, the basic tasks for processing do not change. The *distribution* of tasks may change (e.g., some bulk mail is sorted by the sender), but the tasks must still be performed, and still take precisely the same amount of time for each piece of mail.

The difference in value and cost for the consumer or business is not in the task time for which they are paying, but rather in the transfer time. Bulk mail sits in large lots and waits, while priority mail is expedited through the same channels at a speed an order of magnitude above that used for bulk mail.

Is quality any less a priority for bulk mail? The Postal Service would claim not. In fact, bulk mail is often the result of a *higher* quality process, since it is mechanically sorted and bar-coded to a precise ZIP+4 location.

Time is the ultimate value judgment. Time is the precious resource that you buy, sell, or compete against. For example, FedEx plays up this fact in an advertisement noting that a sender pays the same amount for priority mail irrespective of whether the package arrives at its destination in two, three, or four days. Whether fair or not (and FedEx's statement does not take into account the fact that its services are considerably more expensive than those of the USPS), FedEx makes the point that the cost of doing a service, or almost any service, is not reflected in its elapsed time (i.e., how long it actually takes to do the job), but rather in its ability to eliminate unnecessary time.

That sounds so utterly simple, and yet it is a challenge of major proportions for companies mired in old ways of doing things, excessive hand-offs, and overspecialization.

The single most important reason for understanding and applying TBA is to break through the hidden obstacles that create the white space among tasks, people, and value.

THE IMPORTANCE AND CHALLENGES OF COLLAPSING BUSINESS CYCLES

Suppose your organization is in the midst of a massive reengineering effort and it's your responsibility to determine where the major areas of productivity increase will come from. You have been in and out of interviews and endless meetings trying to figure out where you can restructure the business process.

Three hours into the latest business process reengineering (BPR) meeting, you find yourself wondering how your organization has been able to survive without a cohesive and realistic vision of its business processes. You started off with what appeared to be a straightforward process as your pilot BPR, but for every known rule someone brings up, there is an exception offered by someone else. So it goes for hour upon hour, day after day. You find yourself mired in a never-ending set of assumptions, perceptions, and exceptions, layered one upon the other into an organizational maze even King Minos would have been proud of. You are starting to understand why up to 70% of reengineering efforts fail—few people agree to what the problem is, much less the solution.[1]

It is amazing to witness the degree to which otherwise successful organizations and articulate, competent people can be reduced to apparent chaos and adhocracy when it comes time to describe existing processes and challenge the rationale behind their existence.

Articulating an organization's process components may be one of the greatest cultural and technological difficulties faced by those who undertake reengineering efforts. The problem one encounters is that the memory of most processes is long gone, along with the people and situations forming the many intricacies of the process over time. As Tevye the milkman says in *Fiddler on the Roof:* "I don't know why we do it...but it's a tradition!"

What remains in a business when we institute change is the aftermath, not the rationale, and we are left with a process that has evolved in ways that no one person can clearly understand. And even when we can attest to what we do, we often have few clues as to why we do it.

This lack of a clear process vision needs to be corrected before undertaking any process improvement or reengineering initiative. The alternative is what Edward Marshall calls *an explicit governance process.*[2] According to Marshall:

> The rules that govern most work environments are usually unspoken...In creating a collaborative culture, the unspoken rules are made explicit and agreed to by all parties. In a collaborative culture there are no secrets or hidden agendas. This way, people know what is expected of them; they have bought into the agreements and take responsibility for their full implementation.

Although there are a variety of traditional tools, such as project management, Gantt charts (a task management system developed by World War I General Henry Gantt) and Program Evaluation and Review Technique (PERT) charts, data flow diagrams, computer-aided software engineering (CASE) and written prose, which you can use to capture a corporate memory, they are far too specialized for use by the typical knowledge worker. In addition, none of these tools provides a real-time process metric. In every case they represent the assumed process. These tools obfuscate the process or simply put off most users.

The result of all this is the lack of a shared understanding of the process and many isolated perspectives of what actually makes the process work. It illustrates what the British historian Thomas Macaulay once warned against: "the collective wisdom of individual ignorance." If you are to change a process for the better, you have two options: start from scratch, or start with an understanding of how the process works today. But in both cases you have to end up with a common vision of the new process. So whatever method you use to change, whether radical or incremental, creating a visualization and a shared mind among the users, developers, and sponsors of a process change will be necessary. [3]

TOOLS FOR CHANGE

Change, in most any scenario, requires not only a vision and a commitment to the ideal of change, but a set of Smart Tools that will enable it. These tools are not just the technologies used to implement new systems, but more important, the technologies used to help teams build visual models of existing and planned processes. Visualization allows for collaborative input and constructive analysis—by everyone involved in the process, not just the analysts and the developers.

In their most basic form, these tools offer the ability to visualize a process in intimate detail. That goes beyond just describing or listing the steps of a process. A traditional approach to this, using a drawing or illustration package, is not enough, however. The tools must be capable of capturing certain parameters about the process that can be used for interpretation, analysis, and discussion. Ideally, a visualization both depicts the process and also helps to analyze it. This visualization serves three purposes.

1. It creates a corporate memory of the process.
2. It provides data for analyzing the process.
3. It creates a dynamic framework for a collaborative reengineering of the process.

Visualization is also a basic element of systemic thinking, which provides the context often needed to understand the collection of events that make up a process. Michael McGill and John Slocum, Jr., authors of *The Smarter Organization: How to Build a Business that Learns and Adapts to Marketplace Needs,* describe systemic thinking as "the ability to see connection between event, issue, and data point—to think of the whole rather than the parts."[4] It is this Mount Everest-scale view that so often escapes the grasp of workers and managers, and impedes process improvement.

To understand how these tools work, envision an electronic white board with the ability to spontaneously create a visual rendering of your process as a team discusses the steps and architecture of the process. As conflicting views arise, the process depiction acts as a common storyboard for individuals to agree or disagree on. If decision points arise in a process, multiple nodes are created for each branch, and when the process depiction is close to completion, the times associated with the tasks and information transfer are solicited from the same team. At any point in time, everyone in the room is faced with a single comprehensive view of the process. An immediately responsive corporate memory of the process has evolved, which means no more flipping through several hundred policies and procedures manuals to recall the specific flow of a process; it is all there in front of you and every other participant.

A tool of this type is a necessity for complex processes that have evolved over long periods of time, especially in highly fragmented and specialized organizations. Don't discount the value of a visualization tool until you have actually used one. No amount of analysis can roll back the clock to uncover the myriad decisions that created the current process—visualization included. But a common understanding of *how* the process works will offer an objective baseline from which to challenge assumptions and create a shared vision of change.

HERE ARE SOME OF THE BASIC COMPONENTS TO LOOK FOR IN THESE TOOLS

• Drag-and-drop palette of icons that are representative of the steps in your process. These should be immediately recognizable by the users as depicting familiar events, people, and activities. Ideally, the palette should allow you to create your own icons so that you can reinforce the visual cues that already exist in your organization, or perhaps model the icons after you have chosen a workflow product metaphor.

• A desktop for diagramming complex processes with the icons and a variety of linkages. For example, in some cases the link between two steps in a process is electronic, in other cases it may be paper.

• The ability to drill down and roll up the diagrams (this provides the visual equivalent of flying at a low altitude to see detail or a high altitude to view the overall scene) so that complex processes can be navigated and displayed easily.

Having an electronic tool does not do much for you if you have to print out wall-sized diagrams each time you have to sit down and discuss the process flow.

- The ability to define parameters for each icon, link, and process. For instance, you may want to track pay rates, skill levels, and network IDs for individuals involved in a process.

- The ability to export captured parameters to a database, flat file, or workflow product. Once you have captured all of the relevant information about your process, you may want to use a best-of-breed simulation tool to identify flaws in your process or restructure it. Additionally, you may want to take the final version and import it directly into a workflow product. As long as you have the ability to define the parameters of the visualization tool, you can then map these definitions to the Smart Tools you choose.

A tool of this type is a necessity for complex processes that have evolved over long periods of time, especially in highly fragmented and specialized organizations. It provides a comprehensible, overall view of the big picture. It facilitates a common understanding of the situation and provides a foundation for visualizing proposed changes to the process going forward that is easily understood by all the participants.

This is the essence of the System Schematic.

END NOTES

1   CSC Index. "State of Reengineering Report," 1994.

2   Marshall, Edward M., *Transforming the Way We Work: The Power of the Collaborative Workplace* (New York: AMACOM, 1995), p. 39.

3   The idea of a shared mind is presented in Michael Schrage's first version of *No More Teams, Shared Minds* (New York: Random House, Inc., 1990).

4   McGill, Michael E., and Slocum, John W. Jr., *The Smarter Organization*, p. 19.

CHAPTER 4

THE SYSTEM SCHEMATIC: HOW DO YOU WORK TODAY?

HOW DO YOU WORK TODAY?

The first step in designing a Smart Company is using a tool such as the System Schematic to design smart workflow, and this begins with an understanding of the work environment, the work processes, and the users' needs and requirements.

The System Schematic is the foundation of a well-designed workflow application. It will be used throughout the entire analysis and design process to assist in understanding how information flows through the organization, how it is processed and accessed, and how the proposed workflow environment will be supported by existing or planned hardware, software, and communications infrastructure.

The System Schematic is what Michael Schrage refers to as a "shared space": it provides the common ground needed to arrive at understanding and agreement on the specifics of the process, problem, and opportunities.

The primary objective of the System Schematic is the development of a common understanding of the organization's existing technology, organizational, and process infrastructure among users, evaluators, and implementors. The term *infrastructure* denotes the full range of all computing, communications, software, work habits, workflow, and political boundaries that make up an organization's processes—including even such low-tech items as paper and file cabinets.

The secondary objective of the System Schematic is the development of a value-chain framework that identifies the major areas of concern and potential difficulty in moving work to workers. For example, there may be a lack of sufficient communications between distributed nodes of an organization or individuals. This may be reflected in anything from the geographically dispersed organization to the time that separates two workers. It may even be something as mundane but crucial as the inability to support the variety of end-user computing platforms currently in place.

To appreciate this, however, we also need to acknowledge that in any organization there are at least three basic layers of infrastructure that must be understood in order to analyze and optimize the organization's value chain of activities.

They are:

- Physical layer—infrastructure: this is the way the organization's information systems (electronic and otherwise) support any given process or set of processes. Most often this was created in pieces and is not a cohesive solution.

- Prescribed (process) layer—organization: this is the way an organization defines a process and assumes it should work. Most often this is based on definition from outdated sources or peripheral parties (such as managers and executives).

- Practical (logical) layer—people: this is the way people naturally work together, and often how they work around obstacles and impediments of the other two layers. It is more spontaneous and rarely documented—both for fear of retribution and for job security.

This is illustrated in Figure 4.1.

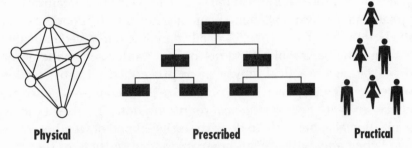

Physical   **Prescribed**   **Practical**

*Figure 4.1: The Three Layers of Infrastructure
in an Organization*

The organization typically exists in three layers: the prescribed
layer is an archaic remnant of the way control was originally meant
to occur; the physical layer is the technology installed to expedite
processes; and the practical layer is the way in which the process
is actually done. Corporate instinct stems from a combination of
the physical and practical layers, while largely obviating the need
for the prescribed layer.

When creating a System Schematic of an organization, all three
layers must be described. Furthermore, any technology, method, or
change must integrate all three layers and consider how they work
for and against each other in achieving any given integration of
people, organization, and infrastructure. Although, ultimately the
prescribed layer may at some point become irrelevant.

The System Schematic is, at first, intended to be an orientation
tool that can set general expectations about the scope of the project and the degree to which existing information systems will support desired results. As we will see in the TBA case study in the
Appendix, the System Schematic, in its final rendering, acts as the
foundation for establishing request for proposal (RFP) requirements for the business system and the development of a project
plan. The reason that the System Schematic works so well in this
capacity is that it is a visual depiction of the process. Do not dis-
miss the process of visually depicting the Systems Schematic as a
trite exercise. It is one of the most important—yet neglected—tasks
in any organization.

It is both interesting and dismaying to find how few organizations already have a System Schematic in place. In a study conducted by the Delphi Group, less than 5% of all companies surveyed indicated that they had a complete and up-to-date graphic schematic of the organization's practical, physical, or prescribed infrastructure in place. Remember, policies and procedure don't count—what we are concerned with here is *graphical* representation. The size of the organization also has little to do with the likelihood of whether a System Schematic exists. Small companies tend to think of this as a superfluous exercise, whereas large companies simply see it as too complex for any one function to create. As a result, IS has its view of the organization process (the network), management has its view (the organization chart), and workers have their view (tacit knowledge). The problem is that the three blocs rarely communicate and are often worlds apart.

Without a System Schematic in place, you are designing your Smart Company or process improvement with a distinct disadvantage: namely, that your assumptions about the company's workflow will be based upon hearsay and fragmented perspectives rather then the actual infrastructure that is in place.*

It is not unusual, however, to encounter resistance to the process of documenting the existing infrastructure. There is a common, if widespread, misperception that by doing this you will be "paving the cow paths," in other words, perpetuating old and outdated ways of doing things. The fact is that a business system, or process, is almost never *fully* supported by the variety of infrastructure components already in place. Some aspects of the current prescribed, practical, and physical layers will work well together and others will practically subvert each other. Without a System Schematic in place, assumptions will be made about the infrastructure and the business process that fail to discern existing inefficiencies.

In addition, there is no denying that much of the legacy in computer applications and data that exist in most organizations reside in the existing infrastructure, which was defined long ago. Ignoring this, will undermine the process redesign. The single largest prob-

---

* My editor originally caught a typo in this sentence. I had misspelled "hearsay" as "heresy." Given the state of many organizations, either term could apply.

lem faced by organizations considering process automation is the support or conversion of these legacy applications. Turning a deaf ear to that may, on the one hand, seem the right thing to do, since we do not want to be saddled by the outdated business process decisions of the past. But this is a key point of the System Schematic. In its initial form, it is simply a touchstone for the process. It does not predict or project what the process deficiencies are. It simply depicts them *as they are*. In itself this may not appear to be much, but it is often the turning point, as we will see in its implementation, in gaining agreement among the varied constituencies of technologists, managers, sponsors, and workers that change *needs* to take place.

Interestingly, experience shows that there is a clear distinction between the United States and other countries in technology investment and legacy applications maintenance. In other countries, there is an unwillingness to invest in technologies that abandon legacy applications. In some ways that may be considered an anchor to the past. It certainly clashes with those proponents of reengineering who advocate radical extrication of old processes. At the same time, the apparent disregard that abounds in the United States when it comes to recreating solutions is almost reckless. This could easily be termed the "Oh hell, we've spent all this money and it looks good on paper, so we'll just plow ahead" syndrome. The wide disparity in attitudes might be explained by socioeconomic factors. For much of the post–World War II era, few nations enjoyed the same levels of technological dominance and economic expansion as those found in the United States American businesses' fetish with the new was possible for the simple reason that they could afford it.

But without regard to its roots, it is probably safe to say that neither extreme represents a reasoned approach to change management. Sound change management weighs not only the cost and benefits of rebuilding, but should also take into account the costs and benefits of preserving the existing process and information assets.

Instead of razing old structures each time we build new ones, the focus should be on the value of preserving the organizational process assets, whether in the form of knowledge or information. There is, of course, the cliché that it is easier to tear down and rebuild than to modify. But this does not fit well in change management and infrastructure redesign in those cases where an business must continue to function as it undergoes change. One executive for a major airline describes the process of changing amid the pressures of business as usual as "trying to replace a jet engine on an aircraft while it is in flight." His point is that you have to suffer downtime to rebuild a process. But it is still downtime of one plane at a time. Grounding the entire fleet, even for a short time, can be catastrophic.

The System Schematic helps to identify those areas where process change can be most beneficial without requiring a wholesale re-creation of the process, technology, and people involved.

For example, at the Mayo Clinic in Rochester, Minnesota, the clinic's patient-records system consists of a variety of paper and electronic documents. In fact, the Mayo Clinic's records managers boast that they still have, and can retrieve, the records of the original patients from the 1880s and 1890s. Although a day-forward patient-records system could be put in place for all new patients, the legacy of patient records would require a decision to either convert extant records to the new system or integrate the old system with the new process. Which is better? Without knowing intimately the nature of the old system, the frequency of readmitting patients with existing records, and the costs and benefits of each approach, it is impossible to tell.

That's precisely the point of the System Schematic. Making an assumption that there is a right answer before evaluating the existing infrastructure and processes, simply because you know where you want to go, is paramount to skydiving without first checking wind conditions, altitude, and your parachute. You'll go in the right direction and arrive at your destination one way or the other, but the condition in which you arrive will be vastly different.

The System Schematic is easily constructed from information gathered by interviewing key individuals participating in the business system. A peculiarity of the approach used to create a System Schematic, which distinguishes it from many other analytical methods, is that the initial interviews are *not* intended to determine the needs and requirements of users for the new system. The first step is to simply develop a better understanding of the existing infrastructures.

This initial System Schematic, as we will see, need not be elaborate; it should simply serve as a framework for validation of assumptions about systems and process infrastructure. By the way, it might just as likely serve to debunk assumptions. There is no need in the early stages of the System Schematic to provide extensive detail about *every* role, rule, and routing instruction involved in the work of the process. This will be undertaken later in the evolution of the System Schematic, when it is used as the baseline for time-based analysis.

PHASE I: THE SPONSOR IS THE ORGANIZATION

Developing the System Schematic is a three-phased process that begins with the definition of a project scope and an assessment of the existing information system's infrastructure. The project scope can be as broad as solving an entire organization's needs or as narrow as the development of an application to help a single workgroup. If multiple parts of an organization are being considered as candidates, the System Schematic must span each of these. The level of detail you are trying to achieve in describing the System Schematic can best be described as a high-altitude view of the infrastructure and process.

The best way to define the term *organization,* in the context of the System Schematic, is to ask the question, "What portion of the organization's infrastructure (as we define it in terms of the *practical* infrastructure) falls under the highest-level corporate sponsor for this implementation?" This is important, since you want to make sure that you have organizational backing for the way people *really* work rather than simply a sponsor of the computer network or a segment of the process (i.e., a department or division). There is a danger of getting a sponsor who is responsible for Part A, and assuming that the sponsor can leverage that change onto other parts of the enterprise. Stated simply, know the boundaries of the area in which change can—or will—occur. Thus, using the definition set out here, the sponsor is for all practical intent the *organization.*

This definition of organization provides a practical scope that can be managed and controlled by the presence of a singular sponsor. It also identifies the success criteria and realistic expectations—both of which are absolutely essential for success. Also, don't confuse *organization* with *enterprise*. Your organization may be only one of a multitude within your enterprise.

There is an obvious temptation here that we need to address. Why not just go for the highest level of sponsorship in any organization, the CEO? If a process is only part of the enterprise, perhaps it could be expanded to cover more ground by gaining this level of sponsor? Be careful; don't confuse sponsorship with endorsement. *Sponsors* are actively committed, *endorsers* are tacitly in agreement. As an analogy, think of charities or organizations that have celebrities or well-known individuals who serve as their chairpersons, but are actually run on a day-to-day basis by a professional staff. One might ask the question, "Does Jerry Lewis *really* run the Muscular Dystrophy Association?" or "Is Elizabeth Taylor *really* in charge of the American Foundation for AIDS Research?"

It is important to strike a balance between both in order to achieve the overall requirements of the enterprise. However, it should be clear that the main objective is to meet the success criteria for the organization and create a successful benchmark for future implementations by other organizations within the enterprise. Do not step out of this scope and compromise the chances for quick, measurable success by constantly deferring to the perceived requirements of peripheral applications and organizations.

Undeniably, this sounds like a fragmented approach, and in fact it is. In most cases, a sponsor's organization is not synonymous with the entire enterprise. Think of it in the following way: each part of the enterprise looks to the initial application as a test bed for its own applications. The success of this initial foray is the greatest testimonial to extending its use to other organizations. Its failure will obviously serve to do just the opposite, and that definitely would create fragmentation as alternative solutions are found.

On the other hand, success may serve to solicit a higher-level sponsor who will spearhead an enterprise-wide or cross-organizational effort. Again, failure would hardly serve that end. The key, then, is to identify the organization by identifying the sponsor. Although this sounds like incrementalism—the ultimate sin in reengineering—it is in fact better described as continuous improvement:

a concept much more established, well regarded, and consistently more reliable than a short prescription for reengineering.

PHASE II: CREATING THE SYSTEM SCHEMATIC

In all cases, the actual process for creating the schematic is the same. The first step is to graphically define an architecture for the physical, prescribed, and practical environment for the new business system. This may mean creating three separate schematics or a single comprehensive model. Doing that can be as simple as a pencil and paper drawing, but in the spirit of relying on Smart Tools to augment the task, there are numerous software packages that provide the same facility in a specialized tool set for business process modeling. The principle benefit of these tools is their ability to depict the business process with vivid detail and to allow real-time changes to be made to the process model. In many ways, the electronic System Schematic becomes a core part of the ongoing corporate memory.

The actual data for building the System Schematic will come from a number of targeted interviews with users, sponsors, developers and any individuals considered representative of the organizational processes that have been targeted. These people are best described as the stakeholders in the process. Mankin, Cohen, and Bikson describe these individuals as:

> those people whose work will be most affected by the changes, whose knowledge and skills are relevant to the change effort, and whose commitment to the changes will play an important role in their success. These people are the *stakeholders* in the development process; they have a stake in the outcomes and are critical to its success.[1]

At this time it is also worthwhile to begin gathering work-routing information. Routing identifies the types of information sources, the way in which information is used, and the path the information takes through the process. The initial routing definition is concerned only with the *existing* business process. It does not consider any potential changes in the way the information is handled. In most cases, this will require expanding the System Schematic to include noncomputer-based tasks and manual or semimanual activities. Once a basic System Schematic has been completed, including a routing definition, you can proceed to the next step.

Note that at this point the System Schematic is far from complete and, in fact, is almost always going to be a misleading representation of the actual and final version. You should resist the temptation to finalize the System Schematic at this stage. Initial interviews can never, and should never, yield all of the information needed to provide a conclusive process description. Don't be concerned about this just yet. If you do attempt to finalize the System Schematic, you will make numerous assumptions and subjective analysis based on incomplete information. This is one of the biggest mistakes made by both novice and experienced business systems analysts: attempting to find "the answers" through extensive interviewing. It just won't happen. What *will* happen is that an enormous amount of time passes, you incur high costs for consultants and their reports, and users tire of being interviewed without seeing tangible results.

A much faster route is achieved by using the System Schematic in a few short iterations of interviewing. You will perform at least two additional iterations of the interview process to complete the System Schematic. Later in the process, during Phase III, we will use a unique approach to collaboratively return to the System Schematic in order to correct the many flaws and incorrect assumptions that have been made thus far.

THE FINE ART OF INTERVIEWING

Interviewing users directly will certainly offer the best insight into their work environment. Without adequate preparation, however, the interviewing process will be frustrating for both the users and the interviewer (whether the interviewer is an outside consultant or an existing employee tasked with the analysis). Without full disclosure from the users, you run the risk of having to repeat the interview process several times before developing even an initial System Schematic. It is also likely that users will, at best, grow irritated by the repetitive questioning, or at worst they will lose confidence in the interviewer's ability to understand the process. This last point is a risk of any systems analysis. However, it is particularly damaging to knowledge-work analysis, due to the level of user buy-in required to successfully implement a system. It may also convince workers that their jobs are going to be radically changed by an outside party or, at worst, eliminated. The worst culprit in any analysis is someone walking in and saying, "We're going to change the way you work. Now, tell me why you're not working well today."

One of the qualities of a good interviewer is a lack of an overt ego. The interviewer should avoid the temptation to stand up and say, "Eureka! I have found the solution!" First, that sort of an approach will certainly sour users; after all, it's *their* process and they have been trying to understand it for years. Who is the interviewer to suddenly open their eyes to it? Secondly, it's *their* buy-in you are looking for. Convincing yourself is easy, but how are you now going to convince them?

Users must not only be a significant source of information for the analysis, they must also believe that they are a strong contributing influence. Without this sense of teamwork, you run the risk of creating a solution that is often circumvented, undermined, ignored, or just plain shortsighted. Again, the objective is in large part to make the people feel like stakeholders in the new process. The value of the System Schematic is that it will provide a common ground for objectively reviewing the collective vision of the process from the very perspective of the participants—not that of the consultant/interviewer.

The goal of the interviewer is to identify weak areas, or potential points for collapsing current business processes, and then present these to the organization as a statement of fact, not opinion. At this stage, it is important to keep in mind that the value of this process is in achieving objectivity and collaboration. It is not uncommon to ask the users/interviewees where they perceive problems and where they would like to see change. The answers provided, however, may only identify *symptoms*—and not the problems themselves. The interviewer's job is to probe beneath the surface by watching for common threads to emerge in the System Schematic, and then using the System Schematic to represent these problems in an objective fashion.

The interview process during Phase II is still dealing at a macro level with personnel who are not necessarily involved with the day-to-day intricacies of the underlying computer systems and technologies used to support the business process. As a result, many users feel the need to respond to questions about the development of new computer-based systems with technical observations about the current system's deficiencies—not unlike the tendency most people have to use a limited medical vocabulary when talking to their physicians. After all, it is pretty natural; people don't want to admit that they don't know what they're talking about.

Most people are also far more retrospective than they are prospective. Thus, their answers are more likely to be based on knowledge of how systems now work, and what is possible within those confines, rather on what they would truly like to see. This limits the value of the user's observations by confining their perceptions to what they believe is possible. In other words, few interviewees will "think outside of the envelope." In the context of traditional systems analysis, this is actually an advantage, because users and developers can establish a common rapport and set of expectations. In the context of a business process analysis, however, user presumptions based upon existing knowledge of what systems can or cannot do is restrictive and counterproductive because it ignores the benefit of changing work models in new ways that have no counterpart in existing systems.

One technique helpful with users who are reluctant to offer an opinion based upon their lack of technical know-how is the "blue sky" approach . When using "blue sky" techniques during an interview with a user, ask that person to set aside his or her preconceptions about information systems and describe an ideal scenario—nothing is too outrageous; the sky is the limit. For example, when asked to describe how to improve a customer support system for a major software supplier, one user replied:

> It would be nice if I could just find out which of my co-workers received the same question. Sometimes you'll get one customer calling several different reps because they don't like the answer they got during the last call. I usually find out about the question later in the day, but by then it's too late.

In this case, the problem was impossible to solve with the existing system, since calls were not logged on-line during the day, but at night—after they had been coded and keyed for retrieval. That same user, when asked for a solution to the problem, responded:

> I would just write down all of the important calls for the day on a bulletin board in the customer support "Bullpen" [the area in which the customer service representatives' cubicles were located] so that you could just glance over to it and then go to the rep who took the call and talk about the problem with him or her immediately.

It would never have occurred to the user that the calls could also be available as they were received. This type of information from a user can be invaluable to an educated interviewer—but to be of any use, it must first be obtained. Phrasing questions in the "blue sky" context may be one way to encourage this. Be careful not to recommend a specific technology solution at this stage. That will serve to set expectations that you do not yet know are reasonable or appropriate, and the ultimate designer of the system will be lured into designing systems based upon the requirements of only one or a few users with whom you have had a good rapport.

Throughout this process, you should be modifying the System Schematic on an ongoing basis with each successive interview. In this way, the schematic slowly evolves to reflect the organization's actual infrastructure and the transfer of information through the organization. It is not meant to be a static document; it is meant as a slice-in-time view, current at any given point in time.

RULES OF GOOD INTERVIEWING

Rules of Interviewing:

- Equality is important. Don't spend unequal amounts of time with different interviewees. The only exception to this is the time you spend with your sponsor in defining the scope and strategy for the process analysis. Although you may find the division chief to be much more interesting than the lowly clerk (or perhaps the other way around), avoid the temptation to play favorites—especially at the outset of the interview process, when your objective is simply gathering a picture, however incomplete, that will be used for later discussion.

- You are not looking for answers.
- Understanding comes first. Insights come afterwards.
- Assess, don't impress.

Focus on all three areas of infrastructure: the physical, prescribed, and practical.

Practical (teams; informal exchange; high-success scenarios)

- How many teams?
- How flat is the organization?
- How tall is it?
- What is the team?
- Who controls the team?

Prescribed (organization chart; policies and procedures; management; auditing)

- How old is it?
- Who originated it?
- Why did it work then?
- Why does it/does it not work now?
- What does it impede now?
- How often is it followed?
- What happens if it is not followed?
- Is it imposed or adopted?

Physical (computer networks; workflow-configuration; transfer mechanisms)

- Has it been designed in advance or ad hoc?
- What is the architecture?
- Where is it diagrammed?
- When did it last change?
- Why did it last change?
- How often is it used?
- How often is it circumvented?

The Three Rounds of Interview Questions

First-round questions: Focus on the perspectives

- What do you...?
- When do you...?
- How often do you...?
- How much do you...?

For example:

Wrong question: How do you do your job?
Right question: What do you do?

Wrong question: Why do you do your job?
Right question: What questions do you have about your job?

Second-round questions: Focus on the "why" as it pertains to the individual

- Why do you...?
- How well do you...?
- How fast do you...?

For example:

Wrong question: Describe the process.
Right question: Describe your role in the process.

Third-round questions: Focus on the spaces between people

- What happens after you...?
- What happens before/after you...?

For example:

Wrong question: What slows down your job?
Right question: What are you waiting on most often?

Wrong question: Can you think of a specific situation that could have been averted if you had done things differently?
Right question: How could the process be improved without changing your job?

By now, it is more than likely that certain trouble spots have begun to emerge as prime locations for automation, augmentation, and streamlining. Again, you must resist the temptation to create a finalized representation of the schematic. You now have a System Schematic that you believe represents the collective view of the organization's existing infrastructure and workflow. You know it is woefully flawed, has gaping holes and loose ends, and in many cases, simply does not make sense. In other words, it is a direct reflection of the fragmented perception most organizations have of themselves and their processes. What do you do with it next? Here comes the fun part.

PHASE III: FINALIZING THE SYSTEM SCHEMATIC AND GETTING READY FOR TBA

The final phase of constructing the System Schematic is the most valuable. Recall that the System Schematic is still far from complete and accurate. There is really only one technique that works in creating a precise definition of current infrastructure and workflow. The process is a simple one—it almost seems too simple to have so much value—yet it is a difficult process to execute because it involves a roomful of humans and all the dynamics attendant in such a gathering. It also requires an objective facilitator who can challenge long-standing assumptions, has confidence in the process, and is experienced in managing group sessions.

What is this simple process? A group session during which you will review the System Schematic created with no more than twenty-five of the individuals involved in the interview process.* The basic premise of the review is that no amount of interviewing—whether group or individual—will provide a complete picture of the organization's full process infrastructure. There are likely to be numerous situations where informal methods have evolved for the transfer and sharing of information that are not adequately reflected until the System Schematic is reviewed by the entire group.

The review of the System Schematic is a dynamic and important part of the overall methodology. In fact, the principal benefit of the System Schematic, as noted earlier, is the development of a *common understanding* of the organization's existing process infrastructure among users, evaluators, and implementors. It is impossible to achieve this without thoroughly critiquing the perceived infrastructure and the perspective—both real and imagined—of the existing infrastructure and workflow.

The review *must* be conducted as a group session consisting of members from each functional group involved with the proposed business application and many of the individuals interviewed during Phases I and II. It is inevitable that many assumptions about the way the existing system works, or is supposed to work, will be invalid. The review will serve to identify the real nature of the organization's infrastructure. The review process also serves as a double-check on the findings of the interviewer/designer, and catches any false assumptions that may have been made along the way.

Ideally, this exercise should be conducted with an electronic white board, software tool, or other automated mechanism for depicting, sharing, and modifying the process with the group simultaneously during the discussion.

The facilitator/interviewer should be prepared to raise constant challenges to assumptions that have been made. When an assumption is found to be incorrect, the System Schematic is changed then

---

* You can try more than twenty-five people, but based on personal experience, as well as feedback received from facilitators at hundreds of these sessions, I would strongly recommend against it.

and there to reflect the correct view of the process infrastructure (this is why an on-line tool for preparing it is probably best). Most important, the facilitator's role is to moderate the many discussions that will ensue and bring digressing attendees back to the focal point of the System Schematic. By doing this, the interviewer can remove almost all traces of his or her own bias, and those of anyone else, from the process by presenting the entire group with a single representation that must be mutually agreed upon.

The result of the review is a completed System Schematic that precisely depicts the computing environment and the obstacles impeding the flow of information within that environment. At this point, we can begin to assess the viability of the existing infrastructure with confidence in the starting point. *This* is the real jumping-off point for the System Schematic; you've checked the wind velocity, direction, altitude, etc. You are ready to make the jump.

As you proceed with the rest of your evaluation, specifically, by using time-based analysis, the System Schematic will continue to change so that it reflects the most current infrastructure. By the time you are ready to implement a business solution—the Business Operation Solution (BOS) discussed in Part III—the System Schematic will have gone through many iterations and incremental changes. But even after having chosen a solution, it is a good idea to continue updating the System Schematic to reflect the changing organization.

Continuing this process of reviewing the Schematic will provide an ongoing system of process validation. It will establish a means of stemming process modifications that may be shortsighted and inefficient. It will offer users a broader perspective than just their own tasks, and will foster an attitude of empowerment, wherein all users can question a process and participate in actively changing it. With this done, the System Schematic will become a cornerstone of a perpetual organization—always ready to change and reconfigure itself for the demands at hand.

END NOTES

1   Mankin, Don, Cohen, Susan B., and Bikson, Tora K., *Teams and Technology*, p. 11.

CHAPTER 5

TIME-BASED ANALYSIS: SEEING HOW YOUR ORGANIZATION *REALLY* WORKS

This chapter discusses the basic components of TBA and how they are used to conduct actual benchmarking. Since the data values used in the TBA come directly from the System Schematic, reviewing the elements of a System Schematic may be helpful at this stage. A TBA case study, involving development of the System Schematic and an actual analysis, follows the chapter. In the Appendix is a TBA self-exercise.

TRYING TO GRAB THE JELL-O WITH CALIPERS

Enterprises are made up of a series of intricately intertwined business cycles. When considering how to streamline an enterprise, the first place to look is the business cycles. The objective of time-based analysis is to redefine and then reconstruct the components of lengthy business cycles in such a way that the queue time required to execute a task is minimized and the transfer time between tasks is eliminated entirely.

For example, a major West Coast banking institution needed to streamline an application dealing with policies and procedures.

Upon examination of the existing system, it became apparent that new policies and procedures sometimes required more than one month to be approved. When the tasks that made up the approval process were listed, however, they totaled only five days. This is the actual task time. The business cycle, on the other hand, averaged fifteen days. The discrepancy was due to the fact that the bank's board of directors met only once a month, and every new policy and procedure had to be read into the minutes and approved by the board members. The result was a process bogged down by a procedure that bore no relevance to the actual needs of the organization.

Processes steeped in history are not atypical. As we will see in Part III, a process retains the memory of its form even after the individuals who shaped it have departed. Because business cycles are often associated with obscure organizational habits, culture, and politics, the solution to uncovering bottlenecks and redesigning the process must include overcoming these organizational obstacles. The application of technology is a secondary issue that may, in some cases, not even be required once the business cycle is analyzed and redefined. It is important to understand and appreciate this when assessing the organization's workflow and recommending technologies to help streamline it.

One of the largest property and casualty insurers in the United States learned this the hard way when implementing an automated workflow solution to expedite its claims processing. Although the system was supposed to result in double digit productivity gains, it did not shorten the process cycle time or increase throughput at all. When the developers of the system examined the reasons, it became clear that the bottleneck was not in how fast the work could be done, but rather in the queue times associated with both paper and electronic transmission of the claims. Basically, each person in the process would wait until a critical mass of claims had accumulated before processing any of them. With the installation of workflow technology, the paper pile in the in box was replaced by an electronic queue of documents waiting to be viewed. In fact, the electronic queue was even more of a bottleneck, since it did not provide a visible reminder of the amount of work needing to be done. It is hard to ignore an eighteen-inch stack of papers on a desk. But ignoring a blinking message indicator on a computer screen is easy.

Such examples may seem laughable, but it is these nuances that make up much of the real work world. And these nuances are particularly susceptible to technology, which may work to mask and bury them deeper in the corporate memory.

To *assume* that huge technology investment is required shows that people involved either (1) did not glean appropriate information during the interview phase or (2) misapplied it—in other words, they saw the trees (technological gaps), but missed the organizational forest.

In another example, Chase Manhattan Bank reviewed its credit card–approval process, which required an average of ten business days from submission of a new application to the approve/deny stage. *The actual time spent in the work of processing the application was two hours.* In other words, 99.75% of the business cycle was dedicated to transfer time and not task time.

Many people are astounded when they first hear stories such as these. But there is a more astonishing fact: *The standard ratio of transfer time to task time, across almost all industries, is nine units of transfer time to each unit of task time.* There is another, more succinct way to state this—and it will make sense to almost any frustrated office worker: 90% of work gets done in the last 10% of time allocated for the task. One way that we can attempt to correct this is to create constant tension in the organization to get work done—effectively, as though every minute were one of the last ten minutes. But this is pure management by fear. It may work for a while, but ultimately it results in employee burnout and poor quality of work.

Stated in simple mathematic terms, the ratio of transfer time to task time in a business cycle is:

(1)Process Time = (0.9)Transfer Time + (0.1)Task Time

Consider carefully what the nine-to-one ratio means. What probably strikes you at first is that, if not for transfer time, organizations could conceivably increase their throughput tenfold, producing more product with less overhead. That is *not* the benefit of eliminating transfer time. If it were, we would have decimated transfer time a long time ago.

Up until the beginning of the second half of the twentieth century, it was a given that increasing output provided a competitive advantage. The manufacturing techniques and substantive advances in productivity during this time were largely the result of growing global affluence. Simply put, business met demand and more people had more money to spend. In fact, today's consumer has twice the buying power of a consumer in 1900, and buys twice as many consumer goods. The so-called leisure dividend has been spent on consumerism. As we have already seen, that equation has begun to shift over the past three decades. Remember that, at present, the world's industrial machine has the ability to produce more hard goods (e.g., cars, stereos, and household appliances) than the world actually consumes. Production has clearly outstripped demand.

So, where is competitive advantage to be found if not in the ability to produce more? Higher quality is certainly one avenue that has been exploited with almost fanatical zeal, but even this playing field is being quickly leveled. The winners are not those who can produce more, but those who can innovate more and faster than their competitors.

Studies conducted by McKinsey & Co. show that, on average, companies lose 33% of after-tax profit when they ship a product to market six months late, as opposed to only 3.5% if they spend 50% more on the development than planned and then ship on time.[1]

The ability to develop new products quickly and continuously outperform competitors is a bastion of competitive advantage, especially when transfer time takes up at least 90% of the time in the innovation, production, and delivery cycle. This is often called time to market, or concept-to-cash time.[2] Both are the time involved in getting from the concept phase of a new product to its actual availability in the market. As the pace of technology quickens, these cycles become increasingly shorter. In the case of knowledge-based products, such as Web services, the concept-to-cash time can be as short as days or weeks. In other industries, such as that of automobile manufacturing, concept-to-cash time has dropped dramatically due to the use of integrated design and production systems.

The dependence of today's enterprises on fast innovation and delivery of product cannot be overestimated. Consider this: 50% of Hewlett-Packard's sales come from products introduced in the last three years.[3] The favorite saying of the company's CEO, Lou Platt, is, "We want to eat our lunch before someone else does." Sony, on the other hand, establishes a sunset date with every new product, effectively planning for its demise before it is even born.[4] This is far removed from the planned obsolescence that once dominated American manufacturing and was roundly criticized as wasteful and manipulative. That practice was driven by suppliers' needs to motivate consumption in limited markets. Today's innovation is driven by business markets that are battling time to beat their competitors to the next product innovation.

A well-known example of innovation at work in establishing clear competitive advantage involves Honda and Yamaha, which in the early 1980s fought fiercely to dominate the global motorcycle market. In the course of one eighteen-month period Honda introduced 113 new motorcycle models, while Yamaha could only churn out 37 models.[5]

In each case, these tacit innovation quotas are an essential part of ensuring future competitiveness.

Perhaps if IBM had taken the same approach with respect to its mainframe computers rather than rely on the stature it gained in the 1950s and 1960s as the industry benchmark, Big Blue would not have to work so hard today to reshape itself by laying off tens of thousands of employees and shedding divisions. The same could be said for Digital Equipment Corporation. Its VAX computers once were the gold standard of computing, but the company largely ignored the PC revolution, and has scrambled furiously to make up for lost time.

This sort of thinking would *not even occur* in a properly constituted perpetual organization. Thinking of change as an event rather than as an *integral* part of the process demonstrates that an organization is still using old paradigms for adapting to its markets.

In many ways, one could say that it is as important to walk away from success and to relearn, or even forget the rules of success, as any other strategic effort.[6] The automation of the innovation cycle is becoming the twenty-first century equivalent of the automation of production cycles that marked the twentieth century.

What we fail to recall, however, is that the Industrial Revolution began over two hundred years ago with the invention of the steam engine and the development of the textile industry. It has taken two centuries to develop the wealth of knowledge about manufacturing techniques, methods, and processes to enable the almost total automation of the factory.

For most of the innovations introduced in the nineteenth and twentieth centuries, it took at least fifty years to demonstrate that the technology represented a quantum increase over its predecessor technologies. This was true of steam power and electricity. James Watt developed the steam engine in the 1760s. Aside from limited use in coal mines, it was largely ignored by most industries. It was not until 1809, when Robert Fulton built the first working steamship, that the true potential of steam power was demonstrated. Electricity had been generated in Leyden jars since the early 1700s. It was not until Edison and Tesla, among others, perfected methods of large-scale generation and storage in the late nineteenth century that electricity became a viable source of wide-scale power.

So why shouldn't it take decades for computers to demonstrate their promise? This seems inaccurate to those people who correctly claim that the power of computing has increased drastically as the cost of computing has dropped. (The often-quoted fact that an automobile would cost a few dollars and get thousands of miles to the gallon if the pace of automobile development matched that of computers is cited as clear evidence of this.) But the enormous leaps in computing power have not gone along with commensurate productivity increases. Paul Strassman, in his book *The Squandered Computer,* convincingly uses extensive statistics to debunk the myth that more spending on information technology has, up to now, resulted in increased return on equity.

The most pressing question at the moment is: What methods exist for achieving these quantum increases in productivity? Even Frederick Winslow Taylor's stopwatch-driven time-motion studies of the early 1900s were intended for rigorous, highly repetitive factory environments, and not for the highly interactive free-form processes that drive today's information-rich enterprise. Using these methods today would be tantamount to trying to grab the Jell-O with calipers.

WHY OTHER METHODS FALL SHORT OF THE MARK

Other methods are equally difficult to use. For example, some organizations turn to business process reengineering (BPR) in their search for improved productivity. BPR ultimately demands a change in the way a company works, whether it be with customers (both internal and external), suppliers, and its employees—or all three. This requirement for change aims to provide faster company response to the needs of the customer, continued growth in revenue streams, and fundamentally lower cost structures.

The commitment to the reengineering effort usually starts with an understanding of the current business cycle processes, and then considers how changes can be made through the use of technology, work redesign, and outsourcing of support services that are not part of a company's core competency. But to understand this current process, analysis of the business cycle is required. That is precisely what TBA does.

If not BPR, then what about project management techniques, computer-aided software engineering (CASE) tools, dataflow diagramming, and systems analysis methods? Don't these qualify as business process analysis tools? Yes, absolutely. And nothing discussed here should diminish the importance of relying on these tools, or others with which the reader is already familiar, as part of a thorough analysis.

However, here's the rub: whatever tool you use must be capable of two things. First, the tool must be comprehensible by the process owners. This is no different than the case of the System Schematic. If process owners are not able to infer readily the efficiency or inefficiency of a business cycle from a visual depiction of the process, they will not be able to participate in redefining it.

Second, the tool must be capable of analyzing three types of process time: task time, transfer time, and queue time (discussed later in this chapter). Amazingly, some tools, such as dataflow diagramming methods, completely ignore the basic element of transfer time and focus exclusively on task time. That's seeing only half the picture. CASE technology, for instance, fails both tests. First, CASE has an acceptance problem. CASE tools are by definition automated software systems, which can only be used with computer-based solutions. Thus, in selecting a specific CASE tool, the people responsible for the project must accept the methodology promulgated by (and embedded in) that particular software vendor. Using CASE requires an odd sequence of comprehension; the methodology must first be understood, and then the software tool itself, and finally its application toward the development of new software systems. It is a tall order to expect anyone but the most sophisticated IS professional to feel comfortable with this.

Second, CASE tools and methods can be used to model the flow of information and process, but the recognition and use of a time factor simply does not exist. This means that the analysis of a business through the use of CASE tools will not provide any objective information regarding the amount of time a process takes to complete, or any indication of how the business cycle can be compressed so as to complete work tasks more efficiently. Quite simply, any solution arrived at through the use of CASE tools will not be an accurate representation of how the business *truly* works.

Yet another long-standing technique that might be used to understand the business process and information flow is data-flow diagramming. This approach is graphical, very visual, and easy for developers to use to see the work in the process, as well as the flow of the information within the organization. But that is about all this technique offers, and it was devised long before the advent of large-scale computer networks. Thus, it is not capable of assessing the enormous transfer times that occur between networked users. Not only are end users reluctant to buy-in to the discipline ("I am a business person, not one of the technology crowd"), but here again the recognition of time is not a focus or strength of this approach. Indicating the task time may be possible, but the *aggregation* of that time, let alone the identification of queue or transfer time, is not feasible with data-flow diagramming.

Lately, a great deal of attention has been paid to activity-based costing (ABC). ABC is intended to provide a measure of the costs attributable to a unit of work. If business processes were completely efficient, and therefore consisted only of task time (which, as noted earlier, is a patently false idea—recall the 90/10 rule), there would be little need for time-based analysis. ABC would work just fine. We simply could define the series of tasks that comprise a process, identify the cost of each task by multiplying the resource cost by the task time, and then associate a cost with the total value chain of activities to produce a given product or service. But any accountant or manager will tell you such a process is much easier said than done.

In most office environments, ABC is virtually impossible. A typical office worker is involved in a variety of tasks at any one time, making the allocation of a specific resource to a specific value chain of tasks difficult even in small organizations. The process cycle time, on the other hand, is an equally erroneous measure of the value-chain duration, since the value-add portion of time in the value chain is always a fraction of the time to complete the business cycle. Think back to the example of Chase Manhattan's credit card–approval process. In that case, the value-chain activities took less than 1% of the time required to complete the approval cycle.

In addition, the identification of "wait time" such as queue or transfer time, is simply not a part of the ABC effort. Thus, the compression or elimination of that time through any type of analysis cannot occur, since the representation of those values does not exist in ABC.

In light of the shortcomings of other tools, the TBA methodology and spreadsheet tool provide a very usable means of analyzing process time for a business cycle. Singular in approach and easy to use, TBA offers insights into questions that other methods and tools cannot easily provide. The most important are: (1) What is the transfer time between tasks? and (2) if a queue exists for a task, how much non-value-added process time does it consume?

AN INTRODUCTION TO THE TBA METHOD

Fundamentally, time-based analysis is a method for quantifying that portion of process time which does not add any value to the completion of a business cycle. The focus of TBA is on eliminating, or at least reducing, the portion of the business cycle occurring between the value-added tasks. TBA is applied through the use of an analytical tool that provides the means for quantifying the three elements of process time: *task time, transfer time, and queue time.*

When an organization makes an effort to understand and analyze its business processes, there is the risk that the method and/or analysis tools used will be incomprehensible to most people, or that they require a certain singular expertise. These methods and tools may simply require too large an investment in time and learning for the analyst to expect even a modicum of success. The result is little, if any, buy-in from the stakeholders in the process.

TBA steers clear of this problem by providing an analysis that is easy to understand and use by the personnel who inhabit the processes, as well as those responsible for making the indicated changes to the business cycle. In this regard TBA is unique.

Although time-based analysis may appear to be like other BPR and analysis tools, it is substantially different—but not to the point of exclusion. You may decide to use TBA instead of, or in conjunction with, other methods and tools.

TBA is conducted in three steps: first, gathering data on work-cells and task times (this is done during the creation of the System Schematic); second, finding and then analyzing nonproductive waiting time; third, devising methods of compressing the business cycle. These will be discussed in detail later in this chapter.

WHAT BENEFITS DOES TIME-BASED ANALYSIS PROVIDE?

With respect to current business processes, TBA:

- identifies both business cycle efficiencies and weaknesses;
- will objectively expose inconsistency and complexity in the existing business cycle;
- makes nonproductive time in a business cycle visible;
- provides a quantifiable basis for separating task time from nontask time (transfer and queue);
- quantifies the waiting time potentially saved by *workflow* technology;
- offers a mechanism for challenging the status quo of existing work processes;
- provides (actually, requires) a detailed understanding of the business cycle process. In the dimension of organizational

participation and support, which is a first step in addressing the issues of cultural resistance issues TBA;

- identifies the workcells affected by the process;
- provides process information understandable by workcells, which begets a sense of ownership.

In addressing new business processes, TBA:

- directly, or indirectly, causes the reengineering of the business cycle;
- supports ideas and direction of process redesign with objective data;
- provides a guide for implementing change in process;
- potentially leads to faster innovation in product life cycle.

WHAT FACTORS WILL TBA EXPOSE THAT ARE NOT ADDRESSED BY OTHER ANALYTICAL METHODS?

First, time-based analysis offers a realistic perspective on the business cycle and the value chain, or the value-add portion of a business cycle, by measuring not only task time but, more important, *the business cycle time between people.* In doing this, time-based analysis also offers a unique benefit for organizations that anticipate cultural resistance to analyzing their processes. Because TBA is based on the premise that 90% of the business process problem lies in the process itself, and not in the tasks performed by the people, it minimizes the threat that workers will perceive that they are being fingered as the problem.

The fact is that tremendous investment in task automation and office computing over the past two decades has made the actual work related with most processes quite efficient. In most cases, the problem is not the people or their work; it is the spaces *between* people and their work.

This is not to say that human factors are not a key aspect of process improvement. It may be that further exploration will demonstrate that there *are* personnel issues that must also be considered. But starting with the premise that people are the problem will alienate both good and poor workers. At the very least, TBA has a definite diplomatic advantage by helping people to focus on the process rather than to dissect their responsibilities. Additionally, many problems with prolonged task times result from deficiencies in the current system's ability to transfer information in such a way as to optimize existing peaks and lows in users' workloads.

Organizations may look upon these as management-related problems that can be solved by increasing the efficiency of the task and worker. This approach often ignores the real problem—transfer and queue time. In many cases, simply eliminating the transfer time or queue time can substantially improve a business cycle. None of this is to say that transfer time and queue time must always be zero for all processes. If they were, there would be no time for unanticipated or necessary downtime. But there is a distinct difference between idle time built into a process by design or spontaneous situations, and idle time that has insidiously filled the dark spaces of the process.

The most incredible aspect of TBA is that it may change the total cycle time without changing a single task; rather, the improvement comes from collapsing the idle time between tasks. Think back to the discussion about process intimacy in Chapter 1 and the effect it has on process efficiency.

Second, time-based analysis provides an *objective measure* of the existing problems. Although it is possible to debate the inefficiencies of work habits, information systems, and infrastructure, the element of time is easily measured and presented. In analyzing a process for potential improvements, it is important to be able to present objective and quantitative metrics, rather than rely on intangible benefits that cannot be readily justified. This is true even when the justification is based on future opportunity. If nothing else, the neutral representations of a TBA will present hard data that tends to mollify the empiricists in the organization. And it can also be used to refute wild claims of workers that are based more on emotion than fact.

Third, the process of defining task transfer times and total business cycle times will expose the full breadth of inconsistency and complexity of the business cycles in question. It is not unusual to find that some business cycles have no consistent duration. In an example found later in this chapter, time required for approval of the organization's policies and procedures varied from two weeks to six months. What appeared to be one business cycle actually consisted of multiple formal and informal cycles. Until time-based analysis was applied, it was impossible to identify the problems with the existing process or the applications for improved workflow.

HOW IS TIME-BASED ANALYSIS IMPLEMENTED?

Time-based analysis can be used by experts with some skill and experience in its methods, but it can just as easily be understood by almost anyone charged with improving a process.

The first step in a time-based analysis is the definition of the tasks involved in a given business cycle and the workcells that actually perform those tasks.

The definition of the business cycle for which you perform a time-based analysis will correspond to the process that you have decided to analyze in your System Schematic. It should be broad enough to include all of the activities for a certain logically connected set of tasks that represent the process. For example, publishing a corporate policy requires, at a minimum, several tasks: authoring and approval of the new policy; checking its consistency with existing policies; obtaining executive-level approval of the policy; submitting it for approval by the board of directors; and typesetting, publishing, and distributing the policy. Don't be overly concerned with getting every single task defined from the outset.

The steps you have created for the System Schematic should be sufficient to begin the TBA. But as with the System Schematic, some dialogue and discussion through several iterations is a better approach than trying to get it all right the first time.

As each task is defined, it is associated with the task time, captured during the System Schematic.

Task time is the total amount of time it takes to complete the task for a given workcell, exclusive of the time spent waiting for information related to the task or subsequently transmitting information to the next task.

For instance, the task time for board of directors' approval of a policy is never more than two hours, since this is the stipulated length of the directors' meeting. It may, however, take up to two weeks to actually approve the policy, because the directors meet only twice each month. This is represented in the second variable, which is the transfer time between tasks.

Transfer time identifies the time required to transfer information from one task to another.

At first this may seem to have only trivial distinction from task time. After all, isn't transfer time part of the task? In the case of the directors' meeting, once the author has written the policy, it's no longer his or her job to get it approved. Instead, approval becomes the responsibility of the directors. As far as the directors are concerned, however, they fulfill their responsibility through meeting twice each month. The problem becomes painfully obvious—transfer time belongs to no one. No one takes responsibility for it. On the other hand, if we arbitrarily say that the onus is on the directors to meet more often, we are suddenly putting someone in the position to defend a piece of the process that he or she cannot control. It's no surprise that business cycles are difficult to collapse if there is no accountability for one of the most time-consuming elements of the business cycle.

Tasks clearly belong to individuals and workgroups. Transfer time, however, *belongs to the process itself and the information systems in place to facilitate the process.* Once we have established that transfer time is a process issue and not a people issue, it becomes much easier to identify problems with the existing process. Transfer time is not associated with one or the other of the receiving or sending workcell, but rather with both.

The point is not simply to look at the total of task time versus transfer time (although this does provide some insight), but rather to identify which tasks are preceded or followed by inordinately long transfer times.

A simple analysis of the policies and procedures approval cycle, described earlier, shows that the transfer and queue times were significantly greater than the actual task time involved.

Queue time does not add any value to work; rather it defines how long information will sit around before someone begins to work on it.

If the process were changed to require the board of directors' approval of only a subset of the policies and procedures, the business cycle could be reduced substantially. In fact, since 95% of all policies and procedures were approved by simply being read into the minutes, the process was being held hostage by the two-week transfer time.

By evaluating the relationship of transfer time to task time we can begin to formulate opinions as to likely workflow candidates for streamlined business processes. For example, if the total transfer time is significantly higher than the task times, there is a great deal of opportunity to reduce information transfer time without necessarily changing tasks. The benefit, of course, is less disruption on the part of users. It may also be the case that transfer times vary dramatically from one set of tasks to another. This may be indicative of a bottleneck situation occurring again and again in the same area, regardless of the information being processed. That may represent a point for automation or augmentation that again minimizes user disruption.

You may similarly be able to draw conclusions about the interaction of workcells. For example, if transfer times consistently appear to be lengthy when transferring information between two workcells, it may be the case that there is a specific situation causing these two groups to experience communication delays. What the problem exactly is, however, cannot be determined from the time-based analysis alone. But it is certain that you will not be pointing a finger of blame at one group or the other from these results alone. Again, this is a key reason for the allocation of transfer time to both sender and recipient of the information.

In every case, the time-based analysis model can deliver a concise assessment of the existing workflow environment and thereby make manifest potential areas of opportunity for a new process.

Keep in mind that throughout our discussion of time-based analysis that we have not said that people are never the problem. That may well be the case, and it may have to be dealt with as part of the workflow analysis.

But starting with the premise that it's the people who are somehow responsible for inefficiency is dangerous and time consuming. The approaches presented in this chapter shift the focus away from people and reorient it toward redefining the process model. Users are much more likely to cooperate, in that case, and the underlying inefficiencies of the business process are much more likely to be resolved. Applying time-based analysis will help you to demonstrate short-term payback that will provide long-term leverage.

BUILDING THE TBA

A Time-based analysis model is nothing more than a simple matrix succinctly indicating the relationship of tasks to workers. From this initial matrix, a variety of charts can be created that act as benchmarks for the process. Benchmark, as used in the context of TBA, is meant to provide an assessment of how different workcells rank against each other's associated task, transfer, and queue times. The benchmarking simply identifies those areas where a particular workcell, or combination of workcells, have protracted transfer or queue times.

It should be stressed that the overall value of doing TBA can be discerned even if an entirely manual application of the methodology is used. In keeping with the belief that ease of use is important, a TBA can, as we noted earlier, even be accomplished with paper and pencil.

Before beginning a TBA, it is useful to become familiar with the terminology used.

WORKCELLS

After the organizational view of the infrastructure and the workflow are determined using the System Schematic, the individual workcells that make up the processes are defined. The concept of a workcell is one of the most important aspects of a correct TBA.

A practical example of a workcell in the traditional hierarchical organization is the formation of a team that consists of representatives from several functions, such as accounting, sales and marketing departments. This workcell approves advertising campaigns, so we will call them "approvers." If one were to list the possible applications for an organization involved with creating advertising programs, it would include the application "new ad program" and the workcell called "approvers." It would also include numerous other workcells, some of which may correspond with traditional departmental groupings, for example, development cell, product roll-out cell, new concept validation cell.

The point of a workcell approach is *not* to obliterate any and all existing structures, but rather to allow for the representation of a process in its most natural form. In reality, most organizations do not follow the boundaries of departments and formal workgroups as often as managers would like to believe.

As a result, processes take shape over time that run contrary to the accepted myth of an organizational hierarchy. This is one of the reasons that our discussion about the various organizational structures is so important to correctly applying either the System Schematic or time-based analysis. Neither of these methods will work if you adhere strictly to a hierarchical model. Many of the incorrect assumptions about process steps are perpetuated by hierarchy. Our objective is to challenge those assumptions by relying on the process structure, not the organizational structure. This will be critical in the use of the time-based analysis tool.

TASKS

Tasks put a name on the work each workcell must complete in the business cycle undergoing analysis. Thus, the identification of each discrete task is often completed in conjunction with the final identification of the workcells. Again, this should be a natural result of the System Schematic.

First, get the tasks listed and then arrange them in the sequence of their occurrence: the first task which must be completed is listed first, then the second task to be completed is listed next, and so on. Be sure the tasks in the list are discrete enough in scope that *no* overlap occurs between Tasks; and that the workcell(s) responsible for all or part of a task can be identified. This is very important to building an accurate model of the business cycle being analyzed.

At this point in the TBA-build process, the foundation data for TBA is almost complete. The workcells and tasks have been identified for the business cycle, so now the times that reflect how long it takes to complete the work must be determined. Remember, once more, that all of this should have been collected while creating the System Schematic.

WORKCELL/TASK TIMES

Since the workcell and tasks are organized as a matrix (as you will see in the case study), the intersection point for these two parts of the business process is where we list the time required for any workcell to complete its portion of the task. This time would be listed in a unit of measure appropriate for the length of the business cycle being analyzed. If the cycle is days in length, then perhaps the time for the task to be completed will be listed in days or hours.

When selecting the unit of measure for the task time, also consider the time which will be determined for the non-value-added process. Should that time be appropriately listed (as explained subsequently) in days or weeks for some reason, then the common unit of measure should perhaps be days with decimal fractions representing less than a one-days time.

Thus, for every task listed down one side of the matrix that is worked on by any of the workcells listed across the top of the matrix, the time for completing this task is listed at their matrix intersection. Then the total time for a task to be completed is summed for each task. Additionally, all the times that a workcell spends on any task are summed for each workcell.

From this allocation of time come the first two data points in the time-based analysis: the total task time for a business process, and the total time a workcell spends on any of the tasks making up this process. These times are generally reflective of value-added time associated with the completion of the business cycle work.

However, the next two steps in the initial building of a TBA for a given business process are key to the unique value of TBA: determining queue time and transfer time. Both of these times are non-value-added activities, and the goal of TBA is to remove these times from the business cycle being analyzed, thus it is import to define these times correctly.

QUEUE TIMES

Queue time is directly associated with the task one or more workcells are responsible for completing. However, this time does not add any value to that work; rather it defines how long information might sit around before someone begins to work on it.

Thus, the next step is to identify any task/workcell combinations which have queues associated with them. Look for a holding time where the work could be started but, for some reason, the workcells do not start working immediately to complete the task with the information when it becomes available.

Queues may not be obvious, as they are sometimes seen by the workcell(s) as a required part of the process. This occurs due to the memory the process and information maintain long after the people in the workcell(s) are no longer involved. The phrase, "but we have always done it that way!" applies to queues that have, in the course of time, become integrated into the process and, therefore, in the people comprising the workcell(s). An excellent example of queue time in computer and electronic-based systems is that of e-mail or voice mail. Both have zero transfer time, but almost always have queue time associated with them.

TRANSFER TIMES

The last, but perhaps most important time, which must be identified for the TBA to be complete is transfer time. Transfer time is entirely non-value-added to the business process.

The problem, as we have already said, is that transfer time is not identified because it is not owned by any workcell or individual. This time is part of the process and not a part of any task or potential queue time associated with a task. Therefore, nobody takes responsibility for how long information from a completed task takes to become available so the next task can get started. Thus, time continues to be consumed by the business process, driving consideration of any efficiencies out of the equation.

When evaluating transfer times, you need to consider two factors: first, the transport method. For example, EDI (electronic data interchange) is fast; FedEx is not so fast. Second, the asynchronous nature of the communication (recall our discussion about the exchanges between Hong Kong and Boston in Chapter 1). The method of information movement and communication will provide the clues needed to determine the extent of transfer time between the tasks.

One of the most critical elements of transfer time is that it is equally attributed to *both* the *sending* and *receiving* workcell. This seems to be counterintuitive at first. However, it only makes sense that to adequately benchmark the relative process problems associated with transfer time we would have to determine every case where a time-to-receive work or a time-to-send-work is consistently associated with a particular workcell or combination of workcells.

WHAT DOES TIME-BASED ANALYSIS INDICATE?

TBA initially provides an objective assessment of the business cycle and process being evaluated. Moreover, TBA provides the means for quantifying nonproductive process waiting time.

Next, the identification of the data for TBA is an ongoing, almost real-time analysis of the process and business cycles. This identification requires that more than work tasks and sequence be understood, but also, what occurs (or, perhaps, falls through the cracks). As the data for TBA is documented, the pattern of the process begins to emerge and a better understanding is gained of how work is performed.

The analysis which is applied to the business cycle has its basis in the nonproductive waiting time. Though task times are a required part of TBA, the focus is *not* on these tasks. The focus is on the relationships between the time tasks require and the time expended during the business cycle where no work occurs. These relationships can provide enormous insight into the details of the process.

Initially, TBA should reflect documentation of the current process being analyzed, as with the process for the System Schematic. This information will provide all participants in the process with a snapshot, or benchmark, of the "as is" situation. Each participant can look at the impact of nontask time on their workcell and also see the larger picture of how they fit into the business process. For many, this may be the first time they have been exposed to the implications of the entire process.

Since the initial TBA reflects the "as is" model, any subsequent TBA can reflect the desired "to be" business cycle. As suggestions and input are received from the team evaluating the TBA model, each iteration of the TBA will provide insight regarding the impact of changes to the process, as well as impact to the workcells. This insight will offer an indication of both the weaknesses and strengths of the "as is" and the "to be" processes supporting the business cycle. Thus, the original benchmark creates a point of reference for any analysis and measurement of the impact of changes to the business cycle.

If all of this can be done in a single integrated tools set, such as a simulation and modeling product, or a workflow solution, the iterations between changing the visualization (a graphical depiction of a System Schematic is found in the case study) and examining the TBA will be that much easier to do. However, it is not unusual to work with several products, including spreadsheets, modeling tools, and workflow to perform the exercise.

END NOTES

1   Hunt, V. Daniel, *Reengineering: Leveraging the Power of Integrated Product Development* (Essex Junction, Vermont: Oliver Wight Publications, 1993), p. 36.

2   Martin, James, *Cybercorp: The New Business Revolution* (New York: AMACOM, 1996), p. 11.

3   For more on how HP accomplished this, see Packard, David, *The HP Way: How Bill Hewlett and I Built Our Company.*

4   McGill, Michael, Slocum, and John W. Jr., *The Smarter Organization,* p. 13.

5   Stalk, George, Jr., "Time—The Next Source of Competitive Advantage," *Harvard Business Review,* July–August 1988, pp. 204–205.

6   Hamel, Gary, and Prahalad, C. K., *Competing for the Future,* p. 60.

PART III

THE EVOLUTION OF A BUSINESS OPERATING SYSTEM

INTRODUCTION

In the first two sections of the book, we have examined the structures and traits of Smart Companies, the role of Smart Tools, and evolution of workers into Smart Employees. We now turn to the concept of the Business Operating System (BOS), which might be considered the physical manifestation of the interaction between these three elements. A BOS is an environment representing vast warehouses of knowledge about the way a business is run and the way people and information come together to add value to a business process.

In other words, a BOS is a repository. It is composed of a common operating environment, a business process library, and enterprise workflow, and is expressed through a consistent standardized desktop metaphor.

A Business Operating System provides:

- a comprehensive work environment;

- a self-service, reflective desktop;

- a reusable library-based repository of business objects;

- an open desktop that integrates the business process with any application;

- a constant and consistent interface allowing a process-centric view;

- a clear focus on process functionality rather than applications (i.e., word processing, spread sheets, databases);

- a repository for the corporate processes memory

Only recently has the commoditization of computers, brought on by plummeting prices, increased portability and power of desktop computers, and the advent of networks made true collaboration possible. In the short span of 1990 to 1995, the desktop has evolved from an isolated personal productivity tool into a networked resource for electronic processes that crisscross organizational boundaries and touch every aspect of the enterprise. Consider this: at the start of the 1990s less than 20% of all desktop computers were connected to a network. Today, it's difficult to find a PC that's connected to only one network. This trend toward connectivity among office workers will undoubtedly prove to be one of the most significant events in the history of white-collar productivity.

There are those who would leave it at that and say that technologies such as workflow and groupware are simply the natural evolution of interconnected desktop computing, but much more is involved. These new desktops will be environments for work. Why is this so radical? Because it represents a level of integration heretofore unknown. Today's desktops are really nothing more than an interface to applications and a separate layer hovering apart from, and below, the processes they facilitate. The new desktops will be the business process.

The traditional organizational hierarchy, with its vertical emphasis on top-down communications as discussed in Chapter 1, has resulted in information systems that do not support the horizontal nature of collaborative, or team-based, communications. Processes do not much care for the arbitrary boundaries of a compartmentalized enterprise. Instead, they must traverse an enterprise's infrastructure both vertically and horizontally. In addition, as enterprises embark on reengineering efforts that eliminate the overspecialized workforce, a keystone of the Industrial Revolution, a new breed of generalist is evolving—one who is no longer constrained by hard and fast departmental boundaries and also has a much higher degree of process intimacy than the specialized worker ever would, or could, have. These generalists work together in extended coalitions of workers that cut across an enterprise's structure, geography, and politics. No longer process components, these individuals are now process *owners,* and in increasing numbers are becoming owners of the business as well.

These extended coalitions of office workers have created new work environments of enormous complexity and interaction. Unfortunately, this has been reflected in ever-increasing fragmentation of information systems, making it that much harder to work as teams across organizations.

Sadly, platform fiefdoms—such as Microsoft's Windows, Apple's Finder, UNIX, IBM's OS/2, WARP, mainframe equivalents, and the many others that litter the information systems of organizations worldwide—have become commonplace and are easily accepted as part-and-parcel of a fast-changing computer industry. We have been led to believe that this diversity is a necessary part of a competitive industry. Yet this plethora of competing systems inhibits the progress of true collaboration by establishing steep barriers between technology and people. Without the commonality of a single operating environment for their processes, workers are forever hemmed in by the boundaries of different platforms, applications, and technologies. The organization is marked by needless atomization.

Nowhere is this more evident than in the advent of new technologies that enable the transfer of work. These represent a logical next step in the use of networked computing to integrate knowledge-based tasks and activities. Yet most enterprises have found that the primary benefit of these technologies—joining islands of automation that use discrete tool sets into enterprise information systems—runs counter to the legacy of noncooperative platforms and applications already in use. In other words, technologies such as workgroup and groupware computing crash head-on into firmly entrenched information systems and traditions.

No matter how many standards, coalitions, and alliances evolve, this fundamental problem of fragmented processes will remain if we do not rethink the very nature of traditional applications and operating systems—namely, their propensity for creating a multiplicity of user environments and splintered processes. Despite the need for each software vendor to differentiate its applications, we have been too easily convinced that these distinctions must also result in the isolation of entire functions within our enterprises. Fortunately, we have begun to rethink this with the advent of Smart Tools such as the World Wide Web and groupware.

But all of this was started, long before groupware was in vogue, by Apple's Finder Operating System, which provided application-independent interface consistency on the Macintosh beginning in the mid-1980s. This set an important precedent for interoperability among diversity (and provided Microsoft with food for thought). But that was principally an interface metaphor. If we carry that theme further, it is possible to envision entirely new operating system architectures based on the groupware paradigm: the Business Operating System. It provides the ideal bridge between the business objectives and technology requirements of an enterprise.

Imagine that such a new Business Operating System environment will be a desktop consisting of agents, each with a set of process rules that ultimately resides in a corporate process library; this is a form of corporate memory. The agents (think of them as sophisticated desktop icons) reference these rules and recombine them in multiple ways, depending on the needs of the user. However, in all cases, the rules are applied consistently and when a rule is changed in the repository, it is automatically picked up throughout the operating environment. In this sense, then, the environment becomes the enterprise memory.

CHAPTER 6

THE THREE PARADIGMS
OF COMPUTING

Global paradigms are images that have become part of humanity's common memory. They effect change by providing an alignment and a context for our actions. Like the image of the earth floating in the void of space, which served as a powerful image for the budding environmental movement of the 1970s, paradigms are simple and singular, yet powerful and pervasive rallying points. While each person can ascribe many personal emotions and meanings to these images, collectively we find a common meaning in them. The meaning of a particular paradigm is often obscure at first, but in retrospect it is easily identified as a turning point (just think of the Internet).

While history cannot always be predicted or anticipated, the significance of a paradigm can become obvious before its (full) effects are realized. For example, in early 1997, over sixty nations signed a global telecommunications pact that guarantees member states greater access to the telecom infrastructures of other signatories, prohibits exclusionary and protectionist measures, and paves the way for increased investment in formerly state-owned telecom systems. We don't know exactly what will happen five or ten years hence, or the tools that will be developed as a result, but we now *think* of global communication and the emerging reality of the global village in a way we could not have imagined twenty years ago. In this way, we can prepare for the impact the treaty will have, and begin to plan ways to utilize the advantages. And, no doubt, we will be faced with the need to find solutions to the obstacles that are sure to emerge. This is no less true of computing than it is for any other social phenomenon.

In the late 1970s John Cullinane, founder of what later became the industry's pioneering applications vendor, Cullinet Corporation, was the first person to suggest the possibility of packaged applications that would embody the collective knowledge of many experts into off-the-shelf application programs. He was considered foolish by most and outright insane by everyone else. Yet the Cullinane model became the standard for applications packaging during the last two decades. Accountants, engineers, marketing professionals, sales personnel, and virtually anyone else looking at new applications would not think twice about using an off-the-shelf or one-off (i.e., a slightly customized version of an existing application) software application over a customized application designed and built from ground zero. That metaphor is now on the verge of changing again—just as radically as it did twenty years ago.

The new model is one that focuses on the next level of knowledge capture: that of encapsulating the building blocks of enterprises, which represent their core competencies, into discrete applications.

For example, an older-generation application might create the forms necessary for processing an insurance claim. But a new application will go one step further and capture the *process* used to expedite a claim. In a similar fashion, other new applications could contain the process memory for submitting a new drug application to the FDA, or running a customer service call center.

With the creation of component-based environments, the user no longer sees, or even cares about, discrete applications such as word processing or spreadsheets; the user sees only a process and the documents that carry the process from worker to worker.

If we consider the evolution of information systems over the past five decades, three distinct paradigms emerge that support the trend toward a BOS.[1] They may be termed the black box, the blue box, and the missing box. These have led to the present-day model of distributed computing, shared information, and the need for a Business Operating System.

It's important to place these computing paradigms in a social context, for they have come into existence at a point when the explosive growth of telecommunications technology and multilateral economic activity heralds a new age of democratization. Today, we are closer than ever before to the realization of the global village that was postulated by Canadian theorist Marshall McLuhan.

- First-paradigm technologies existed from the 1950s until the 1960s and were centered on large-scale computer programs that drove extremely isolated information. This is often called the Von Neumann model of computing (named after early computer theorist John Von Neumann), and was typified by simple input-process-output operations. First-paradigm computer systems were not only isolated from each other but also from the end user, and thus were truly a black box. These systems were the property of the computer scientists and illegible to anyone else.

  Where the computer was once seen as a remote and exotic tool (and often featured in science fiction film and literature as a potentially malign electronic brain—think of the HAL 9000 computer in the film *2001*—the ever-increasing trend toward user accessibility has rendered this archetype obsolete. Once, computers were the realm of scientists and the military; today, not only are they ubiquitous—they are user friendly and increasingly accessible to all segments of society.

- Second-paradigm technologies existed in the early 1970s through the early 1980s. This shifted the focus of computing from input-output models to what were called *data models.* These were highly centralized environments, typified by mainframe computers. If there is a generic icon of this era, it is a large blue IBM mainframe isolated in its own room in air-conditioned splendor, tape drives whirring and lights blinking. Hence, this era it is often called the blue box paradigm.

- The third-paradigm, which began in the late 1980s, brought a shift away from technology toward business processes and the tasks that comprise them. The third-paradigm brings full-range computing into the personal domain of individual workers at all levels of the organization. For the first time, it is possible to create and easily propagate isolated computing environments throughout an enterprise. Hence, the missing box. But—and this is where the contrast with the second-paradigm is at its most stark—these isolated computing environments are linked to one another through the Internet, intranets, and extranets.

Although it would be nice to dispose of paradigms as newer ones come along, not everyone is at the third-paradigm yet. While the first-paradigm has passed into obsolescence, the second-paradigm is still alive and well in many industries and organizations.

Examples of second-paradigm technology are still prevalent in the insurance industry, where fierce competition from inside and outside the industry is forcing incredible pressure to innovate and rapidly move away from the rigid legacy of mainframe second-paradigm computing.

This has prompted significant spending on information technology in the insurance industry, to the tune of $19.5 billion in 1995, a 12% increase over the industry's IT spending in the previous year.[2] This is an enormous effort to introduce Smart Tools into the front office in as revolutionary a fashion as industrial engineering was applied to early-twentieth-century factories.

Add to the insurance industry's woes the dynamic of ever-changing state and federal regulations and you have a business environment as ripe for Smart Tools as any.

Since the principal focus of any insurance company is the customer, Smart Tools such as self-service call centers and transaction systems are being used in areas that would otherwise require extensive staffing with workers who would perform mundane and repetitive tasks. This is similar to the philosophy that drove ATMs into the mainstream of banking, since most bank customers perform relatively simple transactions and usually do not need the assistance of a human teller.

As Michael McKeon, senior VP and CIO of Alexander & Alexander Services, Inc. of New York, one of the companies undergoing this change, notes, "The industry is undergoing white-collar automation on a scale that the manufacturing industry underwent fifty years ago for blue-collar automation."

At Alexander & Alexander, automation gives customers direct access to information that would otherwise have to be dispensed by one or more persons. Mia Shernoff, the firm's director of on-line services (a telling title in itself), describes the process: "Our client now points and clicks for policy data, saving the account executive time for more consultative endeavors."

It is important to note that Alexander & Alexander does *not* say that the automated system eliminates the need for account executives, or replaces them. The key—as with all Smart Tools—is that the technology liberates the people from repetitive and boring administrative tasks, allowing them to focus their energies on creative problem solving and innovation.

The admitted problem most insurance companies face, however, in accomplishing a greater degree of automation is an antiquated information systems infrastructure. At a time when maintenance of a mainframe computer consumes an estimated 55% of the average IS budget, the insurance industry is spending 73% of its IS dollars on mainframe maintenance.[3] The industry is so entrenched in the second-paradigm that it has to literally buy its way out in order to reach the third-paradigm.

In the insurance industry, the legacy of bondage which epitomizes investment in second-paradigm technologies in the 1970s and 1980s is being replaced with efforts to invest in reusable business objects that can be employed across the enterprise on a variety of computer platforms. These business objects are nothing more than extremely small applications, or applets, that know how to communicate with each other. When an organization develops a vast warehouse of these applets, it has in fact created a *knowledge repository.* For example, ITT Hartford has even gone so far as to patent some of its insurance processes that are built on these business objects.

In some cases, insurance companies are even collaborating with their competitors to build foundations for industrywide business solutions.[4] This goes beyond progressive—it is revolutionary thinking. Imagine Henry Ford creating a blueprint for his moving assembly line and handing it over to Alfred Sloan and Walter Chrysler!

This collaborative spirit is not inimical to competition. Rival organizations do not compete on all fronts. There are basic functions that every insurance company performs such as taking policy applications, processing claims, issuing payments and refunds, etc. The differentiation is in how they perform them and how their performance is perceived by their respective customers. Each area of collaboration must be considered separately in a competitive analysis. As one insurance industry executive says, "We realize there are things we do in common from which we can't really derive much, if any, competitive advantage."[5]

Another outstanding example of third-paradigm computing is known as the single point of access business system. A single point of access solution focuses on a user-centric information system that provides support personnel inside of the organization (or customers) access to all information within one interface—an interface that will ultimately make pale the contemporary, two-dimensional displays and window-based metaphors we use today.

An example is the use of single point of access computer systems in call-center applications. The full impact that single point of access will have on today's organizations is virtually impossible to predict. Benefits and drawbacks will arise that cannot be appreciated in the context of current technologies and applications. We can nonetheless speculate as to the changes that will result from this new vantage point and begin to lay the foundation for the Smart Tools we will need in order to prepare ourselves and our organizations for the transformation to come.[6]

CASE STUDY

AT&T Equips Service Representatives with Point-of-Access Desktop Environments to Improve Customer Service

At AT&T, the customer-support workload has been cut in half by using point-of-access technology. At the AT&T call center, everything that a customer service representative needs in order to assist a customer is brought up on a screen—from an icon that indicates an incoming call to troubleshooting information.

When a new call comes into the call center, a "trouble ticket" appears on the customer service representative's point-of-access desktop with customer data already entered, by using caller ID (a feature provided by most current telephone carriers). If the caller's problem cannot be resolved immediately, the trouble ticket goes through an elaborate routing process intended to make sure that problems are resolved in the fastest manner possible. Based on workflow business rules, the routing escalates and balances the work according to the most expedient route available. Through this, the efficacy of the system is easily measured by the number of problems that end up being escalated to the supervisor's level (refer to Momentum Life example, in Chapter 1, where this was one of the metrics used). In the first six months that the application was in place, only one problem was escalated to this level.

The point-of-access interface also has other features that allow workers to route work through the customer support center. In one case, a call can be transferred to a specialist by clicking and dragging the calls icon, along with all files and trouble ticket data, to the icon of another representative. Think of how often you have found yourself repeating the same problem to several customer support representatives— literally bounced from person to person. This is eliminated entirely with the point-of-access system.

It is also important to note that at the same time these paradigms were evolving, the nature of applications development was undergoing a radical shift. Applications that once required sophisticated programming techniques and months of development time can now be created in days or even minutes by using new visual programming languages. The graphical computer-development environments and graphical user interfaces that surround us today are more than the icing on the cake; they represent an entirely new approach to applications development. The success of computing is now contingent on the ability to join individuals and workgroups with radically different computing solutions within a single cohesive and aligned enterprise.

As these independent systems proliferate, they become vast warehouses of information. The information they contain has become the foundation for individualized empowerment and advantage. Systems can be customized to meet the needs of each user. In many cases, the users themselves can customize the systems.

But there is a downside to this success and rapid proliferation. Incompatibility has flourished among applications and data repositories, across vertical and horizontal lines of the organization. The Tower of Babel problem still lurks. The greatest testimonial to this is that office workers are generating more paper than ever before, still unable to communicate work through computer-based systems that cannot talk to each other.

UNDERSTANDING THE STRUCTURE OF THE BUSINESS OPERATING SYSTEM

To fully understand the concept of a Business Operating System, we need to explore it at the basic level of the operating system, which is what most computer users have been dealing with for the last three decades. Operating systems are the basic language of any computer. Notable ones, like DOS (the linchpin of Microsoft's success), made it easy for developers to create sophisticated programs that would run consistently and reliably. As the sophistication of the programs and the end user's demands increased, so did the complexity of the operating systems. Ultimately, graphical tools and metaphors took the place of command line interfaces as layers such as Windows were added to the operating system. Today, for all intents and purposes, the operating system underpinnings and the graphical user interfaces are indistinguishable from one another.

The problem with all operating systems is that they were each created to be singular. They do not coexist very well. And even in the case of more advanced operating systems such as UNIX, which was designed for interoperabilty and standardization, there are many varieties that simply don't work well together. *

---

* UNIX is an operating system originally developed at AT&T. UNIX was long touted as the universal operating system for all computer platforms. Instead it became just one more of many operating systems.

Twenty years ago, we didn't have to worry much about the diversity of platforms, infrastructure, clients and servers. None of that existed. The world was singular from an information systems standpoint. In other words, a company owned an IBM mainframe and all of its applications ran on IBM's operating system.

But then, on top of the operating system, we built applications to run business systems. Simple, straightforward applications did things like perform basic accounting functions. But users quickly realized that applications had to be best of breed. The marketing application had to suit the marketing department. The engineering application had to suit the engineering department. And from that, horribly diverse, fragmented environments arose. This was the beginning of the silos, or smokestacks, of highly compartmentalized, segregated information.

As the number of these silos and smokestacks increased, they were made ever taller. In an attempt to unify that fragmented environment, software vendors created the first stop-gap measures: graphical user interfaces such as Apple's Finder and Microsoft's Windows.

But these applications were, in retrospect, at best a panacea. Their development was an appropriate response to the state of affairs at the time, and it was a step in the right direction. But was this true unification? Of course not. Having twenty windows open on your desktop doesn't allow you to work more effectively with the information. It doesn't create obvious bonds between the processes that underlay the information. Can someone looking over your shoulder appreciate what process you are involved in by glancing at your desktop? Is the desktop reflective—in other words, is it obvious when you look at your desktop what process you are involved in? Unlikely. The process still resides principally in people's minds; it's not embedded in the corporate memory. That means that there is still no meta-memory that serves as a repository. A knowledge of how to do things still depends on specific people or departments. This reflects an *information-centric* view of the world. It is not a *process-centric* view of the world, the goal toward which we strive.

So how do you bind these silos and smokestacks together to create a process-centric view? The answer is not in simply creating a single interface across the compartmentalized information, which is what many computer systems to date have today. In fact, this works against the effort to build a Smart Company by making it even more difficult to change the existing processes. The walls of the silos and smokestacks become harder to break down. The reason is simply that the interfaces we are accustomed to today are not process-centric, but rather application-centric.

The processes in use today were designed years ago to conform with the functions of the applications that were available at the time. The information systems we are using today embody the memory of processes that have long been obsolete. These information systems are the corporate instinct that drives the process. But do you revisit these processes on a daily basis? On a weekly basis? On a yearly basis? In most cases, no. Basically, companies of the 1990s are running on paradigms designed in the 1970s. Retro may be fine for fashion, but it is hardly appropriate for managing information in a competitive, global economy.

Although the concept may far-fetched right now, the concept of the Business Operating System is already taking hold in those organizations investing in building a process memory (synonymous with corporate memory and corporate instinct). These organizations are realizing that the most important asset of their businesses—the process knowledge—must be integrated, preserved, and leveraged throughout their technology infrastructure.

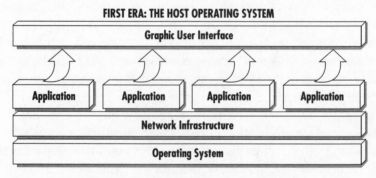

Figure 6.1 The Three Eras of Operating Systems (continued)

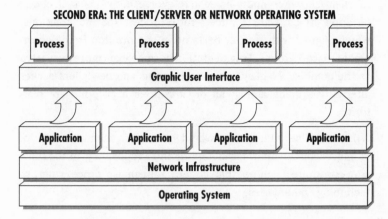

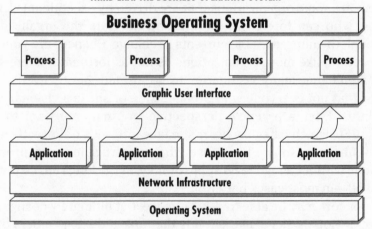

Figure 6.1 (continued)

The evolution of operating systems began with the development of host-based models that supported a common set of applications and networks. This, however, created isolation as extensive application customization became the norm. Departmental solutions began to replace enterprise systems and fragmentation began to take hold. This led to the need for graphical user interfaces that would allow a single metaphor for the use of multiple applications, basic data-sharing facilities, and control panel conventions across differing information systems.

As client/server computing began to evolve, individual collections of applications were bundled into process-specific solutions, which aligned with smaller parts of an organization from departments to workgroups. Fragmentation became even more pervasive as the number of legacy operating systems and new client/server alternatives made almost all organizations a potpourri of platforms.

A Business Operating System would join this fragmentation by providing a common interface metaphor and a repository for the rules and corporate memory that govern a business process across technology boundaries.

TRANSFORMING, NOT REENGINEERING, SMART COMPANIES

There are some organizations that are driven by exceptional visionaries, who can foretell the future and navigate the organization through the unpredictable currents of change. Chances are your organization, like most organizations, is not as fortunate. There simply aren't that many visionaries to go around. In any event, it is clear that not everyone who proclaims he or she is a visionary actually is. From a practical perspective, you may not want to ask your CEO which category he or she falls into—it's not exactly a career-enhancing move. But those who are struggling with process change without a high-level sponsor may, in the long run, be just as well off—in most cases better off.

Sponsors may be able to drive change, but ultimately change is a buyer's, not a seller's, market. It is the rank-and-file members of an organization who will cause change to happen. Consider the fact that for all of Henry Ford's organizational genius, he had great trouble implementing his grand vision in the early years of the Ford Motor Company. In 1913, the turnover of his labor force was 380%.[7] To fully train and retain a hundred workers, Ford had to hire over a thousand. In that year, Ford and his principal business partner at that time, James Couzens, came up with the idea of a $5-per-day wage—a doubling of the existing wage. Ford was roundly attacked; *The Wall Street Journal* thundered that the new wage was "an economic crime," while *The New York Times* dismissed it as "distinctly utopian."[8] But the plan was welcomed by workers—the day after the announcement, ten thousand men stormed the gates of the Ford plant, seeking employment—and profits trebled in the first three years after the initiation of the $5 wage.[9]

Consider this: every successful reengineering project has one thing in common. That common thread is not a crisis; it is not a budget; it is not a cost justification. Rather, the common denominator of success *is a champion who is intent on achieving buy-in from the organization, or at least that part of the organization that will be affected by the reengineering effort.* Notice a subtle distinction here: what is necessary is a champion, not necessarily an overall sponsor. The champion is someone who is committed to effecting change through an organization by demonstrating the value of the reengineering process to the organization as a whole. The champion's vision extends beyond the boundaries of his or her particular turf. And the amazing thing is that champions do *not* have to be CEOs.

Of course, reengineering works best when in fact the CEO is behind the effort. This is axiomatic. But it is often the organization in crisis that must change to survive. And survival is a great justification for participation. But for every CEO at the helm of a troubled company who is committed to massive change, there are many more who say, "Show me, then I'll believe." The latter are not cowards; they are simply prudent business managers who rely on success to breed success.

We hear far too much about the benefits of empowering workers through technology, and not enough about the potential pitfalls of empowerment namely, the burden of even more technology. Many Smart Companies are realizing that the very people in the most need of empowerment are the ones most resistant to change. The net effect is an additional burden on the worker to understand the new technology and an initial decrease in productivity.

One alternative is to motivate people to change by instilling a strong sense of urgency. According to James Belasco, author of *Teaching the Elephant to Dance,* a savvy management team will *"build a sense of urgency."* Belasco notes:

People don't change without pain—lots of it—and anxiety—

lots of it! Bad situations motivate change. *Very* bad situations. Pain and anxiety create the urgency to change, which creates the empowerment for change. Don't create this urgency, and people feel powerless to change."[10]

Belasco's approach may work if there is indeed a crisis, and it may be the principal job of a CEO to see the crisis looming beyond the horizon. But what if there really is no crisis? What if the company is healthy and prospering? That may be as good a time as any to revisit processes that need incremental change. But how do you motivate people to buy into change when things are going well?

The tremendous burden to alter business practices and restructure the basic components of work is creating a new breed of manager. These people are more than change managers; they are *champions of change*. Champions of change don't just tolerate it—they *embrace* it. They risk much—in many cases the integrity of their own careers—to nudge organizations to reevaluate their business practices. And therein lies the key: it's not just a matter of sponsorship; it's finding someone who is willing to drive change and create a track record of success within the functional ranks of your organization. Note that the operative terms here are "track record" and "functional ranks." Why? For the simple reason that few organizations embrace change, no matter who the sponsor is.

So why try to create a champion of change if you already have one—or are one? Let's face it, stepping on the toes of superiors to gain sponsorship may not be the best way to advance a career. Even organizations with a corporate sponsor will probably end up looking for functional champions who are willing to embrace change. In either case, a track record of success will be the leverage that sells upper management on enterprise-wide change and business process reengineering. Nothing speaks louder than success—even a small success.

Unfortunately, most people see this approach of *incremental change* as the ultimate sin. Are we so doubtful of the ability of our functional workgroups and our people on the front line to develop an understanding of the importance of change and to use their best judgment to cause change? Fundamentally, you can only change organizations at the level of the individual. Visionaries and sponsors do not cause change. Rather, their vision is interpreted and internalized by users and champions of change. And in turn, the benefits of change are demonstrated.

Some of the recent thinking in management theory points to the efficacy of change at a workgroup level. It may not be a coincidence that the typical workflow application is found in workgroups of fifty to a hundred people.[11]

However, when workgroups enter the range of fifty to a hundred people, their alignment begins to fall apart and fail. The reason is a breakdown of basic communication. We work best in small teams. Incremental change works best in these same team environments, because change requires unity and common understanding. Try to force change and you are trying to force understanding—more likely than not that is an exercise in futility.

In a study conducted by the Delphi Group, the most often mentioned obstacle to the adoption of any Smart Tools is that of cultural resistance to change.[12] Almost half of the respondents also cited reengineering as part of the cultural obstacle. In many cases, the two issues are considered one and the same. Organizational culture is resistant to change, and sponsorship of change may not be available.

Unlike reengineering, however, the introduction of Smart Tools does not require radical change and exceptional sponsorship in the organization. In fact, reengineering is facilitated by the use of an incremental, or pilot, implementation of technology such as workflow. This provides a tremendous amount of experience to the implementing organization. It also shows immediate results, which in the aggregate provide a leverage point in justifying future enterprise applications. Initially, workflow and reengineering are symbiotic, in that one feeds off the success of the other. As the sponsorship of reengineering and the scope of a workflow application rise within the organization, the two become synonymous.

USING WORKFLOW AS A METRIC FOR TRANSFORMING THE PROCESS

In the turf wars fought over technology, each group of disciples professes that its approach is the magic cure for ailing organizations crumbling under the weight of antiquated business processes and technology. Imaging, EDI, e-mail, workflow, the Internet, and group-ware have each become a fiefdom of technological bigotry. In this quagmire, many companies are turning to the one option that seems to be the only hope for a comprehensive solution—reengineering.

The popular view of reengineering as the obliteration of existing process and systems has its own set of issues and risks First, the level of sponsorship necessary to effect such drastic change within large organizations seldom exists.[13] Second, even sponsorship requires some direction. Where should reengineering begin? Which business processes and information systems are least efficient? What is the measure of efficiency?

Without answers to these questions, any reengineering exercise is no more than a roll of the dice. Workflow can provide these answers and in the process establish the foundation for a sound reengineering effort. But to do this, workflow must be used as more than an automation tool. It must also provide the analytical and reporting tools that help change managers better understand their organization's business processes. In this light, workflow becomes a Smart Tool for restructuring business systems, not just another competing technology.

Although workflow is part methodology and part technology, it is not synonymous with reengineering. The two are complementary methods. Reengineering proposes radically rethinking existing work processes and establishing new business methods based upon new sets of assumptions regarding desired business objectives. It is a comprehensive approach to redefining the organization. Workflow is the analysis, compression, and automation of information-based process models that make up a business. *In short, workflow provides the metrics for reengineering.*

Although workflow appears to represent only one component of total reengineering, no reengineering project should proceed without the use of workflow—at the very least as an analytical tool. The reason is simple: how can we undertake a redefinition of an organization if there is no benchmark against which to measure the efficiency of its business processes? As we have seen, tools such as time-based analysis offer the means by which to establish these benchmarks within your organization.

But measurement alone will not foster change without the application of some form of sponsorship of the reengineering effort. According to Joel Dreyfuss, editor-in-chief of *InformationWeek,* "Technology managers should resist the temptation to use workflow as a quick fix. To realize the benefits of workflow, most organizations need to undergo huge managerial and organizational change."[14]

The specific form of sponsorship, and the motivation behind, it determines one of three methods of reengineering.

THE DIMENSIONS OF REENGINEERING

Reengineering is not a one-dimensional model. Three models of reengineering are commonly used:

- the life-cycle model;
- the crisis model;
- the goal-oriented model.

Although each method may have its appropriate place in an organization, they should not be regarded as interchangeable. An understanding of each approach is necessary to determine which is appropriate for a particular organization.

Life-cycle reengineering results from a strategic initiative to reevaluate existing processes on a continuing basis. Change is incremental and basic processes remain essentially intact, modified slightly to accommodate new requirements. Modification is usually aligned with the critical success factors of the organization. Automation is often applied, but the primary emphasis is on *enhancing and streamlining* the existing process. The sponsorship must be cultural, not mandated. In other words, the workforce must be imbued with the sense of "always look for ways to do it better, smarter, faster."

Crisis reengineering is a response to systems crumbling under the weight of user demands or organizational pressure. For example, a service firm with a cumbersome billing process may have a high percentage of fees that are earned but not billed. The prolonged billing cycle results in a negative cash flow and leads directly to a crisis reengineering of the billing process to speed client invoicing. Sponsorship is not necessary, since *some kind* of change must occur regardless of the solution chosen. Reeducation and technology evaluation are used, rather than a formal reengineering methodology.

Goal-oriented reengineering has defined objectives that may differ substantially from the objectives in place when the system was first developed: "Where do you want to go today?" This is a deliberate attempt to bring existing processes in line with business objectives. Business processes are totally redesigned with new goals and objectives in mind. Sponsorship is inherent. The sponsors must have the clout to drive the application through the organization, often without cost justification. A reengineering methodology such as a time-based analysis tool is almost always used in this case, since the emphasis is on a strategic, long-term implementation with an extended payback.

Life-cycle reengineering is the least disruptive approach because it fosters an opportunistic attitude toward change and an incremental, ongoing approach to modifying information systems. Customization is minimal because the change is spread out over time. The risk, however, is that significant inefficiencies may be overlooked because of the effort required to reengineer them. Also, life-cycle reengineering can be used only if organizational critical success factors (CSFs) are well stated and supported by management and users. Workflow is best applied in this type of reengineering, because the workflow will provide an ongoing measure by which to modify and refine the business processes on a constant and continuing basis.

A good workflow tool offers insight to the workloads, bottlenecks, resource allocation, throughput, productivity, and overall health of the business cycle. By analyzing these, immediate decisions can be made to alter a process by reallocating resources, changing task relationships, eliminating redundancy, or altering priorities of work. The result is a highly adaptive and responsive organization—not unlike the model used to retool factory assembly lines for the purpose of mass customization.

The approach used most often, crisis reengineering, is invariably thrust upon an organization with no other choice. The decision is not, "Should we reengineer?" but rather, "Can we afford not to?" Organizations that rely on crisis reengineering are doomed to encounter reengineering crises regularly. Their organizational life is little more than lurching from crisis to crisis. The prevailing attitude in these organizations is "well enough is best left alone." Entropy increases regularly until the point at which action must be taken. Since reengineering is forced by a particular scenario, the analysis is often biased and rushed. This method has become the norm for reengineering. It is best characterized as a mortgage with a balloon payment option. Hopefully, when the note comes due, you will have the reserves to pay the bill.

During the Industrial Revolution and up to today, technological obsolescence occurred at regular, and if not planned, then at least predictable, intervals measured in decades. In that environment, it was possible to retool and reengineer once or twice each decade. Today, much technology is obsolete in months, not years. Reengineering can no longer be an interval activity—and if it is, the reengineering will always come too late to do any good. Ask the fundamental question, "Does my organization budget a certain amount of money each year for reengineering?" Without that type of commitment—let's say a few hundred dollars for each technology-enabled desktop—reengineering will always be overdue by the time its mandate arrives.

The most enduring approach, goal-oriented reengineering, requires high-level corporate sponsorship. It is driven by the anticipation of *future benefits* resulting from reengineering rather than the cost of an old or inefficient solution, although both should be considered in the cost justification. The primary difference between this approach and the others is the emphasis on business processes rather than technology. It's also worth noting that it requires the sort of management that transcends the standard American short-term, quarter-to-quarter view. In other words, there must the *cultural* foundation for this sort of approach.

Workflow is compatible with goal-oriented reengineering as long as sponsors demonstrate a quantifiable measure of business process improvement. Workflow assists in reengineering through its ability to monitor and report on changing business cycles. Unfortunately, technology is often separated from business process redesign in most reengineering approaches, since the two represent different disciplines in most enterprises. For many, that has meant that workflow is left out of the reengineering effort, in order to avoid compromising business goals. That need not be the case.

As workflow does not impose a specific technology toolset of its own for the actual performance of work—office automation tools, such as word processing, database, spreadsheets, e-mail, and EDI should all work within the workflow environment—it does not alter, impede, or compromise the reengineering effort.

Not only can multiple reengineering approaches exist in a single organization, but there may be elements of any two or all three approaches applied simultaneously to a single reengineering effort. In practice, it is likely that all three aspects will come into play. For example, a crisis may initiate the reengineering effort; management then identifies a long-term goal that provides a context for the initial project and a series of subsequent reengineering efforts intended to achieve a strategic vision; finally, the vision itself is tested repeatedly in a life-cycle approach that continuously validates the vision against the reality.

Weight loss is a striking analogy. Many people struggle their entire lives with weight gain and loss—an endless roller coaster. On occasion, however, a crisis will occur, perhaps a physician's warning of health risks, an actual health crisis, or something as subtle as seeing one's self in a family photo. The impetus is strong enough to cause an individual to take action. In some cases, that action and a bit of success turn into a vision of being on a weight-control and nutrition regimen. That vision needs to be reinforced with success ("Gee, you look terrific!"), since it is not in and of itself a pleasing experience and the urge to lapse into old ways can be great. Results are what drives the vision at this stage. Over time, however, the only successful weight-loss program is that which not only reinforces the vision of a regimen, but also that of a new person and a new lifestyle. At that stage the individual's every decision and future action will have a bearing—not on weight, but rather on lifestyle. The person moves from simply dieting, that is, a period of self-abnegation—toward a new relationship with food and nutrition. By this time, the strict notion of a regimen has been transcended; what exists is simply an ongoing process of checks and balances that act as the measure and countermeasure of success.

Thomas Davenport, author of *Process Innovation,* regards continuous improvement and radical innovation, or reengineering, as necessarily compatible approaches. According to Davenport:

> Although it may not be possible to achieve radical innovation while practicing continuous improvement, companies need to learn how to do both—concurrently across different processes, and cyclically for a single process. Ultimately, a major challenge in process innovation is making a successful transition to a continuous improvement environment. A company that does not institute continuous improvement after implementing process innovation is likely to revert to old ways of doing business.[15]

If an organization can—or has been able to—skip past the crisis and goal-oriented stages of reengineering, it is simply that much further along. Try some basic tests to see where your organization now stands. Keep in mind that these are not guarantees, but *indicators* of where you are today:

FOR THE ORGANIZATION UNDERTAKING LIFE-CYCLE REENGINEERING

- What are the CSFs of your organization? (You should be able to state these no matter what your position, but a little bit of digging is allowed. A lot of digging means that the CSFs, if they exist, are token gestures, not cultural mandates.)
- How much do you budget yearly for reengineering?
- Do you even have a budget line item that mentions reengineering?
- Do you have a title in your organization that contains the term "reengineering" (or a derivative)?

FOR THE ORGANIZATION UNDERTAKING GOAL-ORIENTED
REENGINEERING

- Do you have a clear vision of the new organization or process (the goal) you are trying to create?

- What is the regimen you will follow to achieve this vision?

- Is there a sponsor behind the vision? (Notice that this question was not asked for the life-cycle organization, because sponsors will change on an ongoing basis in life-cycle reengineering.)

- Does the sponsor control the budget or control the person who has the budget?

WHICH APPROACH IS RIGHT FOR YOU?

Which approach should you use? That may have already been decided for you by the culture of the enterprise or the state of your information systems. If you are concerned about the long-term impact of crisis reengineering, it behooves you to find a corporate sponsor who is willing to support a goal-oriented approach and help break the crisis cycle.

Whatever else you do, do not embark on a perpetual journey in search of sponsorship. Far too often, organizations chase their tails in an endless series of good ideas that do not have the backing of a sponsor. Just about everyone would like to have the CEO or chairman behind a particular project, but it rarely happens in real life.

If you can't find a sponsor, maybe you are looking in all the wrong places. If there is a departmental manager, a divisional VP, or a person in any other position willing to stand behind a smaller effort, take advantage of that. It is likely to be the only way to develop higher levels of sponsorship.

Over the long term, the sponsor must establish an ongoing review of the business process. A workflow system that includes management reporting tools will help identify problems and ongoing areas of improvement in the process model. It will also generate data that can be taken to higher level sponsors, perhaps leading to a broader level of sponsorship (i.e., instead of vague promises, those engaged in reengineering can proffer something metrical).

Critical to every reengineering effort's success is the ability to overcome the cultural impediments that one is bound to encounter. Although there are creative ways to deal with these, they are generational to a large degree. To be blunt, there's almost always an Old Guard, and it's likely that this faction will clash with the Young Turks. These differences can only be worked out over time through investment in education, some attrition of staff, a substantive change in the work environment and work tools, and a cohesive commitment to change from management.

Don't expect to reengineer or automate the workflow of an entire enterprise overnight. The battle-worn will tell you of the upheaval an organization goes through to change work patterns and business practices. An incremental approach provides an education for all involved and a demonstration of the benefits to be realized. An approach that includes measurement of the existing and new process models provides the greatest impetus for change and long-term life-cycle reengineering. Workflow makes that possible.

According to Stef Joosten, who is researching workflow:

> The wrong way to change a business process is to use technology to let bureaucrats stifle potential for creativity and reduce staff to pen-pushers, or mouse-movers. I saw a government department's workflow project fail because management took too much time ensuring that procedures were modeled to a very fine level of detail.
>
> The frightening prospect of trapping a business process within a rigid procedure should be treated as one of the risks of workflow projects. Visionary, professional project management should be a key ingredient of a successful workflow automation effort.
>
> The real message of workflow automation is simple: The result of a workflow project does not depend primarily on the technology; it depends on the people who redesign the work processes. If they do a good job, workflow automation can be a blessing, cutting processing times, simplifying procedures, and bringing new market opportunities.[16]

Ultimately, the ability to uncover new potential from business opportunity, and not the application of technology to current problems, makes reengineering worthwhile. This is a common theme in virtually every successful workflow implementation. That potential will seldom be realized without a tool such as workflow, which is able to locate and to measure the extent of problem business processes, at each point along the enterprise life-cycle.

If we sum up the basic principles of reengineering that Smart Tools support, they may be called the *immutable laws of process change:*

- **Reengineering requires measurement.** Smart Tools like workflow provide this.

- **Crises are a great time to reengineer, but they just don't happen often enough.** Smart Tools should be used to improve processes on a continuous basis, rather than change them in a wholesale fashion once each decade. Ultimately, however, both long-term and short-term change will be required.

- **Process redesign is a journey, not a destination.** Reengineering should not just happen once a decade. Process redesign never ends.

- **A small success is infinitely better than a large failure. Even a success that is modest in scale or not readily apparent throughout all elements of the organization is significant,** since it maintains momentum and progress.

- **Don't empower, educate—for change is a buyer's market.** Champions of change are needed even when sponsors are available.

Whichever approach you choose, it is important to keep these principles in mind and to appreciate that process change is not a one-time proposition. Changing an organization en masse is easy for the charismatic (and truly charismatic leaders are rare), but not for the workers, and it is at *their* level that change will ultimately occur—or fail. Manganelli and Klein sum it up nicely in *The Reengineering Handbook.* They note, "We contend that the lure of *the clean sheet is indeed a false one.* We see it as an approach that can produce an exhilarating start on a clear day, followed by too many nights bumping into things in the dark."[17] Indeed! As Chrysler CEO Bob Eaton said to his board of directors shortly after taking the helm, "My personal ambition is to be the first chairman never to lead a Chrysler comeback." In other words, staying healthy is much easier than getting healthy.

USING THE RIGHT METRICS

Workflow applies many of the same basic concepts and benefits of factory automation and industrial engineering to the process of work management in an office environment—without all of the rigidity of factory automation. Workflow, as noted in Chapter 2, is defined as *a tool set for the proactive analysis, compression, and automation of information-based tasks and activities.*

The basic premise of workflow is that an office environment is built around information flows and the transfer of work objects within a defined process. The process, which can exist in a range of formats from paper to electronic form, provides the basic raw material of every office task. The connection of these office tasks creates a value chain that spans internal and external task boundaries. In this architecture, workflow attempts to streamline the components of knowledge work by eliminating unnecessary tasks, thereby saving time, effort, and costs associated with the performance of those tasks and automating the remaining tasks that are necessary to a process.

Treating computerized office systems as a commodity has made this type of analysis and change possible due to their evolution from isolated personal productivity tools into networked resources for electronic process transfer across organizations. This is especially true with the recent advent of the Internet and intranets and extranets, which provide cross-platform solutions for business applications. These solutions can be run across the gamut of computer systems that most companies have been saddled with over the past three decades.

Some would leave it at that and say that workflow is simply the natural evolution of interconnected desktop computing, but much more is involved in the popularity of workflow.

The traditional organizational hierarchy, with its vertical emphasis on communications, has resulted in information systems that do not support the horizontal nature of collaborative, or team-based, communications. In reality, we all know that processes do not much care for the arbitrary boundaries of a compartmentalized organization. Instead, they must traverse an organization's infrastructure both vertically *and* horizontally.

These extended coalitions of office workers have created a new work environment of enormous complexity and interaction. CEOs share electronic dialogues with salespeople, customers become part of the process flow, and suppliers are partners in virtual supply chains. Additionally, processes are amalgamated to create hybrid systems, along the lines of mass customization intended for the delivery of a specific and optimal solution to every problem.* Such complexity requires new tools for the coordination of activities and communications.

Workflow is in many ways a script, or score, for Smart Companies to follow. But unlike policy or procedure, the workflow script changes continuously. It is best described by Peter Drucker's definition of the information-based business:

> Yet a business has no "score" to play by except the score it writes as it plays. And whereas neither a first-rate performance of a symphony nor a miserable one will change what the composer wrote, the performance of a business continually creates new and different scores against which its performance is assessed. So an information-based business must be structured around goals that clearly state management's performance expectations for the enterprise and for each part and specialist and around organized feedback that compares results with these performance expectations so that every member can exercise self control.[18]

As we shall see later, workflow gives this same self-control, the essence of empowerment, to knowledge workers.

---

* We will talk more about this is the section on human factors.

MEASURING SUCCESS

To go even further, workflow may be the only timely method of assessing business process efficiency At first, that statement may sound like a bit of a stretch. What about all of the systems in place to provide managers with reports detailing a variety of volumetrics, such as call volumes, throughput, transaction rates, and the rest? Don't these provide sufficient data to make sound decisions? Perhaps, but only if the data they contain is assimilated in sufficient proximity to the actual events that caused the problem. In practice, this type of data is often woefully outdated.

A management report produced monthly is not only a month out of date, but typically a month and a half to two months out of date by the time data is analyzed and distributed. There is an inherent lack of synchronization in management reporting systems. They report on the *symptoms* of events that have happened in the past, but managers have to solve them in the present.

That presents an almost irreconcilable anachronism. In many ways this points to the fundamental inability of the information systems to work in both directions, both up and down an organization. Stated another way, managers can easily pass down edicts, but processes can not adequately pass feedback up the chain.[19] This is where the workflow control-room metaphor offers a new means of associating problems with their true underlying causes.

THE WORKFLOW CONTROL ROOM

In *Cybercorp,* James Martin talks about the importance of building fast reflexes in today's organizations. He notes that "the Cybercorp should monitor its wealth-generating processes in real time and continuously make adjustments."[20] Another way to look at this is through the metaphor of a process control room, which has the ability to constantly monitor the vital signs of the corporation.

The idea of the control room is particularly suitable. Control rooms, such as those used in a nuclear power plant to monitor vital functions, provide instant access to information about the myriad functions of the reactor in order to give a plant manager ample opportunity to address a potential problem before it becomes a crisis, not unlike the early warning systems that air traffic controllers use to detect possible problems with aircraft routes. Many reengineering efforts today are undertaken in response to a crisis. But even in a visionary organization, the problem remains that the positive or negative impact of any measurement can be assessed only by evaluating it against prior measurements. This adheres to the benchmark principle already described. But if we wait for results to indicate the effectiveness of a process change, we will be perpetually behind the response curve, or responding outside the optimal time frame for the action to have any effect on the problem.

For instance, consider the following problem: The customer support organization of a major software provider notices an increase in complaints about responsiveness to support inquiries. The organization ramps up with additional staffers, but due to the length of the interview and training process, customer complaints increase steadily. After the new trainees are in place, complaints decrease. It would seem that the department has addressed the problem. Six months later, the same event occurs and the same course of action is taken with the same apparent resolution. This continues until the support function of the organization has expanded to three times its original size. The growth is attributed to increased business volume and the cost of doing business as a software vendor. A closer analysis, however, revealed that customer support representatives were spending less time than ever closing calls and more time trying to coordinate specialized routing of calls to the appropriate analyst.

During a period of downsizing, the customer support department is usually one of the first to be targeted. Workflow software is brought in to enable the effective routing of information to specialists. As a result of the workflow software, it becomes apparent that customers are calling in several times to ask the same question of several different analysts, because individual analysts do not have adequate knowledge of the intricacies of the integrated software system to handle more than a sliver of a customer's problem. Redundancy abounds in this scenario, as each specialist repeats much of the work and research done by his or her predecessor. Although the workflow does not initially solve the problem, it makes it obvious—and that is the first step in making process change possible, creating what we earlier termed a reflective desktop or process.

The solution becomes obvious: Generalists take the place of many specialists in the department, leaving behind a handful of individuals able to respond to very specific issues under the guidance of the generalists, who act as conductors of a symphony orchestra.

The actual problem in this scenario was never clear, because cause and effect were not clear. Complaints tapered off after additional hiring, not in response to the new analysts, but because the new staffers started as generalists who took responsibility for gathering all of the information needed to answer a customer problem. Once they became specialists, however, the problem resurfaced, causing the cyclical pattern in customer complaints.

Martin describes this phenomenon as the natural result of process components separated by time or distance. Martin believes that "in the Cybercorp world we increasingly build systems that span long distances, span separate organizations, and span time; hence cause and effect are separated. Managers then do not learn correctly from observable experience. Such systems can give counterintuitive results. A manager does what seems obvious, but it does not produce an obvious outcome."[21]

The solution is not bringing the organization closer together physically, since this is simply not practical in many cases, but rather providing a mechanism with which to eliminate the time delays in communicating problems.

Had a control room been in place, managers would have observed the short-term peaks in call volume and the distribution of calls across analysts in real time through a monitor (by "monitor" we are referring to a real-time feedback mechanism). That monitor would have provided instant information to justify changes in staffing, workloads, information flows, and the reengineering of the support function.

The downsizing imperative and the application of workflow in this organization made evident a problem that would otherwise have been obscured and ignored. Although downsizing is not a pleasant experience for any organization, it is often the only way to uncover problems of this type—problems that often end up labeled as a cost of doing business.

So what is the bottom line? There are organizations with sponsors willing to undertake a reengineering effort. These sponsors have the budget and the clout to enforce change. The metrics for change, however, do not often exist. Even where metrics exist, they may be associated incorrectly with an erroneous cause-and-effect relationship. When implemented to automate existing processes, workflow can establish baseline metrics and long-term monitors for the efficiency of business processes. These metrics can then be used as a stable, sound, and reliable fuel for long-term reengineering efforts.

BEYOND TECHNOLOGY TOWARD INSTINCT

"As the pace of competition quickens, instincts must change faster. If they do not, the price is extinction."

It may sound like heresy, but the most valuable asset of any enterprise is not its people. It is the collaboration among people that endows an enterprise with unique processes. Smart Companies realize that this is the very essence of competitive advantage. It is this collective and collaborative memory that causes Smart Companies to survive while their competitors wither away.

The creation of a collaborative instinct is the natural result of an evolving technology and communications infrastructure that has caused the extinction of traditional hierarchies and the enormous inefficiencies hierarchies entail.

When FedEx delivers a package to your doorstep at 8:00 A.M., it makes no difference who the driver is, what truck he or she is driving, or even how long that person has been on the job. What *does* matter is the sophisticated series of process controls that guide every step of the package delivery, from the satellite telemetry that identifies the status of every package in the FedEx network to the real-time routing of delivery trucks. Drivers can change on a daily basis yet the package still shows up on time, every time.

Does that mean the people are superfluous to the process? Absolutely not. The people *are* the process. They define it, refine it, and reengineer it continuously. But corporate memory must be embodied in more than the gray matter of one or more individuals. If an enterprise is to create a competitive differentiation in an era of constant turnover, downsizing, and restructuring of the workforce, the corporate memory must be part of the very fiber of the enterprise.

This collective process asset is the basis for the concept of *corporate instinct*. Ironically, the existence of instinct is something we most often associate with lower life-forms. Common wisdom has it that intelligence is inversely proportional to instinct. In other words, humans are the most intelligent species and therefore need virtually no instinct.

Why? The answer is simple. The more intelligent a life-form, the more apt it is to communicate explicitly with its peers. In order for human beings to build even a basic structure they must communicate in words. Other animals do not have this capability. Young beavers are not given copies of *Elementary Dam-Building* to read and study. Instinct makes communication innate and implicit.

If we consider the role of the traditional corporate hierarchy in facilitating communications, it becomes apparent that the structure of the hierarchy is intended to provide a vehicle for communicating instructions down a chain of command. Executives instruct managers, who instruct supervisors, who instruct line personnel. Whether this system of communication works well going in the opposite direction, upline, can be debated, but it is very much a human system. One would be hard-pressed to find eight levels of management in the organization of any other species.

It's easy to attribute the hierarchy to the superior intellect of humans. But the hierarchy is a deficient model, fundamentally abhorred by nature and innately inefficient and unresponsive. Let's try another explanation.

What's the alternative? Are we suggesting that human instinct will evolve, that nature will somehow alter our ability or capability to communicate? No. This is not a function of natural evolution, but rather a conscious, deliberate evolution of communication technology capability.

Organizations today are flattening, teams are prevailing, and democratization is spreading because technology makes it possible to communicate in ways that competitively obliterate the arcane nature of the hierarchy. For that matter, they also obliterate the matrix, network, and virtually all other forms of human organization.

This is the very essence of *corporate instinct*.

Imagine, then, that your enterprise is endowed with the benefit of an instinct that allows collaboration based on rules and metrics agreed upon and defined before they are implemented. Sounds familiar you say—a policies and procedures manual. But this is not instinct. Instinct must constantly change to meet the demands of its environment. It must grow and change on demand. If it does not, the result in business, as in nature, is extinction. Darwin's laws of evolution apply to all things, all organizations of intelligence, even your company.

If you're having a bit of difficulty with this concept, take heart; it's not easily accepted, since many enterprises are littered with policies and procedures. But these are in most cases anachronisms. They solve problems that no longer exist or address markets that have since changed.

This is a conditioning response well known to psychologists. In *Competing for the Future,* Gary Hamel and C.K. Prahalad describe a famous experiment in which monkeys were put into a cage and presented with a pole leading to a bunch of bananas. As a monkey climbed the pole in order to get to the bananas, it would be sprayed with a powerful blast of cold water. As one might expect, after some time the monkeys shied away from the bar. This is the simple psychological principle of negative reinforcement.

What was *not* expected, however, was that as new monkeys were introduced into the cage they would naturally begin to make their way up the pole. But before making it up far enough to activate the water, the conditioned monkeys would grab them and pull them down. After several bouts of this, the new monkeys would also shy away from the bar. Eventually, each conditioned monkey was replaced with a new monkey, until the cage contained none of the original monkeys.[22] Yet the new monkeys, who had no basis in experience, also stayed clear of the pole. The memory was there, but its source (that is, the original monkeys) had been lost. Even if the water were now turned off, it would take some time to unlearn the process.

In the same way, your enterprise's old policies and procedures, written memos, and checklists were developed to address real problems in the past, not in the present. What you are left with is the memory of a process that no longer has any basis in today's reality. This is stale instinct and the first step toward extinction.

In an enterprise, instinct is primarily the result of culture. We do things the way we know how to. New employees assimilate slowly, but eventually adopt the party line and policy.

But what if turnover, outsourcing, contract consulting, and market change is happening faster than the rate of assimilation? How do we maintain the continuity of an enterprise's instinct and still allow for the daily decimation of yesterday's instincts for today's, and again for tomorrow's? One way is by creating an enterprise memory accessible to all employees, reflective of the actual process flow, and easily modified to represent the changing business.

HUMAN FACTORS, CORPORATE CULTURE, AND SMART COMPANIES

There also is no parallel in history to the abrupt decline of the blue-collar worker during the past 15 years. As a proportion of the working population, blue-collar workers in manufacturing have already decreased to less than a fifth of the American labor force from more than a third. By the year 2010—less than 25 years away—they will constitute no larger a proportion of the labor force of every developed country than farmers do today—that is, a twentieth of the total. The decline will be greatest precisely where the highest-paid jobs are.[23]

There was a time, not too long ago, when workers were assured of promotion and advancement, time when the upper echelons of the organizational hierarchy created a vacuum for warm bodies. It was not an illusion; the expansion of the mid- to late twentieth century was the beneficiary of a drastic post-World War I decline in birth rates. The sucking sound from the top was not imagined. It was real—and now it is gone.

No matter how we rationalize the use of Smart Tools to help companies increase productivity and profits, we can't sidestep the dual problems of unemployment and underemployment. They are real and they have real human consequences that must be considered as part of technology's effects.

But how do you counter the rational argument that when technology reduces the workload, fewer people are needed? You don't, but it's not the right question to answer. The impatience and frustration of workers that Michael Moore wittingly refers to as "economic terrorism" is not the result of an American, or a global economy, on the verge of collapse. If it were, then we would grudgingly swallow our fate as part of a global depression. The plight would be no different, but the rationalization might ease the pain.

Depending on whom you listen to (or read), the prognosis may be even bleaker than most of us expect. Jeremy Rifkin, in his controversial book, *The End of Work,* claims, "The Information Age has arrived. In the years ahead, new, more sophisticated software technologies are going to bring civilization ever closer to a near *workerless* world" (emphasis added).[24] Even Karl Marx postulated the eventual demise of the worker.[25] Actually, Marx was not so much in favor of abolishing the worker as he was of abolishing the worker *status.*

Workerless? Is that possible to imagine? It stops us dead in our tracks, caught in the headlights of a revolution that may be larger then anything we could have anticipated.

Little wonder that workplace violence has reached epidemic proportions, becoming the third major cause of death in the American workplace.[26] The situation seems absurdly out of whack; downsizing is occurring as profits and returns to stockholders climb, and there is no end in sight.

It seems our zeal for productivity has turned into a feeding frenzy.

What is the alternative? It's what many economists call the denominator effect. Businesses look at the costs of a process as the most important determinant of productivity. Clearly it is not. In *Competing for the Future,* Hamel and Prahalad describe the effect this has had on the British, who are among the best denominator managers in the world:

Take a national example. Between 1969 and 1991, Britain's manufacturing output (the numerator) went up by a scant 10% in real terms. Yet over this same period, the number of people employed in British manufacturing (the denominator) declined by 37%. The result was that during the early and mid 1980s—the Thatcher years—U.K. manufacturing productivity increased faster than any other major industrialized country except Japan."[27]

The price to be paid is high when you consider society a whole— instead of a single industry or, certainly, one company—according to Hamel and Prahalad. Yes, Britain improved productivity and shook off the economic torpor that had gripped it in the 1970s, but at the price of increased social unrest, class conflict, and xenophobia.

The last two hundred years have aptly demonstrated that it is possible to create new markets and new consumers by investing in the innovative and creative ability of people to develop goods and services, and not simply cutting costs and downsizing. The boom in industrialism was the result of a new form of employment and consumption. Each fueled the other. We have recently begun descending in that spiral in the opposite direction. Why not apply the people who technology replaces to new endeavors that can reap new rewards? The short answer is that this does not provide short-term returns. It is clearly a strategic view and a long-term view of the future—not a view shared by the crisis-driven executives who take the easy way out.

It is also a harkening to a greater responsibility that we may share toward the economic welfare of industry and workers. The sort of productivity we are experiencing today has a striking resemblance to that of the 1920s, which according to some economists was the principal cause of the Great Depression. According to Rifkin, "a growing number of economists blamed the depression on the technological revolution of the 1920s that had increased the productivity and output faster than demand could be generated for goods and services."[28] Sound vaguely familiar?

Even the final bastion of opportunity for the unemployed, the service sector, is now seeing productivity take its toll. Ultimately, the hope has to lie in those Smart Companies, large and small, that are tenacious enough to invest in innovation and people.

The basic building blocks of these companies will be their use of Smart Tools to create new opportunities for workers and customers, and greater prosperity.

These results will come in at least three forms:

- one-for-one organizations;
- home work;
- free-agency.

AN ORGANIZATION OF ONE-FOR-ONE

As we have already seen, Smart Tools increase intimacy between workers by bridging time and space to bring workers closer together in collaborative environments. The same is true for the organization's other touch points, namely suppliers and customers. The customer touch point is especially important in establishing competitive advantage. And the most direct way to do this is through increased customer satisfaction. One example is that of the Momentum Life employees (discussed in Chapter 1), who were paid based on their performance in a customer service function. Another is the creation of a one-for-one organization by applying Smart Tools that enable customer service representatives to handle customer inquiries and complaints fully with resources they have at their fingertips.

The objective of such a system is three-fold:

- allow employees to take ownership over customer satisfaction;
- shorten the time to resolution for customer inquiries and complaints; and
- increase the customer's perception of specialized treatment.

Nothing is more disconcerting for a customer service representative than not being able to address a customer's requests. In situations where continued bounces to supervisors and managers are necessitated by customer requests outside of the representative's authority, a general feeling of frustration and antagonism will often result. CSRs are conditioned to expect that their role is to deter escalation of customer requests to the managerial level.

The less authority the representative has, the more antagonistic the relationship between him or her and the customer. Smart Companies provide broad authority to their employees. This entails risk, since customer service representatives have discretion to make decisions with financial consequences for the company. For example, take the policy of many Ritz-Carlton hotels, which allow employees to spend up to several thousand dollars in cases where a guest emergency necessitates fast action. Risky? You bet it is. But isn't it even riskier to chance losing frustrated customers by forcing them to climb an organizational ladder for satisfaction? Also, empowering employees in such a way is a clear sign that management values their insights and judgment. This is even reflected in the corporate motto: "Ladies and Gentlemen Serving Ladies and Gentlemen."[29]

The essence of a one-for-one organization is simple: the first person a customer speaks with is also the last person he or she speaks with. In this case, the customer is left with two distinct impressions. First, that he or she must be awfully special if a request was so important that it was addressed immediately. Second, that the customer is the winner (an impression that may take one by surprise; most of us have been conditioned by experience to expect that the customer usually gets shafted). Employees, similarly, have two perceptions. First, that they must be awfully special to be given such authority. Second, that they are the winners. And employees whose jobs actually make use of higher-level emotions such as self-esteem and self-actualization are likely to be more dedicated and see themselves as integral to the success of the organization; they see their work as more than just a paycheck.[30]

Both parties walk away satisfied that the encounter has increased his or her respective standing—in their eyes and in the other's. All this is well and good, but it often requires the application of some fairly heavy investment in the right smart technologies.

The following two case studies, and the responses these people received, illustrate how powerful Smart Tools can be in achieving customer satisfaction.

CASE STUDY #1

Customer Service at her Fingertips

"I had just brought my Nissan 300Z into the dealer for what I was hoping would be minor repairs to the air-conditioning system. As it turned out the compressor (read $$$) had to be replaced. An inconvenience, to be sure, but I had been wise enough to purchase the third-party insurance option.

"Only minutes after hanging up the phone, having told the dealer to call the warranty company, the dealer called back to tell me the warranty company would not honor the warranty, since a recall bulletin on the compressor had been issued for the car a few months back. Speaking with the warranty company was useless since they would only talk to the dealer. Since I was getting nowhere with the dealer or the warranty company I called Nissan. I was amazed at what followed.

"The customer support representative had on file most everything about me before I even had finished spelling my last name. That a company the size of Nissan knew *me* that well was impressive. I know that I must exist, as do we all, in hundreds—if not thousands—of databases but being at someone's fingertips is another thing altogether.

"She took down the problem and then proceeded to pull up maintenance bulletins on the car that detailed prior problems, the warranty procedure and policy, and the contact information for the dealer and warranty representative. In a few minutes she had the dealer and warranty company on the phone. As it turned out, the warranty *did* fully cover the repair—if I didn't mind waiting five days for the car to be fixed. I couldn't wait. After a few minutes of discussion and exploration of alternatives, she proposed a resolution which effectively reduced my out-of-pocket expense to the cost of parts at Nissan's dealer cost. Nissan would absorb the rest.

"The Nissan CSR then dropped the dealer and the warranty rep from our telephone discussion, outlined the procedure, and then asked me if the resolution was "acceptable to me." Acceptable? She was actually making sure that I was *happy* with the solution. I was, and I didn't contest it. But out of curiosity I asked, 'What if I had said no?' Without a hint of disdain she replied, 'Then we would try to work something else out.'

"Now, one way to look at this is that I could have gotten a better deal. But the better way, I think, is to trust in the sincerity of people (read: customer) when the company (read: support person) is worthy of trust.

"Clearly, I was satisfied, and I will sing the praises of Nissan not only today, but for many years to come."

The role that the Smart Tools played was secondary to the role the Nissan customer service representative played, but both were essential parts of the resolution team. By closing the loop as quickly as the CSR did, the customer had no reason to quibble. The problem did not fester over time. The whole process took less than twenty minutes. This is the sort of customer support that endears customers to a company. Dan Bock, vice president of marketing services at USAir calls this *single-call resolution.* Bock notes, "The customer should never have to call more than once."[31]

Now, contrast the experience noted above with one a colleague of the author's had several years later, involving Nissan's rival, Toyota. Both companies are known for producing high-quality automobiles; it just so happens that in both cases significant problems developed early on in the cars' operating lives. But the resolution in this case was significantly different.

CASE STUDY #2

An A+ for Effort

"My wife's Toyota was towed to the dealer after what we thought was a simple case of a bad thermostat. The car had been overheating regularly and one day just stopped dead in the middle of the road. The news was not good. It needed a new engine. It turns out that Toyota had used aluminum heads in its Supras and that these did not hold up well under extreme abuse—namely, driving a car with an overheated radiator. Now, if I leave the story there, you could well assume that the problem was entirely our own fault. But there's more to it than that.

"You see, the car died while we were driving home from a Toyota dealer who had just dismantled and replaced the thermostat. The cost was in the thousands to replace the engine components.

"The Toyota service rep was nice enough, but of no help. She could do little more than console me. The car was past its warranty period and that was that. I pleaded that it was the dealer's fault for not noticing the problem when we had the car repaired, but that got me nowhere. After a period of much haranguing, she would put me on hold, saying that she was going to speak with her supervisor. When she returned, I would get the same polite treatment (a brush-off, really) and nothing more. At least three of these supervisor conferences ensued during the phone call.

"Sitting at my desk, tapping a pencil, I felt like I was an unwitting subject in some behavioral psychology experiment. The customer service rep, and her boss, were peering at me through a two-way mirror, wondering, 'How long will he hold up?' After what seemed like hours on the phone (it was probably more like thirty to forty-five minutes, but time is relative in these situations), I lost whatever vestige of patience I had left.

"Have you ever heard the term 'empowerment?' I asked. I enunciated with great care, sure that she had never heard the word before.

"'Of course. We are empowered,' answered the rep.

"I launched into a short summary of what empowerment is and why she was not exhibiting any of its characteristics. Well, I might have felt virtuous for a minute or two, but I realized that I'd gotten nowhere. I was actually feeling sorry for her, thinking to myself, 'Poor soul. She clearly doesn't have the options necessary to help me, even if she wanted to.'

"Several days later, I did finally come to a resolution with the dealer who'd done the thermostat work. But I had to wait for him to take the matter up with *his* higher-up, the district representative, before I could get any answers."

What was the difference between the two scenarios? It may appear to be just a matter of the people on the other end of the phone. Both cordial and patient, taking as much time as needed. Ultimately, both car companies did the right thing, in spite of the fine print. And ultimately, both cars were repaired to their owners' satisfaction. But one company did it at a *single point in time* and with a *single point of access,* making that customer's life that much easier, and her satisfaction level that much higher. It's also fair to assume that the Nissan customer service representative felt more satisfaction when she hung up the phone than did her colleague at Toyota. Stated simply, one CSR actually was empowered with Smart Tools and training; the other may well have been told she was, but her actions, training and tools by no means supported such an assertion. In addition, the owner of the Nissan is likely to be more predisposed to buying another car from the company, while the Toyota owner may recall the experience of trying to get it fixed and think twice about making a repeat purchase.

Smart Tools can be used to create these sort of one-for-one environments, but only if the customer remains the focus of the process. Rather than having to traverse an organizational hierarchy, the one-for-one environment creates an organization turned upside-down—here, the point of contact with the customer becomes the top of the organization and everything flows to and from that single point. In effect, the organization chart morphs for each customer, creating an organization of one-for-one.

HOME WORK

Telecommuting, or home work, may be one of the most important social shifts in work since the advent of the Industrial Revolution. It is certainly a prime example of how Smart Tools in the areas of telecommunications and networking have enabled the worker to achieve greater freedom. But one of the more interesting aspects of telecommuting is the widespread preconception that it is something which is best applied to what are traditionally thought of as the higher ranks of an organization. Executives and sales professionals are often considered likely candidates for work at home, but the more operational or tactical functions of an organization are thought to require far too much direct supervision for work-at-home models. The reality could not be further from the truth.

Although just about anyone can be a telecommuter, Smart Companies are realizing that there are significant benefits to home work for many knowledge workers in operational positions. Claims processors, customer support, and a variety of what are traditionally considered back-room functions, can just as easily be done remotely as they can in the office, with far less infrastructure costs and much happier and amazingly more productive employees.

At organizations such as Trigon Blue Cross/Blue Shield, working at home offers an opportunity to provide an additional level of competitive advantage and customer satisfaction by increasing the available workforce.* Trigon's intent was to create home-based claims processing, thereby expanding the labor pool, lowering labor costs, placing satellite offices in less expensive rural locations, and alleviating space constraints in existing facilities.

These sorts of scenarios are increasingly becoming the norm, in large part because of the availability—and constantly dropping costs—of communications technology, but also due to dramatic shifts in demographics and quality of life choices.

---

* From Trigon Blue Cross/Blue Shield case study presentation, winner of the GIGA Information Group 1996 Silver Award for Excellence in Imaging. This award was presented on April 3, 1996, by the Association for Image and Information Management at the AIIM '96 Show and Conference in Chicago, Illinois.

Here are some factors:

- An aging population has forced baby boomers to spend more time at home taking care of aging parents and at the same time assuming parental responsibilities at a later age when their careers are much more advanced. Playing both ends of this role has forced many to consider innovative alternatives to the 9-to-5 workday.

- The National Association of Home-based Businesses estimates that forty-five million people worked at home in 1995, up from six million in 1984. Of those forty-five million, only fifteen million are entrepreneurs running home businesses.[32] The leading occupation of these home workers? Anything computer related. No surprise that the same industry creating Smart Tools is the one applying them most.

- Home workers have also been shown to be 15% more productive than their office counterparts, working later hours, eliminating commuting times, and generally indicating that they are more motivated.[33] This last point presents an interesting and contemporary argument for telecommuting: employee retention. It goes without saying that the happier someone is with his or her job and its environment, the more likely that person is to stay with the company. Jose Antonio Valencia, assistant vice president for business services at Alabama-based St. Vincent's Hospital, points to retention of St. Vincent's transcription staffers as a key argument for telecommuting.[34] "When you have good people working for you, you don't want to lose them," he says. "You have to consider the cost of looking for a replacement and training someone who doesn't have the same skills and experience. I would rather let a good employee take their workstation home and work from there."

- In 1938, the Congress passed the Wages and Hours Act, which mandated eight-hour work days and a forty-hour work week. However, the introduction of overtime pay created an interesting dynamic that has haunted the American worker and created an impossible temptation to take pay over leisure time. This was one of the fundamental building blocks of the American middle class and mass consumerism, but many also claim it undermined the family and a healthy work ethic.

- U.S. workers, especially, are getting tired of the impossible rat race of the past century. Increasing productivity for American workers, almost twofold since 1900, has been met by a twofold increase in consumption.[35] Recently, attention has once again been paid to the issue of striking a balance, or at least an option for balance, between the two extremes of pay and time off. President Clinton has advocated a bill that would provide the option of compensatory time off in lieu of overtime. Home work at least offers an option for overworked Americans to re-establish some balance in their lives.

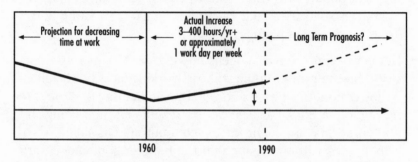

Despite projections of decreasing work hours, actual time at work has increased steadily since the mid-sixties beyond the 40 hour "standard" work week. The result is that any leisure dividend we have received in terms of higher standard of living has been spent.

Figure 6.2 Projection for Increasing Time at Work

During the 1960s, predictions were that the amount of work time would decrease dramatically for blue- and white-collar workers. In fact, well in advance of that, in 1938, Congress passed into law the overtime wage bill, which limited the work week to forty hours and further stipulated time and a half for hours over forty. In the years that have followed the forty-hour work week has expanded consistently. The difference between the forty-hour work week and the current work week can be construed as a leisure dividend not taken but rather used up by increasing twentieth century consumerism. Overtime pay and the pressure to compete have raised work hours steadily. The vast majority of this work has been hours spent "at the office." Without a means by which the workload this represents can be distributed over a more integrated style of life and remote work, workers are facing an future of unprecedented job stress as their personal lives occupy an increasingly lower percentage of their overall available time.

Smart Tools are as opportune to the advent of the home worker as factories were to generations of immigrants, with the distinct difference that the conditions for home workers are clearly preferable.

Today we regard underemployment as a departure from normalcy and stigmatize it as the state of society's downtrodden. Workers who have been laid off, are between jobs, or work less than normal hours hide in their homes for fear that the neighbors will notice their plight. There is the story, often told, about a senior executive who turned to consulting after being let go by his employer of twenty years. One day, while working out of his home, he noticed a terrible accident on the street outside his house. He ran to help and as he arrived at the scene, he found his next-door neighbor at the curb. Looking at each other, there was flush of embarrassment until one spoke, "You too, huh?"

We are soon approaching the stage of any epidemic when it is more likely than not that everyone knows someone who has been touched by the plague. The definition of normalcy changes then, as does the stigma attached to deviating from it. At least that opens the door to a more positive outlook, and a new level of acceptance becomes the societal norm. Rather than fight the forces reshaping work and workers, exploit the opportunity the new rules present: the opportunity of free agency.

FREE AGENCY

"The lukewarmness [by which change is greeted] arises from the incredulity of mankind who do not truly believe in anything new until they have had actual experience with it."

Niccolò Machievelli, *The Prince* (1532)

The final chapter of the Industrial Revolution begins with the realization that people are much more valuable than any technology. It ends with the reintegration of people into the workforce as free agents.

Free agency is not an entirely new concept; entertainers, sports figures, writers, and entrepreneurs have been using it for some time. The basic premise that draws these people to free agency still holds true for virtually every worker, from CEO to mailroom clerk—quality of life. How it does this is less familiar to those of us who have had careers in an office setting or as part of a large structured corporation, but it is no less important to developing a Smart Company than any of the other technologies and methods we have discussed.

Free agency is founded on three basic tenets of the modern organization, which we have talked about extensively:

1. the transportability of work.
2. the transposability of skills.
3. the immediate accessibility of information.

Fundamentally, these three tenets allow workers to develop core competencies which are portable, transferable, and measurable. It also provides the greatest form of equity and control of any work model, and it is heavily contingent on Smart Tools. By equity we are referring to the ability of the worker to define his or her own best mode of working, and its integration with his or her life.

Don't misconstrue this to mean that under free agency people no longer work together. In fact, the greatest limitation to free agency is the lack of sufficient Smart Tools to overcome the importance of collaboration in a face-to-face setting. Real-time methods are still the best to resolve and respond to most creative team efforts. However, as we have already seen, the modern enterprise is already fragmented geographically and functionally.

We are forced to spend more time at work, as well as more time going to and from work. The questions, as noted in Chapter 1's discussion of an integrated rhythm of work, are, "Where is the work?" and "How do we find it?" It is simply naive to expect that people can continue to work and lead meaningful and rewarding lives by spending more and more time at the office, on airplanes, and in the chaos that defines today's competitive corporate culture.

Free agency is not "work all-over-the-place-all-the-time." Rather, it is simply *working at the right place and time.* Without Smart Tools, such as those described in this book, that becomes impossible to coordinate and manage.

The fact is, as we saw in the discussion of time-based analysis in Chapter 5, the tasks we are involved in represent a relatively small part of our work lives. It is time waiting and planning for waiting that makes up the vast majority of our on-the-job time. Eliminate this and we eliminate much of the time needed to do just about any job.

The downside in this is no different that that imposed by the federal overtime legislation passed in 1938. We can decide to take the dividend in two ways: quality of life, or more work.

As noted in *The Workflow Imperative,* "In tomorrow's enterprise the knowledge worker will be freed to release creative energy that will result in an era of enormous innovation and discovery, fulfilling the potential and promise of the human mind. Then we can say the revolution is over."[36]

Will Smart Tools be the foundation for that vision, or simply the way to an even more overworked workforce?

One can wish for a definitive answer, but any attempt to answer the question smacks of hubris. The variables—both human and technical—are so vast, and the permutations so endless, that it is impossible to make any sort of an accurate prediction.

The undeniable fact is that Smart Tools are just that—tools. The way they are used will change from one organization to another. Methodologies and technologies are not meant to be cults; they are not dogma; and they are not panaceas. Be leery of anyone who tells you otherwise, and exceptionally leery of any management fad that claims the answer is there, hidden from all but the fortunate few.

The simple conclusion is that an education awaits all of us, and the only way to begin is to start today. Start large, start small, but start and don't ever expect to stop. Smart Companies, like smart people, never cease looking for the answers, even after they have found them.

23 LESSONS FOR BUILDING A SMART COMPANY

WHAT SMART COMPANIES DO: A SUMMARY

1. Building a Smart Company requires emphasis on seven distinct traits: an integrated rhythm of work independent of organizational structure; fostering a high degree of process intimacy among employees; the use of asynchronous communications to bridge time and geography; applying technology to leverage, rather than eliminate, people; a strong emphasis on return-on-time as the principal success metric; an extended enterprise that encourages nontraditional employment; heavy technology investment in touch points both inside and outside the organization.

2. Smart Companies are as adept at transferring work to any location as they are in coordinating its performance.

3. Smart Tools such as workflow are required to more easily integrate work with the general quality and rhythm of our lives.

4. One of the most basic problems in today's highly specialized workforce is that of process intimacy. Simply put, this means that specialization increases isolation and a lack of shared purpose and understanding. Smart Companies focus on tools that increase intimacy.

5. Smart Tools increase return-on-time, the most valuable resource during periods of fast innovation.

6. Smart Companies focus their technology investment heavily on three touch points: employees; customers; suppliers. By collapsing the time between the enterprise and these touch points, Smart Companies are able to increase their responsiveness and agility.

7. Smart Companies ensure that monitoring metrics, which measure the efficacy of employees, are agreed to by the process participants. Contrast this with the industrial era model, where these metrics were arbitrarily determined by management.

8. The way an organization is structured affects the performance of the individual and the responsiveness of the enterprise. There are four basic organizational structures: vertical; horizontal; virtual; perpetual. Smart Companies adopt the perpetual model because:

- Vertical organizations are intended to provide rigid conduits for communication and control. They move slowly and impede evolution. The instincts of a vertical organization do not change quickly enough to respond to fast-changing markets. Since Smart Tools replace the hierarchical purpose of communication, they also obviate much of the rationale behind an extensive enterprise hierarchy.

- Horizontal organizations are built on team-based models, which rely on minimal hierarchical management and respond quickly to change, but their reliance on interpersonal communication can easily cripple them in a time of free agency.

9. Smart Companies realize that communication alone will not provide a foundation of collaboration. The application of Smart Tools is not an excuse for poor management in the absence of a shared common vision.

10. Since no single structure is right or wrong, Smart Companies realize that in a perpetual enterprise all of the structures have a place, but for limited time frames. In many cases all can exist simultaneously in a single enterprise solving different problems.

11. As organizations embark on efforts that eliminate overspecialization in the workforce, a new breed of generalist is evolving. The new generalist is one who is no longer constrained by hard and fast departmental boundaries. These individuals need Smart Tools to survive the complexity of their interactions.

12. The key to creating a boundaryless enterprise lies in sharing not only information but processes across the entire value chain of activities, from production to consumption, through a single universal interface, thereby collapsing transfer times and creating a new level of intimacy with customers, suppliers, and teams. That, in essence, is the role of the intranet in Smart Companies.

13. Providing methods of collaboration across disparate time zones is a strategic advantage for Smart Companies. We refer to this as P2P communication, where the Ps stand for process or person. This allows for three separate interactions: person to person; person to process; or process to process. This is a fundamental change in the nature of communication, since we are no longer communicating with people but with the process itself. That is a key competitive advantage for the Smart Company, allowing it to compete far more effectively by bridging traditional barriers of space and time.

14. The intranet Magna Carta threatens to radically alter the way in which applications are deployed, the way software companies make money, and the availability of technology, by commoditizing Smart Tools. Smart Companies are taking advantage of this by investing heavily in intranet business solutions.

15. In any organization there are at least three basic layers of structure that must be understood in order to analyze and optimize the organization's value chain of activities: the prescribed; the practical, and the physical. Without the exercise of the System Schematic, these layers are often out of sync with each other and hidden from process participants—making change an effort in the dark.

16. Coordinating the three layers of structure requires that the people most likely to understand the process are empowered with the Smart Tools to change it and modify it as it changes—in many cases too fast for developers, who are one removed from the process, to keep up.

17. Smart Companies realize that the most valuable asset of any enterprise is the collaboration among people, which endows an enterprise with unique process assets.

18. Your enterprise's old policies and procedures, written memos, and checklists were developed to address real problems in the past, not in the present. What you are left with is the memory of a process that no longer has any basis in today's reality—stale instinct and the first step toward competitive extinction. But capturing instinct across disparate computing environments is not possible due to incompatibility and the resulting silos of computing architecture. The answer to this is Business Operating Systems, which cross platform boundaries.

19. Smart Companies use Business Operating Systems to replace traditional computer interfaces and applications. BOS environments are collections of agents that represent the vast knowledge of how an organization is run and the way people and information interact.

20. Smart Companies build their business solutions around third-paradigm computing, which is epitomized by single-point-of-access interfaces that allow workers to access and route all work-related information from their desktops.

21. Process data must be assimilated in sufficient proximity to the actual events that caused a problem. In practice, this type of data is often woefully outdated. Process control rooms are Smart Tools that create an immediate monitor of process metrics, allowing immediate action to be taken.

22. Smart Companies develop their instinctive reactions by eliminating the layers of fat between themselves and their market.

23. Smart Companies don't look for the one management fad that will solve their problems. Instead, they consistently look for answers to help reshape their enterprise and renew their knowledge.

TWELVE WAYS IN WHICH SMART TOOLS WILL BE USED TO CREATE SMART COMPANIES

There are myriad ways in which the Smart Tools of tomorrow's organizations will alter the paradigms that today hold true for the human, technology, and market elements of an enterprise. Here we've defined at least twelve of the technology changes that are the most radical and yet plausible for determining the corporate landscape and the work environment of tomorrow's Smart Companies.

The order is not relevant and the explanations are direct, and concise, with much of the background being materials in the book itself. What's important is to grasp fully how far along your company is in embracing these new attitudes, methods, and practices. Your ability to compete and even to survive will be determined by just that.

SMART TRACKERS PROFILE CONSUMER BUYING HABITS

One of the ways in which Smart Companies are already using the Internet to help better serve their customers and compete is by capturing information from customers' buying and browsing habits. Popular on-line services now monitor the interests and nuances of their consumers behavior while on-line and then create profiles that present each consumer with a unique view of the enterprise.

PUSH OR PULL? RECEIVERSHIP TECHNOLOGIES CREATE DEMAND-DRIVEN ORGANIZATIONS

Information creation ultimately makes it much more difficult to communicate until you radically change the information distribution paradigm.

Marshall McLuhan coined the phrase, "The medium is the message." He was right for his time. The publishing industry was built on the premise that control of media is control of minds.

But that message has been turned inside out. We have moved from a distributorship society to a receivership society. One of the best examples is the Internet.

The Internet is a receivership model. I decide what's valuable to me and pull it down. As Nicholas Negroponti, director of the MIT Media Lab, is fond of saying, "You will not have five hundred channels in the future. You will have one. It will be yours." That's receivership. I define what has value. I define what's important. Information comes to me as I require it to, not as others dictate and demand it. (That is a very different way of looking at the world than we are accustomed to.)

Today you surf, in frustration, the eighty-plus cable or satellite channels at your disposal because there is not much of an alternative. TV guides, on-line or paper, are of little value since they cannot adequately depict in a timely fashion all of the alternatives that are available for you to view.

The reason many people still don't see the promise of technology, and instead remain convinced that the technologies we are surrounding our organizations and our people with are more of a burden than a blessing, is that they are stuck in the distributorship model. Distributorship is in fact the root cause of much of the tremendous press about the stagnation of the white-collar workforce; despite decades and trillions of dollars of rampant technology innovation, it's easy to see why.

Today information is inflicted on us. Information is an infectious disease. It ravages the organization because we have too much of it. It consumes our time because we can't sift through it quickly enough.

The most important question is, "How long will people allow themselves to be held hostage by the distributorship paradigm?" As long as they don't have the tools to do otherwise.

In a receivership model, this is a very different picture. In a receivership model, the only information that comes to you is that information you deem to be important for your particular function, for your particular task.

WORKFLOW CREATES BROKERS WHO PROVIDE 80% OF THE SOLUTIONS TO THE MARKET

The 1990s could also be termed the decade of the integrator. Large consultancies, from EDS and TRW to Big Six accounting firms, turned IT advisers and custom-solution developers have made a lucrative business out of the need for integrated solutions. These organizations have grown rapidly due to their ability to bring large bodies of knowledge and manpower to organizations desperately in need of business solutions.

But the advent of new technologies such as workflow are allowing a new class of solution provider to emerge, one that may well obsolete much of the need for classic systems integrators: the solutions broker.

The basic premise of solution brokers is that they offer a fully integrated solution for most business applications, which integrates the component technology, plugs it into an existing hardware infrastructure, and significantly minimizes the risk factors associated with the technology integration. This is a natural function of the technology market's maturation and will soon become a standard business model for a new cadre of large technology vendors. This new market will represent a $20 billion market by the turn of the century.

As component software becomes more standardized the value-add will be found in three places:

- the integration of the components;
- the creation of core-competency integrated applications for specific verticals;
- the customization of core-competency applications and ground-zero applications.

The solutions broker will play in the first two areas.

NETWORK COMPUTERS DELIVER APPLICATIONS WITHOUT THE HEADACHES OF ADMINISTRATION AND TIMELY UPDATES

The network computer, or the NC, will be one of the Smart Tools that propels the wide-scale portability of work. Although the personal computer is not going away anytime soon, there is a significant share of most organizations that have limited access or archaic access to the leading-edge technologies that are found in the pages of this book. Moving work to anyplace, anytime means being able to move the power of the work engine as well. That costs extraordinary amounts of money. In fact, a minimum of $10,000 per worker is typically budgeted for today's desktop computers. Contrast that with the potential $100 cost (or less) of NC over the next two years and the possibilities become endless.

It is easy to imagine that even the seatback phones on airplanes will be replaced by NCs.

UNIVERSAL, CHEAP ACCESS TO INFORMATION SOURCES ELIMINATES PAPER STORAGE

As difficult as it is to imagine paper going away as a vehicle for storing and preserving knowledge, it's already happening. As a temporary transport vehicle, paper will no doubt remain, but this is significantly different from using paper as the vehicle of choice in storing information.

The result will be a dramatic increase in just-in-time access to information, which will actually serve to streamline processes and work. Today we hoard information for just-in-case scenarios: what if I need this piece of paper and I don't have it?

The difference between just-in-case and just-in-time is value added hours per employee. In a just-in-case situation, value add is very low and workloads are not balanced since many people are likely to be hoarding the same information for their individual safety nets. In a just-in-time scenario, work is balanced and value add is much higher.

TOOLS SUPPORTING THE SCALE OF THE PERPETUAL ENTERPRISE

BUSINESS DEFINITION TOOLS MAKE PROCESS SHARED MEMORY

The diversity, dispersion, and complexity of organizations makes understanding even the simplest process outside of the domain of any single knowledge worker an impossibility. The result is not only fragmentation but redundancy and wasteful repetition. The use of business definition tools will allow workers across a process and an enterprise to understand the extended nature of their interactions and their implications.

THE WEB MAKES ORGANIZATIONS SEAMLESS ACROSS AN ENTERPRISE

When we talk about the Web, we often think of the highly graphical and interactive computer screens that have dominated the Web's presence so far. But the true value of the Web is in its ability to use sophisticated standards to make transparent the complexity of underlying applications, information, and connections. This ultimately eliminates the need for proprietary interfaces for different parts of an organization. The impact of this can't be underestimated in those companies that are struggling to create process continuity across their enterprise.

In a recent study 97% of all new applications development was being developed specifically for the Web. That is an incredible statement about how radically the computer desktop of tomorrow may depart from that of today.

EXTRANETS PROVIDE TRUE FORM MARKETING DISINTERMEDIATION

To call it the death of marketing may be an exaggeration, but with the ability to directly interface internal processes with customers and to incorporate their desires, perceptions, and habits into marketing instinct may well obviate the better part of what we considered marketing during the second half of the twentieth century.

Focus groups, market surveys, and demographics all required extraordinary time and effort to do, draining marketing resource from its core function of meeting consumer needs rather than defining them.

Extranets are extended versions of the intranet that allow customers, suppliers, and business partners to effect change in a company's processes without the layers of marketing blubber that get in the way today.

MERGERS AND ACQUISITIONS INCREASE AS OBJECT-ORIENTED TECHNOLOGY MATURES

One of the most pronounced trends in global business today is that of mergers and acquisitions. During the 1990s this trend has created not only a frenetic atmosphere on Wall Street but has also wreaked havoc on the IT departments, as disparate technologies used for similar business purposes have been brought together under one roof. For companies merging as a continual way of business, this has become the hardest part of bringing together organizations—even more so perhaps than the human impediments of different company cultures.

On a level playing field, where all companies face the equally daunting task of merging separate information systems, this is less an issue of competitive advantage than it is of customer perception. For example, two well-known Boston banks recently merged under a single name, yet nearly a year after their much ballyhooed merger, which now includes the display of a common logo on all of their joint ATM machines, it is impossible to gain access to your balance in one bank's account from the other bank's ATM machine.

Mergers and even acquisitions do not necessarily mean losing the identity of independent business units operating as one. But the long-term liability of perpetuating the walls that stand between realizing shared processes and a shared perception of the market can create confusion inside and outside of the origination.

Object-oriented technology is a way to minimize the impact of these situations, and ultimately to eliminate them altogether. Object-oriented technology, or OO, provides a set of standardized ways by which business objects (basically, small pieces of applications that define rules about how a certain transaction is performed) can communicate with each other. Organizations such as the Object Management Group, which is now over ten years old, have proposed ways in which to do this. But it is a Herculean undertaking due to the mass of technology vendors that must adhere to the standards before they are a viable foundation for integrating information systems.

The reality is simple, however. For organizations to support common missions and markets, they must share common processes. Without strong support and adoption of OO methods and technologies, the infrastructure of mergers and acquisitions is severely limited and flawed.

SELF-SERVICE COMPUTING MAKES REENGINEERING OBSOLETE

The ability to rapidly alter business processes by involving workers in the change effort on an ongoing basis has been a difficult task. With the advent of the self-service desktop, the likelihood of processes going stale is virtually eliminated. Users begin to take control of the processes that they inhabit and thereby allow less room for the processes to go stale.

REFLECTIVE COMPUTER DESKTOPS MAKE COMPUTING REALLY PERSONAL

The trend toward personalization will continue to the desktop of each individual. There is no more reason why your personal computer workspace cannot resemble your idiosyncrasies than your office environment does today.

SMART AGENTS ALLOW PEOPLE TO COMMUNICATE WITHOUT THE BARRIER OF TIME AND PLACE

The model of asynchronous communicating that we laid out early in Part I is essential to the global nature of today's enterprise. Ultimately, the smartest companies are those who invest in technologies and methods that leverage the single most precious resource of any organization, person, or process—*time*.

END NOTES

1 Also see, Koulopoulos, Thomas M., *EDMS: A Portable Consultant* (New York: McGraw-Hill, 1995).

2 According to G2 research of Mountain View, California, as reported in *InformationWeek,* Issue 596, September 9, 1996.

3 Foley, John, "Rethinking Old Policies," *InformationWeek.* Issue 545, September 18, 1995, as reported by Deloitte & Touche.

4 Ibid.

5 Ibid. p. 54.

6 Koulopoulos, Thomas M., *EDMS,* p. 197.

7 Halberstam, David, *The Reckoning,* p. 84.

8 Ibid.

9 Ibid.

10 Belasco, James A., Ph.D., *Teaching the Elephant to Dance: The Manager's Guide to Empowering Change* (New York: Plume, 1990), p. 20.

11 Delphi study of workflow, *Workflow: The State of the Industry* (Boston: The Delphi Group, Inc., 1995).

12 Ibid.

13 This view was popularized by Michael Hammer in his seminal article, "Reengineering Work: Don't Automate, Obliterate," *Harvard Business Review,* July–August 1990.

14 McCormick, John. "Workflow: Go Slow." *InformationWeek.* Issue 544, September 11, 1995.

15 Davenport, Thomas H. *Process Innovation: Reengineering Work through Information Technology* (Boston: Harvard Business School Press, 1993), pp. 24–25.

16 Joosten, Stef, "Reengineering—Behind The Workflow Hype," *Final Word.* Issue 551, October 30, 1995.

17 Manganelli, Raymond L., and Klein, Mark M., *The Reengineering Handbook: A Step-by-Step Guide to Business Transformation* (New York: AMACOM, 1994).

18 Drucker, Peter F., "The Coming of the New Organization," *Harvard Business Review,* January–February 1988.

19 Davidow, William H., Malone, Michael S., *The Virtual Organization,* p. 57.

20 Martin, James. *Cybercorp,* p. 10.

21 Ibid., p. 198.

22 Hamel, Gary, and Prahalad, C.K., *Competing for the Future,* p. 55.

23 Drucker, Peter F., *Managing for the Future,* p. 158.

24 Rifkin, Jeremy, *The End of Work,* p. xv.

25 Ibid., p. 16.

26 Ibid., p. 196.

27 Hamel, Gary, and Prahalad, C. K., *Competing for the Future,* p. 9.

28 Rifkin, Jeremy, *The End of Work,* p. 25.

29 Heil, Gary, Parker, Tom, and Stephens, Deborah, *One Size Fits One,* pp. 162–163. It is also interesting to note the appreciation Ritz-Carlton Hotels have of database management. Once a guest has stayed at a hotel, his or her preferences (such as hypoallergenic pillows, extra blankets, and even the preferred types of

complimentary cookies delivered to each room at night) are stored in the computer. When that guest makes a new reservation, that information is retrieved, and the guest's stay is custom-tailored.

30 Ibid., pp. 206–207.

31 Stahl, Stephanie, "Information Is Part of the Package," *InformationWeek,* Issue 596, September 9, 1996.

32 Jacobs, April, [Abstract] *Computerworld.* 30:29 (July 15, 1996), p.1. Other estimates vary on this point. For example, Framingham, Massachusetts-based IDC estimates approximately six to nine million home workers, but this may represent only the information systems portion of the work at home population. The discrepancies seem to be part of the fast-changing work-at-home paradigm.

33 Liebmann, Lenny. [Abstract] *LAN Magazine,* 11:6 (June 1996), p. 121.

34 Ibid.

35 For more on the effects of work on leisure time and work habits, see Schor, Juliet, B., *The Overworked American: The Unexpected Decline of Leisure* (New York: BasicBooks, a division of HarperCollins Publishers, 1991).

36 Koulopoulos, Thomas M., *The Workflow Imperative,* p. 214.

Appendix

TBA CASE STUDY

It is easiest to understand time-based analysis by actually working through a case study involving an actual company. This exercise will illustrate each step of TBA, from development of the System Schematic to several simple iterations of the TBA workcell/task matrix. A self-exercise may be found at the end of the Appendix.

You may w.ant to review the discussion of TBA in Chapter 5, especially the terminology used, before proceeding. Remember also that the principal reason for doing a TBA is to increase your return-on-time. Used in this way, a TBA can be one of the most powerful justification tools in any change-management effort and investment.

I. THE BUSINESS PROBLEM: MANUFACTURING DOWNTIME

The company this case study is based on is a well-established defense contractor that creates unique, highly customized equipment for existing and new customers. Existing customers have tended to provide the bulk of business revenues.

223

The process the company is concerned with represents its lifeblood—responding to its existing customers' Requests for Proposals. These are extensive documents, sometimes numbering in the hundreds of pages, that specify requirements for new products. Customers' RFPs are issued to several contractors for competitive bids.

In addition to its home office, the company has a number of branch offices throughout the United States, which are intended to support the customer base in different geographic regions. RFPs submitted by customers arrive at the branch offices. However, all equipment is built at the home office.

Since each piece of equipment is custom-built and requires the resources of the complex production facilities of the home office, confirming orders and completing contracts expeditiously supports the continuous use of the central manufacturing plant.

The problem lies in the down-time at the central manufacturing facility. Since equipment cannot be built without a processed order, which in turn grows out of an RFP, the focus of the reengineering process should be on the methods in which RFPs are completed. Quite simply, RFPs are not completed quickly enough to maintain any sustained manufacturing throughput.

II. PREPARING TO CONDUCT THE TIME-BASED ANALYSIS

The initial steps in defining the data for the TBA are:

1. identification of the business cycle to be analyzed;
2. identification of the groups of people (workcells) involved in support of the business cycle;
3. defining and sequencing the tasks to be performed.

The business cycle to be analyzed is the company's response to and processing of customers RFPs.

Identification of the workcells is done by first completing the system schematic (see System Schematic in Figure A-1).

225

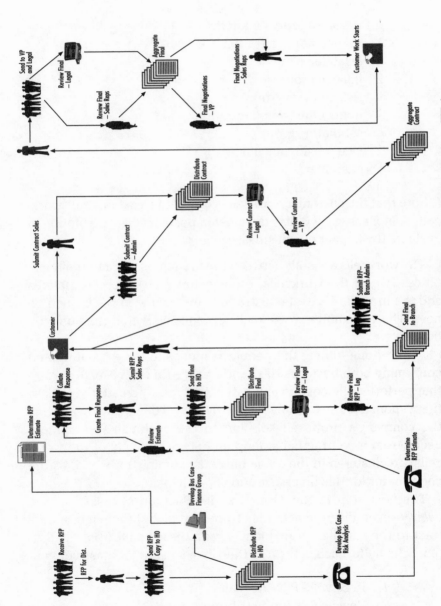

Figure A-1: System Schematic#1 The Business Cycle Before TBA

This reveals eight workcells involved in support of the business cycle. They are:

1. the sales representatives
2. branch administration
3. legal department
4. finance group
5. risk analysis group
6. home office administration
7. estimating group
8. vice president's office
9. customer*

(*Note that the customer workcell is one of the least obvious work-cells in most cases. It is also the most important when attempting to evaluate the impact of a business cycle.)

The workcells are split between the branch offices and the home office. Two of the workcells, the account (sales) representatives and the branch office administration, are located in the branch offices. The remaining six workcells are located within the home office.

At the home office, the people responsible for estimating and confirming both business risks and finance (in this case, the group that performs the costing and estimation tasks) create the bulk of the response to the customer's RFP. The legal department confirms the company's proposed solution to the customer's equipment needs from a contractual standpoint. Since so many of the workcells are clustered in the home office, an administrator acts as the coordinator for this diverse group of participants.

The next step in the TBA, the identification of tasks, reveals twenty-seven discrete activities to be completed to deliver a contract to the manufacturing plant. Again, these result from the System Schematic. Each of these is then listed on the TBA task column.

1. Receive RFP in the mail.
2. Review RFP for distribution.
3. Send copy of the RFP to the home office.
4. Distribute the RFP in the home office.

5. Develop business case.
6. Determine RFP estimate.
7. Review estimate.
8. Collate response to RFP.
9. Create final response to RFP.
10. Send final response to RFP to the home office.
11. Distribute final response to RFP.
12. Review of final response to RFP by legal department.
13. Review of final response to RFP by vice president.
14. Send final RFP to branch office.
15. Submit response to RFP to client.
16. Client awards/provides contract*
17. Submit contract for RFP work.
18. Distribute contract for RFP work.
19. Review of contract by legal department.
20. Review of contract by vice president
21. Aggregate contract reviews.
22. Negotiate contract.
23. Send contract to vice president and legal depart-
    ment.
24. Review contract—final.
25. Aggregate final contract reviews.
26. Final negotiations on contract.
27. Contract work begins.

(* Note that this workcell and activity is performed by an external party, namely, the customer.)

The resulting task sequence and the responsibility for their performance is illustrated in Figure A-2.

The next step is to enter the task times, so that value-added task times and non-value-added waiting time, specifically, transfer time or queue time, can be understood.

To recapitulate the overview presented in Chapter 5, the components of cycle time are:

- **Task time** is the total amount of time it takes to complete the task for a given workcell, exclusive of the time spent waiting for information related to the task or subsequently transmitting information to the next task. Task time adds value to the fi-

TASK NAME & SEQUENCE	Sales Reps.	Branch Admin.	Legal Dept.	Finance Grp.	Risk Analysis	H.O. Admin.	Estimating	V.P	Customer
1. Receive RFP in the mail	X								
2. Review RFP for distribution		X							
3. Send copy of the RFP to the Home Office		X							
4. Distribute the RFP in the Home Office						X			
5. Develop business case				X					
6. Determine RFP estimate							X		
7. Review Estimate								X	
8. Collate Response to RFP	X	X							
9. Create Final Response to RFP		X							
10. Send Final Response to RFP to Home Office		X							
11. Distribute Final Response to RFP						X			
12. Review of Final Response to RFP by Legal			X		X				
13. Review of Final Response to RFP by V.P.					X			X	
14. Send Final RFP to Branch Office						X			
15. Submit Response to RFP to client	X	X							
16. Client Awards/Provides Contract									X
17. Submit Contract for RFP work	X	X							
18. Distribute Contract for RFP work						X			
19. Review of contract by Legal Department			X						
20. Review of contract by Vice President								X	
21. Aggregate contract reviews						X			
22. Negotiate contract	X								
23. Send contract to V.P. and Legal Dept			X						
24. Review contract—final								X	
25. Aggregate final contract reviews						X			
26. Final negotiations on contract	X							X	
27. Contract work begins									
Number of tasks workcell must complete	6	7	3	1	2	6	1	5	1

Figure A-2: Task Sequence and Responsibilities of Workcells

nal product (as it usually represents physical or intellectual labor).

- **Transfer time** is the time required to transfer information from one task to another. Transfer time belongs to the process itself. In the case of electronic communication, transfer time can be practically zero; if information must be transferred by a physical medium (e.g., mail or personal delivery), transfer time can be hours, or even days. Transfer time does not add value to the final product.

- **Queue time** is directly associated with the task one or more workcells are responsible for completing. It may be described as the length of time information might sit around before work is started on it. For example, the transfer time of electronic information from workcell 1 to workcell 2 might be nanoseconds. But it is quite possible that the individual(s) in workcell 2 do not access their e-mail for several hours. So, for example, if workcell 1 sends information electronically at 1:00 P.M., but the receiver in workcell 2 does not become aware of it until 3:00 P.M., the queue time is two hours.

Initially, the task times are entered for each task/workcell combination at that intersection of the matrix area within the TBA spreadsheet. Then, the transfer time between tasks is identified and entered against the second in any sequence of two task/workcells. However, it will be applied to both, the sending and receiving workcell.

It is important to remember that even though the task time is always associated in the spreadsheet with the second of any two tasks, this is process time which is owned by *both* tasks, not just the initiating task/workcell or the following task/workcell.

Lastly, the queue time associated with any receiving task/workcell is input to complete the population of the spreadsheet with raw data. Note that only receiving, or in box, queues are considered, while outbound queues are included in transfer time. The reason for this is simply that an inbound queue is actually more a part of the task than the transfer, since inbound queues are often used to set the workload priority and acknowledge certain planned delays in work.

For example, many people will sort their inbound queues based on priority of the work. Outbound queues, on the other hand, are not part of the task. Once the work is done it is in transit as far as that particular worker is concerned. While a delay caused by an outbound queue is not ignored, it is generally associated with the transfer time, which is attributed to both the sender *and* receiver. The inbound queue, however, is entirely the responsibility of the receiver. This will become clearer as the analysis progresses.

At this point, a calculation function is performed (either manually or with an automated spreadsheet). These results are simply the summation and allocation of task and transfer times. Remember that transfer times are allocated to both the sending and receiving workcells, although the transfer time appears on the spreadsheet only once for the receiving workcell. This is critical to using and understanding TBA.

In order to make it easy to follow the TBA analysis, a series of bar charts is used to display the relative differences in task, transfer, and queue times. These bar charts were created from a spreadsheet that is shown in Figure A-3 (iteration 1).

Although there are many ways to evaluate a TBA spreadsheet, the two basic types of bar charts generally relied upon are:

1. Relative times for tasks, transfer time, and queue time;
2. Relative percentage for tasks, transfer time, and queue time.

III. THE FIRST ITERATION: HOW THE BUSINESS NOW WORKS

Looking at the extreme left column of the TBA Iteration 1, we see that the transfer time on three separate occasions is significantly larger than the balance of transfer times (in these three instances, the transfer time is 32.00 hours). In other words, three out of twenty-seven discrete transfer times account for *two-thirds* of the total transfer time. Many tasks have negligible transfer times, while others account for anywhere from 1% to 6% of the overall transfer time. This discrepancy acts as an initial benchmark, which indi-

Transfer Time	Queue Time	Task Time	Task Nameame	Sequence Number	Sales Reps	Branch Admin	Legal	Finance Group	Risk Analysis	Home Office Admin.	Estimg.	Vice Pres.	Cust.
		0.50	Receive RFP in Mail	1	0.50								
	2.00	16.00	Review RFP for distribution	2	16.00								
		1.00	Send Copy of RFP to Home Office	3		1.00							
32.00		2.00	Distribute RFP in Home Office	4						2.00			
2.00	1.00	24.00	Develop Business Case	5				16.00	8.00				
		40.00	Determine RFP Estimate	6				16.00	8.00		32.00		
1.00	4.00	4.00	Review Estimate	7								4.00	
32.00	3.00	8.00	Collate response to RFP	8		8.00							
		2.00	Create Final Response to RFP	9	2.00								
		0.50	Send Final Response to Home Office	10		0.50							
32.00		2.00	Distribute Final Response	11						2.00			
2.00	1.00	3.00	Review Final RFP Response	12			3.00						
2.00	0.50	1.00	Review Final RFP Response	13								1.00	
		0.50	Send Final RFP to Branch	14						0.50			
8.00		2.50	Submit RFP Response to Client	15	2.00	0.50							
			Client Awards / Provides Contract	16									
		2.50	Submit Contract for RFP Work	17	2.00	0.50							
8.00		0.50	Distribute Contract for RFP Work	18		0.50				0.50			
		8.00	Review Contract	19			8.00						
	1.00	4.00	Review Contract	20								4.00	
1.00		0.75	Aggregate contract Reviews	21						0.75			
8.00		4.00	Negotiate Contract	22	4.00								
		0.25	Send Contract to VP & Legal	23		0.25							
8.00		5.00	Review Contract – Final	24			4.00					1.00	
1.00		0.50	Aggregate Final Contract Reviews	25						0.50			
8.00		4.50	Final Negotiations on Contract	26	4.00							0.50	
			Contract Work Begins	27									
			Work Cell Total Task Time		30.00	11.25	15.00	16.00	16.00	6.25	32.00	10.50	0.00
			This Work Cell % of Total Task Time		22%	8%	11%	12%	12%	5%	23%	8%	0%

Total Task Time	137.00
Total Transfer Time	145.00
Total Queue Time	13.50
Total Cycle Time	295.50

Figure A-3 The First Iteration

cates that there may be a problem with the process used to transfer work to and from the tasks that bound these transfer times.

It is important to remember that the objective is not initially to assess the task but rather to scrutinize the "white spaces" *between* the tasks. These three high transfer times are each bounded by two tasks and two workcells (those that occur before and after the transfer time). Now, the job of the person or persons conducting the TBA is to determine the significance of these findings.

The total transfer time—145.00 hours, which is larger than the total task time of 137.00 hours by a factor of 1.06—is another indicator that the overall process provides room for improvement. However, it should be noted that many of the companies that undertake a TBA find a 10:1 ratio of transfer to task time, so this company's process appears to be relatively well off.

Yet another indicator of a potential problem is that the standard deviation for transfer time (in other words, the degree of deviation from the central tendency) is very large, 13.50 hours, reflecting a wide range of values for transfer time, as compared with the average transfer time of 10.36 hours. (Standard deviations and averages are calculated using the data within the spreadsheet shown in Figure A-3. For example, dividing the total transfer time of 145.00 by the total number of steps with a transfer time, 14, yields the figure of 10.36.

This wide range means is that there is little or no consistency in the transfer time, regardless of where it occurs.

Although the spreadsheet approach is fairly easy to understand, TBA results are easiest to visualize in the form of a bar chart or line graph that depicts the times side by side. A quick glance at any of the charts below helps to visualize the transfer and queue times for the various workcell (percentages of total transfer, task, and queue times). It is clear that the branch administration, home office administration, and vice president all have a very large time factors associated with them. More specifically, the percentage of time to send is very large for branch administration; percentage of time to receive is very large for the home office administration; and percentage of queue time is very large for the vice president.

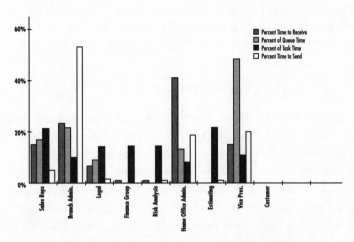

*Figure A-4: Percentages of Total Transfer, Task,
and Queue Times*

Also, notice how the percentage charts are valuable in the analysis. For example, on the *actual* time chart (actual time for transfer, task, and queues), branch administration send time and home office receive time seem to account for the lion's share of the problem, whereas in the *percentage* time chart the vice president queue time is an obvious problem.

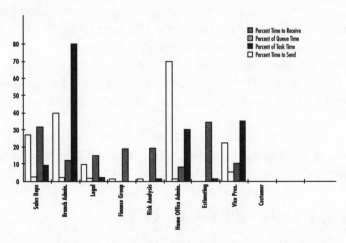

Figure A-5: Actual Time for Transfer, Task, and Queues

Admittedly, the example is simple so far, but even in complex TBAs immediate correlations can be drawn from the data—even at this early stage in the analysis. But more digging is needed.

IV. WALL CLOCK TIME VERSUS BUSINESS TIME

Although the observations appear straightforward, some very serious mistakes have already been made, and incorrect conclusions could be drawn from these preliminary results.

TBA can be elusive for two basic reasons. First, recall that transfer time is not owned by anyone, and therefore is often ignored in lieu of improvements to task times. Second, most business cycles are measured in "business hours" and not in "wall-clock time." That creates an unrealistic perception. Clients and prospects are interested in the wall-clock time, not business schedules, holidays, vacations, and all of the other ancillary factors that are usually applied to costing a business process. You may be paying for your process by the hours worked, but your customer is paying by the hours waiting. TBA is therefore *always* evaluated based on wall-clock time.

In this case, the company made *both* mistakes by calculating its process transfer times in business hours rather than wall-clock time. Whenever an organization uses business hours to determine process cycle times, it is clearly focusing on task-based analysis and largely ignoring transfer times and their impact on the customer. This is a natural tendency, and is not done with devious or dishonest motives, but it does not recognize the importance of the customer as part of the business cycle—and every business cycle's value is ultimately measured by its effect on the customer, not the organization.

If wall-clock time is used, as it should be, the TBA model now looks considerably different (Figure A-6). Total transfer time has jumped to 417 hours, slightly over three times that of total task time.

V. BACK TO THE INVESTIGATION

Upon investigating the largest transfer times in the business cycle, those between the home office and branch offices, it was deter-

Transfer Time	Queue Time	Task Time	Task Name	Sequence Number	Sales Reps	Branch Admin	Legal	Finance Group	Risk Analysis	Home Office Admin.	Estmg.	Vice Pres.
		0.50	Receive RFP in Mail	1		0.50						
	2.00	16.00	Review RFP for distribution	2	16.00							
96.00		1.00	Send Copy of RFP to Home Office	3		1.00						
2.00		2.00	Distribute RFP in Home Office	4						2.00		
	1.00	24.00	Develop Business Case	5				16.00	8.00			
		40.00	Determine RFP Estimate	6					8.00		32.00	
1.00	4.00	4.00	Review Estimate	7								4.00
96.00	3.00	8.00	Collate response to RFP	8		8.00						
		2.00	Create Final Response to RFP	9	2.00							
		0.50	Send Final Response to Home Office	10		0.50						
96.00		2.00	Distribute Final Response	11						2.00		
2.00	1.00	3.00	Review Final RFP Response	12			3.00					
2.00	0.50	1.00	Review Final RFP Response	13								1.00
		0.50	Send Final RFP to Branch	14						0.50		
24.00		2.50	Submit RFP Response to Client	15	2.00	0.50						
			Client Awards / Provides Contract	16								
		2.50	Submit Contract for RFP Work	17	2.00	0.50						
24.00		0.50	Distribute Contract for RFP Work	18						0.50		
		8.00	Review Contract	19			8.00					
	1.00	4.00	Review Contract	20								4.00
1.00	1.00	0.75	Aggregate contract Reviews	21						0.75		
24.00		4.00	Negotiate Contract	22	4.00							
		0.25	Send Contract to VP & Legal	23		0.25						
24.00		5.00	Review Contract – Final	24			4.00					1.00
1.00		0.50	Aggregate Final Contract Reviews	25						0.50		
24.00		4.50	Final Negotiations on Contract	26	4.00							0.50
			Contract Work Begins	27								

| | | | Work Cell Total Task Time | | 30.00 | 11.25 | 15.00 | 16.00 | 16.00 | 6.25 | 32.00 | 10.50 |
| | | 137.00 | This Work Cell % of Total Task Time | | 22% | 8% | 11% | 12% | 12% | 5% | 23% | 8% |

Total Task Time	137.00
Total Transfer Time	417.00
Total Queue Time	13.50
Total Cycle Time	567.50

Figure A-6: TBA Using Wall-Clock Time

mined that the U.S. Postal Service was being used to send documents between the branch offices and the home office.

Realizing that these mailing activities constituted a bottleneck, the company initially decided to make a simple change and use overnight mail service as its standard approach for sending information between branch offices and the home office. Since RFPs tend to be rather bulky documents and cost more to send, regular next-day delivery was considered acceptable. Contracts, on the other hand, tend to be more compact and the packages weigh less, so next-day morning delivery was used for that information flow. With the commitment to overnight delivery for these documents, economies of scale could also be applied to achieve lower unit mailing costs for all the offices.

Concluding the first iteration of the TBA, the ninety-six hours for sending RFPs became twenty-four hours, and the twenty-four hours became eight hours. Thus, there has been some improvement in the method of transferring information within the company without the process tasks changing at all, But there is still considerable room for improvement.

VI. THE SECOND ITERATION: SOME REDUCTION IN TRANSFER TIME, BUT PROBLEMS REMAIN

In Figure A-7, total transfer time is now 121 hours, as opposed to 417 hours in the first iteration. In addition, the standard deviation for transfer time has dropped to 9.81 from 41.82, reflecting greater consistency with the average transfer time of 8.64 hours, as opposed to 29.79 hours in the first iteration. Thus, average transfer time has been reduced by nearly a full day.

Some readers may look at this and wonder, "But what have we really gained if the amount of work is still the same?' In other words, the task times have not changed. It's a reasonable question. First, the transfer-times result in internal idle time spent not only waiting for work but, more importantly, planning around the unpredictability of work. Large transfer time deviations, as shown by the standard deviation metric, often lead to frustrated workers who cannot plan their work in advance, since they often have no idea of when the information needed to perform a task will arrive.

Transfer Time	Queue Time	Task Time	Task Nomeome	Sequence Number	Sales Reps	Branch Admin	Legal	Finance Group	Risk Analysis	Home Office Admin.	Estmg.	Vice Pres.	Cust.
		0.50	Receive RFP in Mail	1		0.50							
	2.00	16.00	Review RFP for distribution	2	16.00								
		1.00	Send Copy of RFP to Home Office	3		1.00							
24.00		2.00	Distribute RFP in Home Office	4						2.00			
2.00	1.00	24.00	Develop Business Case	5				16.00	8.00				
		40.00	Determine RFP Estimate	6					8.00		32.00		
1.00	4.00	4.00	Review Estimate	7								4.00	
24.00	3.00	8.00	Collate response to RFP	8		8.00							
		2.00	Create Final Response to RFP	9	2.00								
		0.50	Send Final Response to Home Office	10		0.50							
24.00		2.00	Distribute Final Response	11						2.00			
2.00	1.00	3.00	Review Final RFP Response	12			3.00						
2.00	0.50	1.00	Review Final RFP Response	13								1.00	
		0.50	Send Final RFP to Branch	14						0.50			
8.00		2.50	Submit RFP Response to Client	15	2.00	0.50							
			Client Awards / Provides Contract	16									
		2.50	Submit Contract for RFP Work	17	2.00	0.50							
8.00		0.50	Distribute Contract for RFP Work	18						0.50			
	1.00	8.00	Review Contract	19			8.00						
	1.00	4.00	Review Contract	20								4.00	
1.00		0.75	Aggregate contract Reviews	21						0.75			
8.00		4.00	Negotiate Contract	22	4.00								
		0.25	Send Contract to VP & Legal	23		0.25							
8.00		5.00	Review Contract – Final	24			4.00					1.00	
1.00		0.50	Aggregate Final Contract Reviews	25						0.50			
8.00		4.50	Final Negotiations on Contract	26	4.00							0.50	
			Contract Work Begins	27									

Total Task Time		137.00	Work Cell Total Task Time		30.00	11.25	15.00	16.00	16.00	6.25	32.00	10.50	0.00
Total Transfer Time		121.00	This Work Cell % of Total Task Time		22%	8%	11%	12%	12%	5%	23%	8%	0%
Total Queue Time		13.50											
Total Cycle Time		271.50											

Figure A-7: The Second Iteration

Secondly, many people make the mistaken assumption that eliminating transfer times will simply make automatons out of the workers as work is delivered to them rapid-fire with no breathing room. The fact is that the problem associated with the rhythm of work is easier to manage without transfer times, since the work to be done can more easily be integrated with existing work. In other words, it's easier to deal with juggling work and setting priorities once it's in a queue than it is when it is in transit.

But the question remains: Does the model of tasks and workcells in this case reflect the best process for moving work toward the rapid completion of the RFP and contract signing?

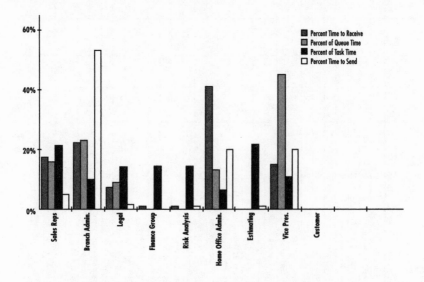

Figure A-8: Percentages of Total Transfer, Task,
and Queue Times

It is clear from looking at the percentage values in Figure A-8 and the summary numbers in Figure A-9 that the *same workcells—branch office, home office administration, and vice president—*still display the same high values for percentage of time to receive, percentage of time to send, and percentage of queue time as found in Iteration 1. Since transfer time sending and receiving for any workcell is based on transfer time for the process between the tasks and workcells, it is now appropriate to analyze just how this transfer time occurs.

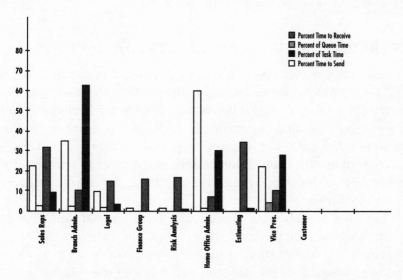

Figure A-9: Actual Time for Transfer, Task, and Queue Times

This is an essential part of TBA, which can be likened more to a compass needle pointing to the general direction where change is indicated rather than a road map dictating how to change.

When this case is evaluated, it is discovered that transfer times exist in the business cycle on fourteen separate occasions. Every transfer time could be considered independently by looking at the tasks framing each transfer time and then examining the workcells responsible for those tasks.

Not only would this be time-consuming and laborious, but, as noted earlier, some transfer and/or queue time is required in any business cycle. This accommodates the necessary chaos of most knowledge environments and the prioritization of work in a work queue. A more reasonable approach is to use the TBA column charts to identify *the workcells that should be considered first,* based on their relatively high transfer times.

Of the fourteen occurrences of transfer time, eight occur when information is sent between branch administration and the home office administration workcells. While these eight instances of transfer time were addressed in the first iteration (changes in mail service), there were no changes made in the process—only in the transfer *times* associated with the process.

VII. RETHINKING INTERNAL DELIVERY MECHANISMS

The company recognized that moving paper and hard copies of the RFP and contract documents internally was time consuming and required the efforts of at least two administrative workcells in branch office and home office locations. In addition, the company understood that the customer required responses in paper form. Thus, it was determined that any modifications of the process could only be *internal*. However, these would still result in faster overall response to the customer.

Given the overall requirements, the company decided to use a technology solution to modify its process. Since there was already electronic communications capability between all branch offices and the home office, the decision was made to use this infrastructure, along with workflow software, to support the internal work process involving RFPs and contracts. The workflow system would be used to route work packages through the process and to rearrange the responsibilities of several workcells.

The two documents forming the basis for an order from the customer are the RFP and the contract. Both documents can be scanned as electronic images and used by all workcells, eliminating the need for physical transfer of the work.

VIII. THE THIRD ITERATION: WHITTLING DOWN TRANSFER TIMES THROUGH ELECTRONIC DOCUMENT DELIVERY

With the implementation of electronic document processing, the transfer time between branch offices and the home office administration becomes very small—practically nonexistent.

Each of the eight transfer times from a branch office to the home office can be set at a nominal 0.25 hours, which accounts for the outbound queue time to schedule an electronic transfer (Figure

241

Transfer Time	Queue Time	Task Time	Task Nameame	Sequence Number	Sales Reps	Branch Admin	Legal	Finance Group	Risk Analysis	Home Office Admin.	Estmg.	Vice Pres.	Cust.
		0.50	Receive RFP in Mail	1		0.50							
	2.00	16.00	Review RFP for distribution	2	16.00								
		1.00	Send Copy of RFP to Home Office	3		1.00							
0.25	1.00	2.00	Distribute RFP in Home Office	4						2.00			
2.00		24.00	Develop Business Case	5				16.00	8.00				
		40.00	Determine RFP Estimate	6					8.00		32.00		
1.00	4.00	4.00	Review Estimate	7								4.00	
0.25	3.00	8.00	Collate response to RFP	8		8.00							
		2.00	Create Final Response to RFP	9	2.00								
		0.50	Send Final Response to Home Office	10		0.50							
0.25		2.00	Distribute Final Response	11						2.00			
2.00		3.00	Review Final RFP Response	12			3.00						
2.00	0.50	1.00	Review Final RFP Response	13								1.00	
		0.50	Send Final RFP to Branch	14						0.50			
0.25		2.50	Submit RFP Response to Client	15	2.00	0.50							
			Client Awards / Provides Contract	16									
		2.50	Submit Contract for RFP Work	17	2.00	0.50							
0.25		0.50	Distribute Contract for RFP Work	18						0.50			
		8.00	Review Contract	19			8.00						
1.00	1.00	4.00	Review Contract	20								4.00	
		0.75	Aggregate contract Reviews	21						0.75			
1.00		4.00	Negotiate Contract	22	4.00								
0.25		0.25	Send Contract to VP & Legal	23		0.25							
		5.00	Review Contract – Final	24			4.00						
0.25		0.50	Aggregate Final Contract Reviews	25						0.50		1.00	
1.00		0.50	Final Negotiations on Contract	26	4.00							0.50	
0.25		4.50	Contract Work Begins	27									

Total Task Time	137.00	Work Cell Total Task Time	
Total Transfer Time	11.00	This Work Cell % of Total Task Time	
Total Queue Time	13.50		
Total Cycle Time	161.50		

Work Cell Total Task Time: 30.00 | 11.25 | 15.00 | 16.00 | 16.00 | 6.25 | 32.00 | 10.50 | 0.00

This Work Cell % of Total Task Time: 22% | 8% | 11% | 12% | 12% | 5% | 23% | 8% | 0%

Figure A-10: The Third Iteration

A-10). Thus, we can see the decrease in total transfer time through the first three iterations:

First iteration: 417.00 hours

Second iteration: 121.00 hours (implementation of overnight mail service)

Third iteration: 11.00 hours (implementation of electronic transmission)

But it is still worth noting that the *process* has not yet been addressed in any meaningful way. Total task time remains the same through the first three iterations, at 137.00 hours.

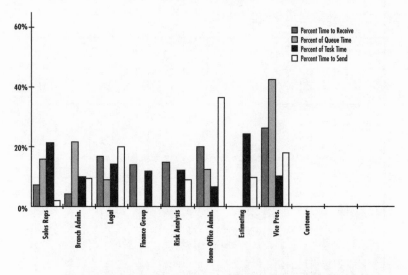

Figure A-11: Percentages of Total Transfer, Task, and Queue Time

Although the percentage time to send and receive for the branch offices and the home office, respectively, has dropped dramatically (Figure A-11), the time to send for the home office workcell and the queue time for the vice president workcell is still relatively high. And this will be more difficult to solve than simply eliminating the transfer time, as will be noted in the final iteration.

IX. THE FOURTH ITERATION: EFFECTING A DROP IN TOTAL TASK TIME

Compared to process change, cutting transfer time is fairly easy to achieve. Other simple reductions in task time follow from the specific reductions in transfer time. For example, with the ability to send and receive documents electronically, the branch office administration's total task time of 11.25 hours can be trimmed. Of this time, approximately 1.5 hours are considered of value to the process: 0.50 hour each to scan each RFP and the contract, and 0.50 hour to create paper copies of the company's response to RFP.

The total task time of the branch office administration workcell has now been cut to 3.00 hours as a result of the electronic document processing. Two tasks previously required when using paper documents—sending final response to the home office (number 10) and sending the contracts to vice president and legal department (number 23), have been eliminated altogether. The time associated with receiving the mail could also be shortened if that task were analyzed only for the RFP portion of the effort. (This is reflected in the modified System Schematic Figure A-12.)

The queue time of 3.0 hours for collation of the response to RFP can be shortened to 1.0 hour, due to the fact that all the responses from the home office now arrive via electronic means, rather than in multiple paper copies via overnight courier.

Thus, the total queue time for the business cycle, which remained at 12.50 hours through the first three iterations, now drops to 11.50 hours, *and for the first time we see a drop in the total task time,* from 137.00 hours in iterations 1 through 3 to 128.75 hours in Figure A-13.

Still, these changes are trivial, and there have not been any marked changes in the process model or the output. Transfer times have dropped dramatically across the board, but the percentage time to send for the home office administration (Figure A-14) is still quite high when compared with all of the other workcells. Examining the tasks in the matrix area for home office administration, one sees that this workcell still acts as the coordinator for all the workcells in the home office and then sends work which has been completed to the branch offices.

244

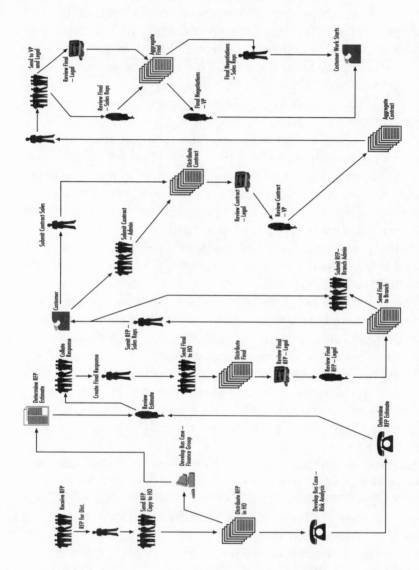

Figure A-12: System Schematic #2 The Business Cycle After the Introduction of Electronic Document Processing

Transfer Time	Queue Time	Task Time	Task Nameame	Sequence Number	Sales Reps	Branch Admin	Legal	Finance Group	Risk Analysis	Home Office Admin.	Estmg.	Vice Pres.	Cust.
		0.50	Receive RFP in Mail	1		0.50							
	2.00	16.00	Review RFP for distribution	2	16.00								
0.25		1.00	Send Copy of RFP to Home Office	3		0.50							
2.00	1.00	2.00	Distribute RFP in Home Office	4						2.00			
		24.00	Develop Business Case	5				16.00	8.00				
		40.00	Determine RFP Estimate	6					8.00		32.00		
1.00	4.00	4.00	Review Estimate	7								4.00	
0.25	3.00	8.00	Collate response to RFP	8		1.00							
		2.00	Create Final Response to RFP	9	2.00								
0.25		2.00	Distribute Final Response	11						2.00			
2.00	1.00	3.00	Review Final RFP Response	12			3.00						
2.00	0.50	1.00	Review Final RFP Response	13								1.00	
		0.50	Send Final RFP to Branch	14						0.50			
0.25		2.50	Submit RFP Response to Client	15	2.00	0.50							
			Client Awards / Provides Contract	16									
		2.50	Submit Contract for RFP Work	17	2.00	0.50							
0.25		0.50	Distribute Contract for RFP Work	18						0.50			
	1.00	8.00	Review Contract	19			8.00						
	1.00	4.00	Review Contract	20								4.00	
1.00		0.75	Aggregate contract Reviews	21						0.75			
0.25		4.00	Negotiate Contract	22	4.00								
0.25		5.00	Review Contract – Final	24			4.00					1.00	
1.00		0.50	Aggregate Final Contract Reviews	25						0.50			
0.25		4.50	Final Negotiations on Contract	26	4.00							0.50	
			Contract Work Begins	27									
			Work Cell Total Task Time		30.00	3.00	15.00	16.00	16.00	6.25	32.00	10.50	0.00
			This Work Cell % of Total Task Time		23%	2%	12%	12%	12%	5%	25%	8%	0%

Total Task Time	128.75
Total Transfer Time	11.00
Total Queue Time	13.50
Total Cycle Time	153.50

Figure A-13: The Fourth Iteration

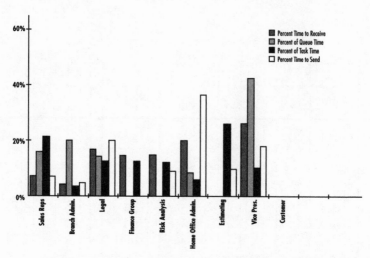

Figure A-14: Percentages of Total Transfer, Task,
and Queue Times

X. INTRODUCING WORKFLOW TECHNOLOGY TO TRIM THE BUSINESS CYCLE

With the introduction of workflow technology in the branch offices and its ability to significantly augment existing tasks that are primarily entered on distribution of work, the perceived need for a home office coordinator can be significantly altered.

By implementing the routing function of a workflow system, which can be defined to intelligently route work to corresponding roles, the company realized that eliminating the requirement of a coordinator could streamline the total cycle time, as the workflow system sends the correct document to the appropriate person. Notice the changes as represented on System Schematic Figure A-15.

It is important not to forget the distinction between augmentation versus automation, discussed in Part I. In this case, it would appear that the process has eliminated a person, but that is not the case. What has been eliminated is a *task performed by a person.* In the actual case study, the person doing the task was thrilled that one of her roles would no longer be the mundane task of routing paperwork. She could instead apply more of her time to the quality contribution of her abilities in the RFP process. Remember, the

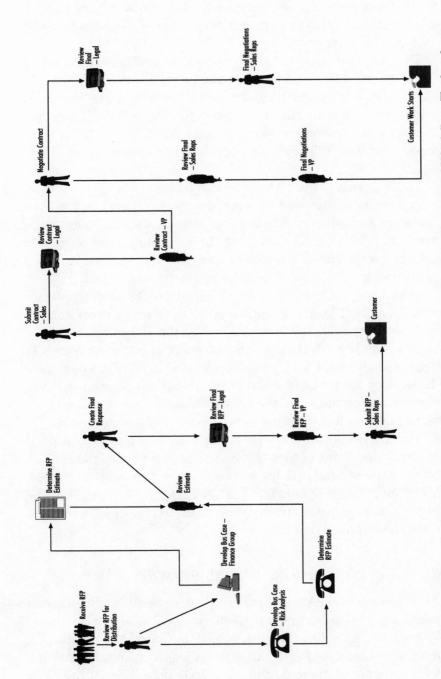

Figure A-15: System Schematic #3 The Business Cycle After Introduction of Workflow Technology

Smart Company employs technology and people where each is used best. TBA helps to point out where that is, in an obvious and indisputable manner.

Thus, the next changes to the TBA model entail the elimination of the home office administration workcell and eliminating the tasks in the branch offices, which can easily be handled by the workflow. Additionally, due to this automated routing function, previous transfer times between workcells within the Home Office with values greater than 0.25 hours are decreased to a minimal value of 0.25 hours.

The final step in the TBA is to focus on the home office, specifically the knowledge and information transfer between the vice president and other workcells within that location. Looking at Figure A-16, it becomes obvious that the percentage time to receive and the queue time for the vice president need additional study—a polite way of saying that this individual is the final logjam.

In the case study this ended up being one of the most significant findings of the TBA. It may appear odd, but this type of result is actually quite typical. The team developing the TBA model needed a way to show the VPs that their queue management was severely in need of an overhaul. Vice presidents tended to let RFPs sit on their desks, even though all that was needed was their signatures. When they were presented with the final analysis, it became patently obvious that they had to revisit their queue management process.

The final results are shown in Figure A-16. Task time has dropped to 120 hours. Transfer time is now 8 hours, and queue time is 9.50 hours. A substantial ROT for our case company has been effected. More important, the column chart in Figure A-17 shows that the process now almost entirely consists of task time, with minimal queue and transfer times.

XI. WHAT CONCLUSIONS CAN BE DRAWN?

As we have seen, TBA is not a crystal ball. It is simple, obvious, and easily adopted by even those with minimal analytical abilities. Therein lies its value. Complex tools will put off the people you need to involve most in your analysis—those workers who have the least amount of time to develop new analytical skills. At the same

Transfer Time	Queue Time	Task Time	Task Nameame	Sequence Number	Sales Reps	Branch Admin	Legal	Finance Group	Risk Analysis	Home Office Admin.	Estmg.	Vice Pres.	Cust.
		0.50	Receive RFP in Mail	1		0.50							
	2.00	16.00	Review RFP for distribution	2	16.00								
2.00		24.00	Develop Business Case	5	0.00			16.00	8.00				
		40.00	Determine RFP Estimate	6					8.00		32.00		
1.00	4.00	4.00	Review Estimate	7								4.00	
		2.00	Create Final Response to RFP	9	2.00								
2.00	1.00	3.00	Review Final RFP Response	12			3.00						
2.00	0.50	1.00	Review Final RFP Response	13								1.00	
0.25		2.00	Submit RFP Response to Client	15	2.00	0.00							
			Client Awards / Provides Contract	16		0.00							
		2.00	Submit Contract for RFP Work	17	2.00		8.00						
1.00	1.00	8.00	Review Contract	19								4.00	
		4.00	Review Contract	20	4.00								
0.25		4.00	Negotiate Contract	22			4.00						
0.25		5.00	Review Contract – Final	24								1.00	
0.25		4.50	Final Negotiations on Contract	26	4.00							0.50	
			Contract Work Begins	27									

| | | | Work Cell Total Task Time | | 30.00 | 0.50 | 15.00 | 16.00 | 16.00 | 0.00 | 32.00 | 10.50 | 0.00 |
| | | | This Work Cell % of Total Task Time | | 25% | 0% | 13% | 13% | 13% | 0% | 27% | 9% | 0% |

Total Task Time	120.00
Total Transfer Time	8.00
Total Queue Time	13.50
Total Cycle Time	137.50

Figure A-16: The Fifth Iteration

time, TBA is a powerful mechanism for streamlining the route to a Smart Company by providing a tool for the measurement of the most critical gap in today's business processes: transfer and queue times. Used wisely, it can be one of the most powerful tools in a Smart Company's arsenal for process improvement and competitive advantage.

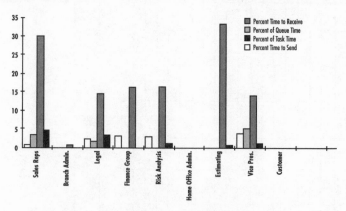

Figure A-17: Percentages of Total Transfer, Task, and Queue Times

---

TBA SELF-EXERCISE

ABOUT OUR CASE SUBJECT COMPANY

An international manufacturer employs five thousand people on four continents and supplies product for resale through leading distributors and retailers. Customers range from Fortune 500 corporations to general consumers. It is probable that most readers of this case study have been, or are, users of the company's product.

THE PROBLEM

The company's U.S. manufacturing facilities are located in seven

U.S. cities. Orders are received and delegated in only one of the cities, Boston. In January customer service functions were transferred to Boston from the individual plants to improve control, increase efficiencies, and improve customer service. This was mainly due to an increase in customer complaints about service on outstanding orders.

The decision to consolidate was based on management's determination to provide superior services to clients and customers and to gain the strategic/competitive advantages associated with excellence in customer relations. It was thought that only through a centralized function could customer support be adequately managed for consistent improvement.

Over the six months following the move to Boston, however, the customer service department grew from ten to fifty people, as management attempted to address the paper-chase problem by adding personnel. The complexities of communication and document tracking soon became overwhelming, driving overtime efforts beyond acceptable budget limits.

The problem stemmed from the company's policy of expedient fulfillment of a customer's order. To meet this objective, the customer service department must be able to access information concerning an order from sales, order entry, manufacturing, and accounting departments at any time during the fulfillment process. Accomplishing this had become impossible. A tightly integrated method of information exchange among the departments was considered key to the probability of the company's continued successes.

Following the consolidation of its customer service department, the company assembled a task force to assess the needs and directions the company would take to meet its goals of information exchange and improved customer service. A team headed by the vice president of IS initiated an investigation of available technologies and systems to support and maximize the opportunities of centralized customer service.

The requirements identified by the team called for a solution that would provide a method of managing the various parts of an active order. These parts are currently distributed across the order entry, customer support, sales, and manufacturing functions. Orders are initiated by mail, fax, or telephone. Data is entered into and output is received from a central computer server. Corrections, modifications, and annotations are made to the active order throughout its processing and manufacturing life. A primary concern was the timely communication of order specifications and status to and from the seven manufacturing plants. Many new solutions were assessed included workflow, imaging, EDI, and various ways to automate paper flow.

AN ASSESSMENT OF THE EXISTING PAPER-BASED PROCESS

Orders fall into two categories: custom and stock. Customer orders typically contain four to five pages: one order, one art, one instruction, customer correspondence, and labels/packing slips. Stock orders average five pages. Rush orders have limited options and are designated as a twenty-four–hour turnaround guarantee. Average order volumes often double during peak season. This creates a serious customer support burden, since inadequate staffing levels will result in poor fulfillment and increased customer support call volume. Although every effort is made to expedite customer orders, an order is active (in process, shipping, or response to customer inquiry) for up to three weeks.

The assessment of the process of receiving and servicing a customer order revealed a number of trouble spots. The primary concerns about this system included:

- the difficulty in identifying the status of work in process;
- time spent searching for order documents;
- the compounding of paperwork required to flow the order accurately;
- the duplication of paperwork by separate departments;
- the difficulties of supporting continued growth;
- the overlapping of staff who process, control, and check the job;
- the effect on rapid customer service;

- the long-term impact on the company's ability to maintain competitive advantage.

PROCESS DESCRIPTION

1. An <u>order is received</u> by mail, fax, or telephone at the receiving desks in the order processing department. About 30% of the orders arrive by fax, 20% by phone, the remaining 50% by mail.

2. The <u>order is date stamped, logged, and placed in due-date order</u>. Rush orders are identified.

3. All <u>orders are coded</u>; account codes, product numbers, plant, ship date, and prices are entered on the order. <u>Coders manually reference a product code book</u> to identify the appropriate numbers.

4. <u>Questions about an order are entered onto a customer correspondence sheet and routed for clarification</u> to the salesperson, artist, or customer.

5. <u>Orders are entered into the AS/400, printed, and matched with the original customer fax or paper order; matching is not required for phone orders</u>.

6. All <u>customer documents are photocopied and sent to manufacturing for order fulfillment. Rush orders</u> containing limited options <u>may be faxed to the plants</u>.

7. One set of documents is retained in the office; plant documents are sent to the plant via overnight service.

8. A <u>copy</u> of the documents <u>is temporarily filed in an order-processing suspense file</u> until the order is processed by the plant and additional paperwork is returned to order processing. It is then refiled by customer and a copy of the file is sent to customer support for future reference in their files.

9. Packing and shipping documents are printed in the manufacturing plants. After production, orders are checked for completion and changes in billing information. Invoices are printed and matched with the order. The orders are packed into one or more boxes and readied for shipment. Box shipping labels with the shipper's control number are attached. Copies of the shipping document with control number and labels are filed in the plant. Documents are sent back to the main office via overnight delivery.

10. Order documents are received at the main office. <u>In-process files are purged of office copies and the order set is filed</u>.

11. <u>An order acknowledgment</u> (part of the printed set) <u>is</u> detached from the packet and <u>sent to the customer by a customer support representative</u>.

SOLVING THE EXERCISE

Given what you now know about the company's process, answer the following questions (make sure to jot your answers down briefly so that you can refer to them later). Try doing this based only on what you have read in the case study and don't jump ahead yet to use either a system schematic or a TBA.

1. What department is the problem in this company?

2. Is there a problem with the process that they are using to define good customer service?

3. Where are the major gaps in the process?

   Now let's try answering the same questions with the TBA toolset.
   Follow these instructions and use the blank TBA spreadsheet provided. Note that you will not need to worry about transfer times, task times, or queue times. This exercise is intended to show you how rapidly a TBA can demonstrate a problem in the contemporary logic used to address a business process problem.

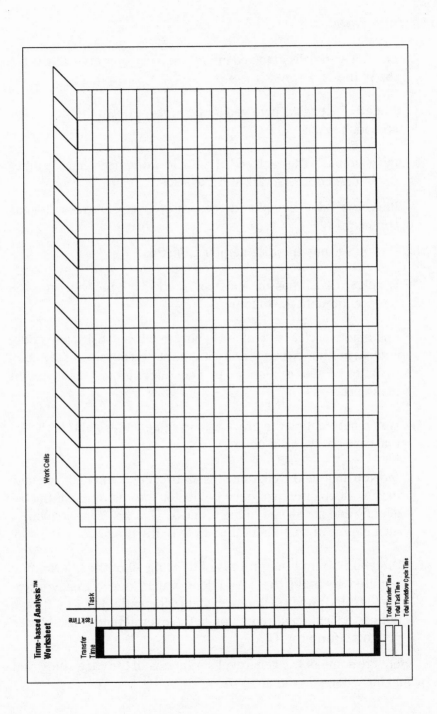

Time-based Analysis™ Worksheet

Work Cells

Transfer Time

Task Time

Task

Total Transfer Time
Total Task Time
Total Workflow Cycle Time

INSTRUCTIONS

1. List the workcells involved in the company's process across the top of the TBA spreadsheet.

2. List all of the tasks involved in the process down the side of the spreadsheet.

3. Put a simple "x" in each cell of the TBA worksheet that identifies the intersection of a task and a workcell.

When you have completed these steps answer the following questions:

1. Do you see any trends emerging from this?

2. Which workcell has the most "x" marks? It's probably not the one you thought it would be.

3. Customer service is involved in only two basic tasks, and oddly enough neither corresponds with the stated mission of the company "to be able to respond to a customer inquiry at any point in the process."

4. Would automating the process help achieve this goal? In the actual case study, it did not.

5. Did you include the customer as a workcell? If you had, you may have noticed only two touch points for the customer: at the beginning and at the end of the process. That hardly represents a high degree of customer intimacy with the process.

6. Did you also find the process of defining all of the information required to build the TBA taking much longer that you expected? Had you first done a system schematic, you would have noticed a significant reduction in the overall time it would take you to perform the TBA.

Here are some of the general observations of the case study that would have helped your analysis:

1. The company's customer is in many cases another company, likely to be using an information system, which could easily be tied to the company's internal product-tracking systems to allow for instantaneous access to status information without any need for an intermediary—in the same way that you can now track a FedEx package. This sort of disintermediation is a central theme of Smart Companies. Put another way, it increases customer intimacy.

2. Decentralized manufacturing with centralized support and ordering only works if the geographic diversity is transparent to the process. As with our RFP case study, this was clearly not the case.

3. Service is key, but it is not obvious how it is measured. Smart Companies always have a measure for good service.

4. The problem seems to be centered around C/S, when in fact order entry seems to own the vast majority of information and tasks. Customer service is isolated.

5. It's good that the IS department is participating, but who is the sponsor? Remember that we said the sponsor must straddle the entire process you are trying to improve. The general problem of communication across the enterprise may indicate that this is much more than a customer service or manufacturing problem; it is an enterprise problem that requires high levels of sponsorship, not just IS.

6. Documents seem to be constantly held in wait for some action to take place. The documents must be constantly monitored to determine if a specific task is overdue or in need of attention. This may be an ideal case of augmentation that would free the people in the process to spend more energy on customer support than paper tracking.

BIBLIOGRAPHY

Ackoff, Russell L. *The Democratic Corporation: A Radical Prescription for Recreating Corporate America and Rediscovering Success.* New York: Oxford University Press, Inc., 1994.

Barker, Joel Arthur. *Paradigms: The Business of Discovering the Future.* New York: HarperBusiness, a division of HarperCollins Publishers. 1992.

Belasco, James A., Ph.D. *Teaching the Elephant to Dance: The Manager's Guide to Empowering Change.* New York: Plume, 1990.

Blasi, Joseph Raphael, Kruse, Douglas Lynn. *The New Owners: The Mass Emergence of Employee Ownership in Public Companies and What It Means to American Business.* New York: HarperBusiness, a division of HarperCollins Publishers, 1989.

Brown, Dee. *Hear That Lonesome Whistle Blow: Railroads and the West.* New York: Touchstone Books, 1976.

Buderi, Robert. *The Invention that Changed the World: How a Small Group of Radar Pioneers Won the Second World War and Launched a Technological Revolution.* New York: Simon & Schuster, 1996.

Burke, James. *The Pinball Effect: How Renaissance Water Gardens Made the Carburetor Possible.* Little, Brown and Company. 1996.

Chang, Richard Y. *Continuous Process Improvement.* Irvine, California: Richard Chang Associates, Inc. Publications Division, 1994.

CSC Index. "State of Reengineering Report," 1994.

Davenport, Thomas H. *Process Innovation: Reengineering Work through Information Technology.* Boston: Harvard Business School Press, 1993.

Davidow, William H.; Malone, and Michael S. *The Virtual Corporation: Structuring and Revitalizing the Corporation for the 21st Century.* New York: HarperBusiness, a division of HarperCollins Publishers, 1992.

Davis, Stan, and Davidson, Bill. *2020 Vision: Transform Your Business Today to Succeed in Tomorrow's Economy.* New York: Simon & Schuster, 1991.

Davis, Steven J., Haltiwanger, John C., and Schuh, Scott. *Job Creation and Destruction.* Cambridge, MA: MIT Press, 1996.

Denna, Eric L., Cherrington, J. Owen, Andros, David P., and Hollander, Anita Sawyer. *Event-Driven Business Solutions: Today's Revolution in Business and Information Technology.* Homewood, Illinois: Business One Irwin, 1993.

Doctorow, E.L. *Ragtime.* New York: Bantam Books, 1976.

Drucker, Peter F. *Managing for the Future: The 1990s and Beyond.* New York: Truman Valley Books/Dutton, 1992.

Drucker, Peter F. "The Coming of the New Organization," *Harvard Business Review,* January–February 1997.

Feitzinger, Edward, and Lee, Hau L. "Mass Customization at Hewlett-Packard: The Power of Postponement," *Harvard Business Review,* January-February 1997.

Florida, Richard, and Kenney, Martin. *The Breakthrough Illusion: Corporate America's Failure to Move from Innovation to Mass Production.* New York: BasicBooks, a division of HarperCollins Publishers, 1990.

Foley, John. "Rethinking Old Policies," *Information Week*, September 18, 1995.

Garson, Barbara. *The Electronic Sweatshop: How Computers Are Transforming the Office of the Future into the Factory of the Past.* New York: Simon & Schuster, 1988.

Gascoyne, Richard J., and Ozcubukcu, Koray. *Corporate Internet Planning Guide: Aligning Internet Strategy with Business Goals.* New York: Van Nostrand Reinhold, 1996.

Gilmore, James H., and Pine, Joseph B. II. "The Four Faces of Mass Customization," *Harvard Business Review*, January–February 1997.

Goldman, Steven L., Nagel, Roger N., and Preiss, Kenneth. *Agile Competitors and Virtual Organizations: Strategies for Enriching the Customer.* New York: Van Nostrand Reinhold, 1995.

Gouillart, Francis J., and Kelly, James N. *Transforming the Organization.* New York: McGraw-Hill, Inc., 1995.

Halberstam, David. *The Fifties.* New York: Villard Books, 1993.

Halberstam, David. *The Reckoning.* New York: Avon Books, 1987.

Hamel, Gary, and Prahalad, C. K. *Competing for the Future.* Boston: Harvard Business School Press, 1994.

Hamel, Gary, and Prahalad, C. K. "The Core Competence of the Corporation," *Harvard Business Review.* May–June 1990.

Hammer, Michael. "Reengineering Work: Don't Automate, Obliterate," *Harvard Business Review*, July–August 1990.

Hammer, Michael, and Champy, James. *Reengineering the Corporation: A Manifesto for Business Revolution.* New York: HarperBusiness, a division of HarperCollins Publishers, 1993.

Heckscher, Charles. *White-Collar Blues: Management Loyalties in an Age of Corporate Restructuring.* New York: BasicBooks, a division of HarperCollins Publishers, 1995.

Heil, Gary, Parker, Tom, and Stephens, Deborah. *One Size Fits One: Building Relationships One Customer and One Employee at a Time.* New York: Van Nostrand Reinhold, 1997.

Helgesen, Sally. *The Web of Inclusion.* New York: Currency/Doubleday. 1995.

Hunt, V. Daniel. *Reengineering: Leveraging the Power of Integrated Product Development.* Essex Junction, Vermont: Oliver Wight Publications, 1993.

Interview with Michael Schrage. *Virtual Workgroups,* September–October 1996.

James, Geoffrey. *Business Wisdom of the Electronic Elite: 34 Winning Management Strategies from CEOs at Microsoft, COMPAQ, Sun, Hewlett-Packard, and Other Top Companies.* New York: Times Business Books, a division of Random House, Inc., 1996.

Joosten, Stef. "Reengineering—Behind the Workflow Hype," *Final Word,* October 30, 1995.

Kash, Don. *Perpetual Innovation: The New World of Competition.* New York: BasicBooks, a division of HarperCollins Publishers, 1991.

Koulopoulos, Thomas M. *The Workflow Imperative: Building Real World Business Solutions.* New York: Van Nostrand Reinhold, 1995.

Koulopoulos, Thomas M., and Frappaolo, Carl. *Electronic Document Management Systems: A Portable Consultant.* New York: McGraw-Hill, Inc., 1995.

Lynd, Robert S. and Helen M. *Middletown.* New York: Harcourt, Brace & World, 1929.

Manganelli, Raymond L., and Klein, Mark M. *The Reengineering Handbook: A Step-by-Step Guide to Business Transformation.* New York: AMACOM, 1994.

Mankin, Don, Cohen, Susan G., Bikson, and Tora K. *Teams and Technology: Fulfilling the Promise of the New Organization.* Boston: Harvard Business School Press, 1996.

Marshak, Ronni T. *The Workgroup Computing Report.* Boston: Patricia Seybold Group, 1996.

Marshall, Edward M. *Transforming the Way We Work: The Power of the Collaborative Workplace.* New York: AMACOM, 1995.

Martin, James. *Cybercorp: The New Business Revolution.* New York: AMACOM, 1996.

Masaki, Imai. *Kaizen: The Key to Japan's Competitive Success.* New York: McGraw-Hill, 1986.

McCormick, John. "Workflow: Go Slow," *InformationWeek,* September 11, 1995.

McGill, Michael E., and Slocum, Jr., John W. *The Smarter Organization: How to Build a Business That Learns and Adapts to Marketplace Needs.* New York: John Wiley & Sons, Inc., 1994.

Moore, Michael, *Downsize This!* New York: Crown Publishers, Inc., 1996.

Morris, Daniel, and Brandon, Joel. *Re-engineering Your Business.* New York: McGraw-Hill, Inc., 1993.

Ohno, Taiichi. *Toyota Production System.* Cambridge, MA: Productivity Press, 1989.

Packard, David. *The HP Way: How Bill Hewlett and I Built Our Company.* New York: HarperBusiness, a division of HarperCollins Publishers, 1995.

Penzias, Arno. *Harmony: Business Technology & Life after Paperwork.* New York: HarperBusiness, a division of HarperCollins Publishers, 1995.

Peters, Tom. *The Pursuit of WOW!: Every Person's Guide to Topsy-Turvy Times.* New York: Vintage Books, a division of Random House, Inc., 1994

Porter, Michael E. *Competitive Advantage: Creating and Sustaining Superior Performance.* New York: The Free Press, a division of Macmillan, Inc., 1985.

Porter, Michael E., and Millar, Victor E. "How Information Gives You Competitive Advantage," *Harvard Business Review,* July-August 1985.

Rifkin, Jeremy. *The End of Work: The Decline of the Global Labor Force and the Dawn of the Post-Market Era.* New York: G.P. Putnam's Son's, 1995.

Schor, Juliet, B. *The Overworked American: The Unexpected Decline of Leisure.* New York: BasicBooks, a division of HarperCollins Publishers, 1991.

Schrage, Michael. *Shared Minds.* New York: Random House, 1990.

Smye, Marti, Ph.D. *You Don't Change a Company by Memo: The Simple Truths about Managing Change.* Toronto: Key Porter Books, 1994.

Stahl, Stephanie. "Information Is Part of the Package," *Information-Week,* September 9, 1996.

Stalk, Jr., George, "Time—The Next Source of Competitive Advantage," *Harvard Business Review,* July-August 1988.

Stamp, Daniel. *The Invisible Assembly Line: Boosting White-collar Productivity in the New Economy.* New York: AMACOM, 1995.

Strassman, Paul. "Will Big Spending on Computers Guarantee Profitability?" *Datamation,* February 1997.

Tichy, Noel, and Charan, Ram. "Speed, Simplicity, Self-Confidence: An Interview with Jack Welch," *Harvard Business Review,* September-October 1989.

Treacy, Michael, and Wiersema, Fred. *The Discipline of Market Leaders.* Reading, Massachusetts: Addison-Wesley Publishing Company, 1995.

Winslow, Charles D., and Bramer, William L. *FutureWork: Putting Knowledge to Work in the Knowledge Economy.* New York: The Free Press, a division of Macmillan, Inc., 1994.

INDEX